D1737449

The Vermont Non-GMO Cookbook

Map of Vermont 1814 Amos Doolittle from Carey's General Atlas of the World Library of Congress www.old-maps.com

The Vermont Non-GMO Cookbook

125 Organic and Farm-to-Fork Recipes from the Green Mountain State

TRACEY MEDEIROS

Skyhorse Publishing

Skyhorse Publishing books may be purchased in bulk at special discounts for sales promotion, corporate gifts, fund-raising, or educational purposes. Special editions can also be created to specifications. For details, contact the Special Sales Department, Skyhorse Publishing, 307 West 36th Street, 11th Floor, New York, NY 10018 or info@skyhorsepublishing.com.

Visit our website at www.skyhorsepublishing.com.

10 9 8 7 6 5 4 3 2 1

Library of Congress Cataloging-in-Publication Data is available on file.

Cover design by Jane Sheppard
Cover photo credits: top row left and right by Brent Harrewyn, Hoverfly Photography; top row center, courtesy Wood's Market Garden; bottom row center, courtesy Evi Abeler; all other images by Oliver Parini

Print ISBN: 978-1-5107-2272-9
Ebook ISBN: 978-1-5107-2273-6

Printed in China

I dedicate this book to my mother, Sheridan, for your guidance and intuition, which are always spot-on. Everything that has inspired my culinary journey started at home. Thank you for giving me the strength to reach for the stars and follow my dreams.

crunchy, crispy, mild & delicious
RADISHES
$2.50/bch
HEAD LETTUCES
$2.50/ea
BABY SQUASHES
SALE! $6/pound

Contents

Acknowledgments

It is my hope that those folks who read *The Vermont Non-GMO Cookbook* will not only enjoy its mouthwatering recipes, interesting profiles, and beautiful photographs, but also gain a new awareness and respect for those who toil long and hard to give us a product that benefits both the land and consumer. A wholehearted thank-you to all of the organic farmers and the chefs, as well as the non-GMO food producers for their strong sense of community and unshakable love for Vermont's land and its bounty.

Thank you to the entire team at Skyhorse Publishing that helped me to put this book together, particularly editorial director Abigail Gehring and my editor, Brooke Rockwell, for giving me the wonderful opportunity to bring the vision for this book to fruition. A special thank-you to Tony Lyons, president and publisher of Skyhorse Publishing, Inc.

A huge well done to Oliver Parini and all of the other very talented photographers whose stunning work graces these pages. Food stylist Natalie Wise for making the food look delectable. To my enthusiastic recipe tester, Sarah Strauss, who had such an important job and did it well. My beloved husband, Peter, for your supportive spirit as well as your invaluable taste testing feedback. Finally, my amazing son, Peter, who inspires me every day. It is a joy to see the world through your eyes. Always remember that I love you to the moon and back!

A portion of the proceeds from the sale of this book will be donated to Rural Vermont.

Rural Vermont

Rural Vermont is a nonprofit, grassroots, membership organization founded in 1985. One of our primary goals is to ensure that farmers and the people they feed, which is pretty much all of us, have a voice in the creation of public policies that affect our lives.

Rural Vermont was one of the first organizations in the U.S. to raise concerns about the introduction of genetically engineered crops into our food system back in the early 1990s. We were vocal advocates for requiring labels on milk produced from cows treated with genetically engineered bovine growth hormone. Although the labeling law Vermont passed then was overturned by the courts, it launched a consumer movement that led to voluntary labeling by much of the dairy industry in the northeast.

In 2012, Rural Vermont was a founding member of the Vermont Right to Know GMOs Coalition, which included the Northeast Organic Farming Association of Vermont (NOFA-VT), the Vermont Public Interest Research Group (VPIRG), and Cedar Circle Farm, and led a huge, statewide grassroots effort that resulted in the passage of Vermont's historic GMO Food Labeling law in 2014. This statewide campaign also collaborated with the then growing national effort to pass labeling laws in many states. Only Vermont was successful in passing a "no-strings-attached" food labeling law, which went into effect on July 1, 2016.

Just a few weeks later, Congress passed a national GMO labeling bill that would nullify Vermont's Labeling law. However, Vermont's successful campaign, and dozens of other state-based, citizen-led labeling campaigns have created a national movement that has forever changed what Americans know about their food. The fight for true transparency in our food system continues!

—Andrea Stander,
Executive Director, Rural Vermont

Foreword

Do you love making delicious, healthy food for your family and friends? Does it make your heart sing when your food choices also help your community, its local farmers, and this beautiful planet that we all share? Then you have chosen the cookbook that is just right for you!

Tracey Medeiros shines when it comes to cookbooks that highlight recipes that feature healthy, locally grown foods. With this exciting new book, she is adding to her delicious body of work by spotlighting the benefits of choosing non-GMO food. Travel with her throughout the state of Vermont to visit the people who are working to make non-GMO products a part of our everyday lives.

Why is the theme of this book so important? Why do so many people care enough to insist that non-GMOs be part of a healthy diet focused on natural foods? Throughout time, humans have bred new strengths into plants through the natural process of developing hybrids from cross-pollination. With genetic engineering, technicians in labs insert genes from other organisms into the DNA of seeds. Those modifications then show up in every cell of the plant, from its roots and flowers to the fruit and grains we eat. The majority of the genetic modifications either add Bt (*Bacillus thuringiensis*) toxin, which acts as an insecticide into plant DNA, or gives the plant the ability to resist herbicides such as glyphosate, and in some cases both can occur.

As a safeguard, a growing number of people in the United States want to know what is in their food so they can make their own decisions about what foods to buy. Meanwhile, other countries are also taking a precautionary approach to GMOs. More than sixty countries ban or severely restrict the use of GMOs, including Germany, France, the United Kingdom and the rest of Europe, Australia, China, Russia, India, Greece, and Mexico.

If you are from Vermont or, like me, love the Green Mountain State, you can take special pride in the fact that Vermont passed the first U.S. mandatory GMO labeling law. Unfortunately, it was preempted by a much weaker federal law, which leaves us all waiting to see what kind of regulations will be created to implement that law. We have to wonder, with no U.S. regulations yet in place to address the labeling of GMOs, which would allow people to know what's in their food, what exactly is the extent of the GMOs in the foods we eat? The Grocery Manufacturers Association estimates that 70–80 percent of the packaged foods you can buy on grocery store shelves today contain GMOs. Why? Because about 90 percent of the most common ingredients used in processed foods are GMO corn, including high fructose corn syrup; soy, including soy lecithin; sugar beets, the most common form of sugar after corn syrup; canola, a common oil used in packaged foods; and cottonseed oil.

There is even more of a problem when we examine the issue of GMOs and animal feed, which is primarily corn and soy. In the United States, almost all of the diet of dairy cows, beef cattle, hogs, and chickens includes GMOs. Animal feed drives the agriculture system, and in the U.S. almost half of all corn and 90 percent of all soy is grown for animal feed. If we want a healthier food system, we need to insist that our food, dairy, and meat products are produced more sustainably.

That's why Tracey is calling all this to your attention in her new cookbook, encouraging you to make more of your own food using simple, wholesome, locally purchased, and non-GMO ingredients. The delicious, healthy food you create from these great recipes will *not* include GMO ingredients. Don't panic, you *can* avoid GMO foods! When shopping, look for non-GMO certified foods—the Non-GMO Project butterfly is now on over 45,000 products. Also watch for the USDA organic label—organic does not allow GMOs in food or animal feed.

Turn the pages of this delightful book to find the very best ideas and recipes for serving delicious, healthy food that will make a difference in your own life and help this extraordinary planet as well. You can change the world with your fork! Enjoy!

To your health,
Alisa Gravitz, President, Green America
www.GreenAmerica.org

As president of Green America, a nonprofit advancing a just and sustainable economy, Alisa Gravitz has worked for an organic and non-GMO food system for more than thirty-five years. She co-chairs Green America's GMO Inside program, which provides consumer education and advocacy for a healthy food system (www.GMOInside.org). She also co-chairs Green America's Sustainable Food Supply Working Groups, which help companies build sustainable and non-GMO supply chains as part of Green America's Center for Sustainability Solutions (www.CenterforSustainabilitySolutions.org). She also serves on the Non-GMO Project board, which provides non-GMO certification and verification for foods and animal feed (www.NonGMOProject.org). Please reach out to her at alisa@greenamerica.org if you'd like references to any of the statistics cited in her forward.

Introduction

I am continually amazed by the evolving face of Vermont's agricultural community. It is truly astonishing to see what a large impact this small state has had on both the local and national organic and non-GMO scene. Vermont became the first U.S. state to pass the historic GMO Food Labeling law, forever changing the way Americans eat.

With farmers, food producers, and chefs in agreement that it is of paramount importance for consumers to know where their food comes from, how it is grown, and what is in the food they eat—these folks are jumping in with their boots on to practice what they preach.

The Vermont Non-GMO Cookbook takes you on a culinary journey through the tiny villages, quaint towns, and bustling cities of our Green Mountain State to meet the people that have helped to make this book a reality. From farms to bakeries; ice cream, candy, and maple producers; cafés and restaurants; co-ops and general stores; wineries, canneries, and learning centers, these special people share their personal stories to explain why they do what they do. This cookbook celebrates all the folks who are doing their utmost to connect communities to healthy food through the use of organic farming practices and non-GMO products.

It is important to note that the term "organic" refers to a product that was grown without the use of synthetic fertilizers, industrial pesticides, antibiotics, growth hormones, or artificial ingredients. The use of genetically modified organisms (GMOs) is prohibited in organic foods. To carry the USDA organic seal, a product must be made up of 95 percent organic ingredients. In comparison to certified organic, Non-GMO Project Verified focuses specifically on GMOs. The verification mark indicates that a product has achieved compliance with the Non-GMO Project's Standard, North America's most rigorous standard for GMO avoidance. The Standard includes ongoing testing for major GMO risk ingredients, along with rigorous segregation and traceability measures.

The recipes found in the cookbook were generously contributed by a number of Vermont's hardworking organic farmers, non-GMO food producers, chefs, and restaurant owners who are working tirelessly to change the face of food as we know it. All of the farms featured in my book are certified organic, and their owners are members of the Northeast Organic Farming Association of Vermont (NOFA-VT). Feeling that farming should be more about responsibility than profitability, their message rings forth loud and clear, "To ensure good health, you must know where your food comes from and how it is grown. Know what is in your food!" Each eatery featured in this book strongly supports their fellow organic farmer and non-GMO food producers by using only the freshest locally sourced ingredients in the dishes they serve. By doing so, they are encouraging and sustaining Vermont's agricultural community for today and all the tomorrows to come.

There is a sense of reciprocity between Vermont's network of farmers, chefs, and food producers and the communities that they serve. Perhaps, it is born out of their belief that quality, not quantity, is the secret to good health. I have made the pursuit of healthy eating, through the support of sustainable food systems, my life's passion. The inspiration for all of my cookbooks stems from the desire to promote community wellness by showcasing foods that are grown in the healthiest, most responsible way. This cookbook is a tribute to all of the folks who have dedicated their lives to doing just that. Hats off to all of them!

Photograph by Tristan Von Duntz

CHAPTER 1

BREAKFAST AND BRUNCH

Coconut Banana French Toast with Strawberry Ginger Butter and Maple Syrup

Serves 6

"This recipe is dairy-free and gluten-free. Turmeric and banana work together in this recipe to mimic eggs that are normally the basis for French toast batter. The bananas act as a binder, and the turmeric gives the batter a yellow tint. At the café, we use a millet bread, which works great and smells amazing when it's cooking." —*Trevor Sullivan, owner, Pingala Café & Eatery*

Batter

Makes about 7 cups

2 medium bananas, peeled and coarsely chopped, preferably Fair Trade
¼ cup organic coconut sugar
1 12-ounce can unsweetened organic coconut milk
1 cup unsweetened organic shredded coconut
2 tablespoons organic ground cinnamon (start with 1 tablespoon)
½ teaspoon organic ground nutmeg (start with ¼ teaspoon)
1 teaspoon organic pure vanilla extract
½ teaspoon organic turmeric
4½ cups organic soy milk

8–12 1-inch-thick slices day-old bread, such as millet or country bread
Pure Vermont maple syrup
Strawberry Ginger Butter **(see page 55)**

Preheat the oven to 200 degrees Fahrenheit. Lightly grease an ovenproof baking dish. Set aside.

Place all ingredients for the batter in a blender and blend until smooth. Pour the batter into a large bowl, cover with plastic wrap, and chill in the refrigerator overnight.

Pour half of the batter into a 9-by-13-inch baking dish. Working in batches, place the bread slices in a single layer in the batter and gently press on the bread to allow it to absorb the liquid. Add additional batter to the dish as needed.

Generously spray a large, nonstick skillet with cooking spray and heat over medium heat. Shake off the excess batter from the bread, then place the bread slices in the skillet in a single layer. Cook until golden brown on both sides, about 3 minutes per side. Transfer to the prepared baking dish and keep warm in the oven. Repeat this step with the remaining bread slices. Serve with strawberry ginger butter and maple syrup.

Recipe from Pingala Café & Eatery
Photograph (page xxiv) by Oliver Parini

Ben & Jerry's Homemade, Inc.

PROFILE

Ben & Jerry's has long been known for its support of environmental issues, sustainability, and social justice, so is it any wonder that they are now on the front lines backing the labeling of genetically engineered foods. The company believes that food is a personal choice, with the use of mandatory GMO labeling ensuring consumers the freedom to choose healthy, non-GMO products. It is the company's strong conviction that everyone deserves to know what is in its food.

By the standards laid out in the new Vermont labeling law, animal feed is unaffected by the non-GMO ruling. Ben & Jerry's is striving to build a sustainable dairy chain in the Northeast that does not use GMO feed. The company is working with the dairy industry and major commodity chains to accomplish this goal. It is the company's desire to be part of creating a healthy agricultural network.

Consumers will be happy to know that Ben & Jerry's has been able to make the switch to non-GMO without discontinuing any of its unique flavors. Going non-GMO is about the bits of candy, nuts, and baked goods that are used in their products, rather than the ice cream itself. Their taste gurus have had to make a few flavor alterations here and there, with positive results. All of the ice cream sold in pints, quarts, and at scoop shops has been made with non-GMO ingredients since 2014.

A majority of the brand's ice cream—four million gallons a year—is made at its St. Alban's, Vermont, factory. All pints are labeled, "We source non-GMO ingredients." This stamp is found right above the company's Fair Trade certification icon. Ben & Jerry's has always been about the spirit of transparency.

The company's goal is to assist other businesses in sourcing non-GMO ingredients, while also helping farmers to remain sustainable. Ben & Jerry's is much more than just a scoop of delicious ice cream with a fun name; the company is an integral part of the community, doing its part to effect positive change. With a mission of protecting the earth and the goal of making the best ice cream possible, they continue to address social and economic issues, proudly standing up for what they believe in. Ben & Jerry's is, without a doubt, a force to be reckoned with!

French Toast Casserole with Ben & Jerry's Vanilla Ice Cream

Serves 6–8

This rich and creamy custard casserole was created in the kitchen of Ben & Jerry's by Flavor Guru Eric Fredette. This super easy dish is delicious whether served for breakfast or dessert.

Note: The bread needs to soak in the custard 1 day before you intend to bake the casserole.

1 pint of Ben & Jerry's vanilla ice cream, melted
½ cup organic ginger spread, or fruit spread of choice, plus extra for garnish
6 large eggs, lightly beaten
1 cup milk
1 day-old baguette, cut into ¾- to 1-inch-thick slices
Pure Vermont maple syrup

Lightly grease an 11-by-7-inch baking pan. In a large bowl, whisk together the melted ice cream, ginger spread, eggs, and milk.

Place the bread slices in the pan in a single layer, slightly overlapping them. Pour the custard evenly over the bread, then gently press on the bread to allow it to absorb the liquid. Cover with plastic wrap and refrigerate overnight.

Preheat the oven to 350 degrees Fahrenheit. Remove and discard the plastic wrap and place the pan in the oven. Bake until golden brown and the custard is set, about 55 minutes. Let cool slightly. Drizzle with maple syrup and top with ginger spread, if desired, and serve.

Recipe from Ben & Jerry's Homemade, Inc.
Photograph by Oliver Parini

Tip: The best way to melt the ice cream is to refrigerate it overnight. Make sure to put the container of ice cream on a plate or in a bowl to catch any leakage.

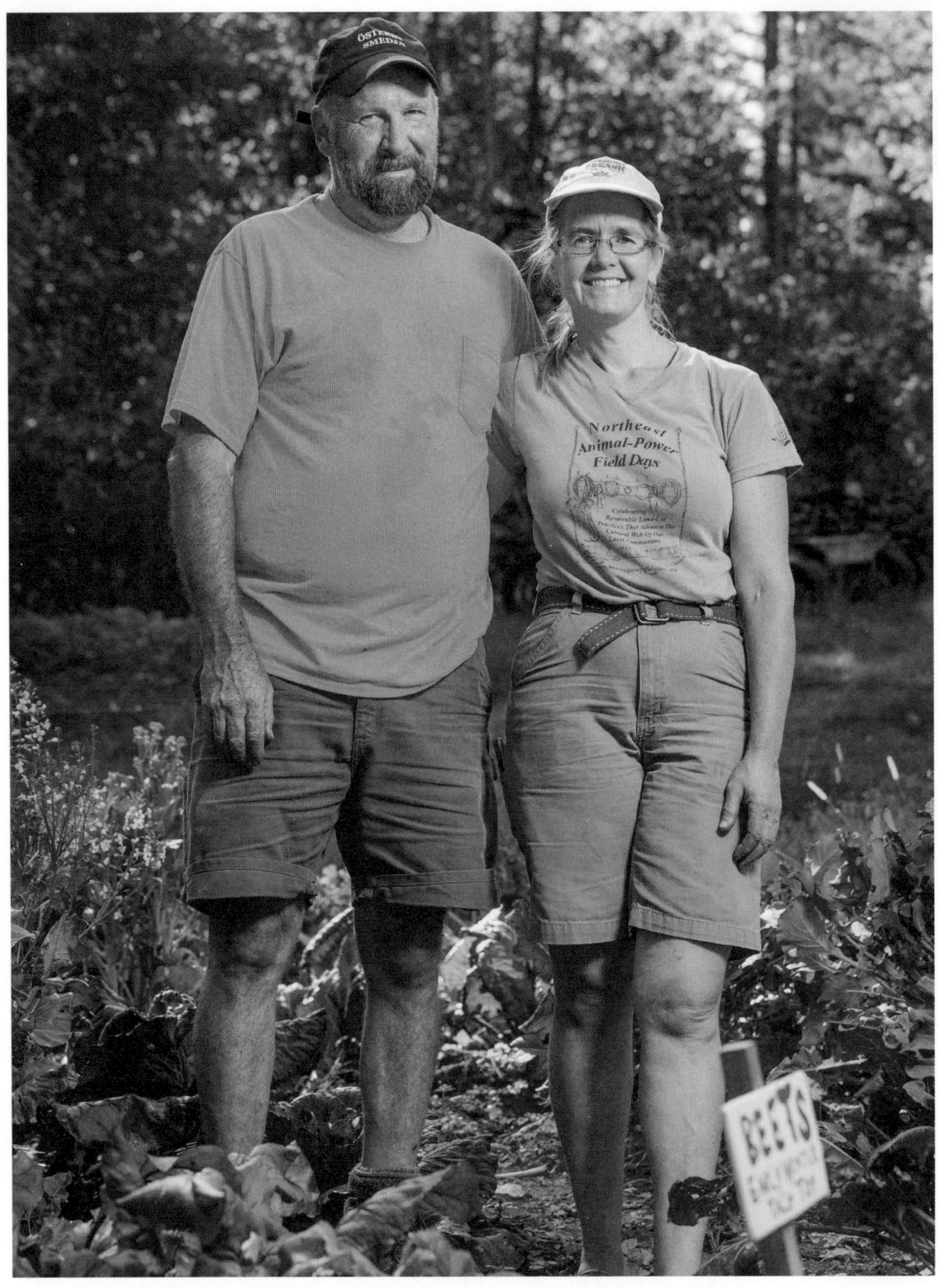
Northeast
Animal-Power
Field Days
BEETS

Earthwise Farm and Forest

PROFILE

Carl Russell and his wife, Lisa McCrory, started Earthwise Farm and Forest approximately sixteen years ago. The property has been in Carl's family since 1938, when his grandfather, Charles Russell, purchased it with the hope of turning it into a working farm. Because of his poor health in the 1950s, he decided to instead plant thirty acres with softwood timber species. Little did he know that his grandson, Carl, would continue his legacy. It wasn't until 1986 that Carl bought the first draft horse for his logging business, making his dream of working the land a reality.

When Carl met Lisa in 2000, they soon realized they had many common interests and beliefs, one being to live within the means of their own resources. After they married, the log house they designed took three and a half years to build. It is powered by photovoltaic panels. They heat with wood, and a gravity-fed well provides water for the household.

Located in Bethel, Vermont, Earthwise Farm and Forest is a certified organic, draft animal-powered family farm. Carl and Lisa strongly believe that the food they have access to should support their principles about health, the environment, economics, and social beliefs. To this end, they explain, "The name of our farm points to our belief in the inherent wisdom of established processes of the earth, as we work to secure what we need from the land, we also need to validate those processes as our most valuable resources."

Carl and Lisa try to use natural systems when possible, such as horses instead of tractors and rotating pasturing livestock rather than spreading manure. They hand-milk their cows, producing three to eight gallons of certified organic raw milk per day. The small farm store found on the property sells certified organic garlic, potatoes, raw milk, flowers, herbs, cabbage, perennials, and whole, packaged (frozen) chicken and turkey meat. Their GMO-free eggs and pork are raised organically, but not certified. The farm's draft horses are used to harvest logs, which are sold as custom-cut lumber and fuel wood. There are approximately one hundred and twenty-five acres of actively managed forests, which range from northern hardwood to mixed softwood species.

The hardworking couple are available to speak at conferences or give workshops on a number of ecological and forestry subjects, including small-scale homestead farming (growing food for personal use). They are also prepared to work with school groups, campers, children, and adults. Carl and Lisa maintain, "Farming in the twenty-first century should not be just about profitability or affordability, it should also be about responsibility."

Farm Fresh Quiche with Potato Crust

Makes one 9-inch pie; serves 8

"We use a lot more eggs in our quiche compared to the quiche recipes that I often find in cookbooks, giving it less of a custard texture and more of an egg soufflé. Oftentimes, our goal is to find creative ways to use up our surplus of eggs. I modify this recipe with garlic and vegetables from the garden; meats from our farm, such as bacon; and some of our farmstead cheeses, whenever they are available." *—Lisa McCrory, co-owner, Earthwise Farm and Forest*

Potato Crust

1½ pounds potatoes, such as Yukon Gold, peeled
1 large egg, lightly beaten
2 tablespoons organic all-purpose flour
1 tablespoon minced fresh basil, optional
Salt and freshly ground black pepper
Extra virgin olive oil, for brushing the crust

Filling

½ pound sweet or hot artisan Italian sausage (casings removed) or ¾ cup chopped ham
1 tablespoon butter
½ cup chopped onion
6 eggs, lightly beaten
¾ cup plain yogurt, such as Butterworks Farm
¾ cup heavy cream
Salt and freshly ground black pepper
1½ cups shredded Vermont cheddar cheese, divided

Preheat the oven to 375 degrees Fahrenheit. Lightly grease a 9-inch pie plate. Set aside.

To make the potato crust: Grate the potatoes into a strainer, pressing out any extra liquid. In a medium bowl, mix together the grated potatoes, egg, flour, basil, if using, and salt and pepper to taste. Press the potato mixture gently into the bottom and sides of the prepared pie plate. Bake for 20 minutes, then brush the crust with olive oil and continue to bake until the crust is light golden brown, about 15 minutes. Set aside.

To make the filling: Heat a medium skillet over medium heat. Add the sausage and cook, crumbling with a fork, until browned, about 8 minutes. Using a slotted spoon, transfer the sausage to a medium bowl. In the same skillet with the reserved sausage drippings, melt the butter over medium heat. Add the onion and cook, stirring often, until soft and translucent, about 5 minutes. Using a slotted spoon, transfer the onion to the bowl with the sausage and mix until well combined. In a separate medium bowl, whisk together the eggs, yogurt, cream, and salt and pepper to taste.

Spread the sausage mixture evenly over the bottom of the pie crust. Sprinkle ½ cup of the cheese on top of the sausage mixture, then carefully pour the egg mixture over the cheese. Sprinkle with the remaining 1 cup of the cheese. Place the quiche on a baking sheet and bake until the egg mixture is set in the center, about 40 minutes. Serve warm or at room temperature.

Recipe from Earthwise Farm and Forest
Photographs by Oliver Parini

Spelt Pound Cake with Sourdough, Pumpkin, and Nuts

Serves 8

"Spelt is one of the ancient grains that humans have been eating for thousands of years. In Greek mythology, spelt was a gift to the Greeks from the goddess Demeter, and I can understand why! The taste is almost nutty-sweet, but at the same time is robust and flavorful. I buy mine from the Lazor family of Butterworks Farm, because I know that their spelt is grown with care and integrity. I wanted to develop its full flavor with a recipe that would make the spelt shine, so I used a bit of mild sourdough and even a pre-ferment in this cake. The end result is sure to please!" —*Heike Meyer, bakeress, Brotbakery*

Sourdough Starter Culture

Refresh your sourdough starter culture the night before you intend to bake the pound cake. You will have ¼ cup ripe culture the next day.

Poolish Pre-ferment, optional

Starting 4 to 5 hours before you intend to make the pound cake, prepare a pre-ferment. Combine 1½ tablespoons water and 1½ tablespoons all-purpose flour. Add ⅛ teaspoon instant dry yeast and let rise in a warm environment for 3 to 4 hours, until bubbly. Although this not a necessary step, it will enhance the flavor of the cake.

Pound Cake

1 cup fresh or canned organic pumpkin puree*
⅓ cup real buttermilk or kefir (cultured)
¼ cup sourdough culture
2 tablespoons pure maple syrup
3 tablespoons poolish pre-ferment, optional
2 large eggs, lightly beaten, at room temperature
1 teaspoon pure vanilla extract
½ cup whole wheat pastry flour
½ cup whole grain spelt flour (you can substitute sifted whole wheat or wheat flour)
¾ cup organic cane sugar or maple sugar, plus extra for topping
2 teaspoons aluminum-free baking powder
1 teaspoon baking soda
½ teaspoon ground cinnamon
½ teaspoon fine sea salt
⅓ cup unsalted pastured butter, cut into 1-inch pieces and chilled
1 cup pitted dates, finely chopped
¾ cup walnuts or hazelnuts, chopped roughly

Preheat the oven to 350 degrees Fahrenheit. Spray a 9-inch loaf pan with nonstick cooking spray and line the bottom with parchment paper. Set aside.

In a large bowl, mix together the pumpkin puree, buttermilk, sourdough culture, maple syrup, pre-ferment (if using), eggs, and vanilla extract.

In a separate large bowl, sift together the flours. Add the sugar, baking powder, baking soda, cinnamon, and salt, then mix until well combined. Cut in the butter with a pastry cutter, two butter knives, or with your fingers, until the mixture begins to form pea-sized pieces. Using your fingers, mix in the dates and nuts.

Using a rubber spatula, fold the flour mixture into the wet ingredients, being careful not to overmix. Pour the batter into the prepared pan and sprinkle additional sugar over the top, if desired.

Bake until a toothpick inserted into the center of the cake comes out clean and reaches an internal temperature of 200 degrees Fahrenheit, about 80 minutes.

Let the cake cool in the pan on a wire rack for about 30 minutes, then turn it out onto a cooling rack. Let cool completely before serving.

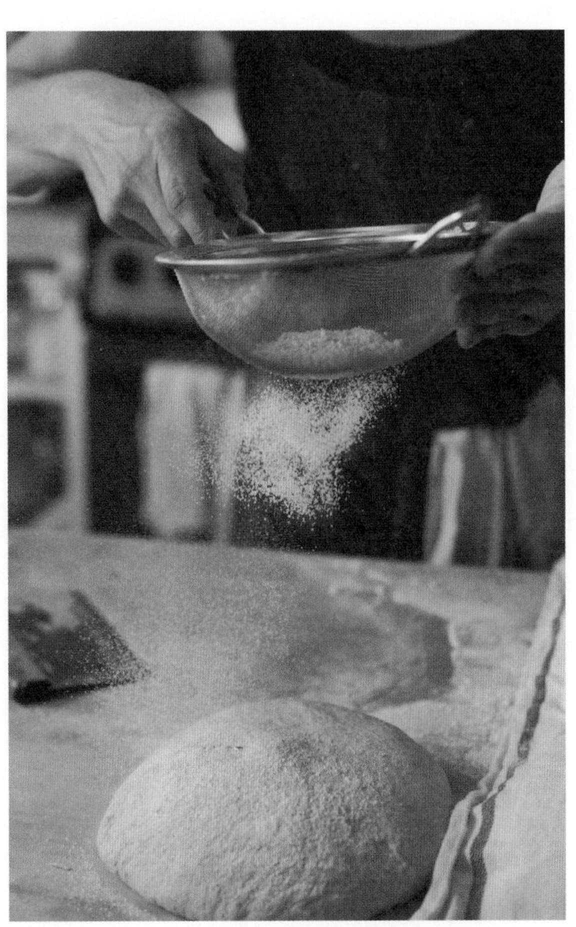

**When using canned pure pumpkin puree, be sure not to use pie filling, which is spiced and sweetened.*

Note: A pre-ferment is a combination of flour, water, and sometimes yeast that is prepared in advance (as in pre-fermentation) and then mixed into the main body of the dough as an additional ingredient. Poolish is one of the most common preferments that use commercial yeast.

Recipe from Brotbakery
Photograph by Evi Abeler

Spring Breakfast Tacos

Makes 4 tacos; serves 2–3 people

"If adding hot sauce, I recommend using the Roasted Garlic & Carrot Cayenne Pepper Sauce from Vermont Pepper Works. The pepper sauce is made from our organic cayenne peppers. It has a nice balance with a medium heat level." —*Eli Hersh, owner, Shadow Creek Farm*

Filling
4 slices uncured bacon
1 cup red radishes, trimmed and thinly sliced, about 5 radishes
¼ cup chopped ramps
Salt and freshly ground black pepper

Eggs Over Easy
4 eggs
Salt and freshly ground black pepper

Tortillas
4 6-inch white corn tortillas

1½ cups loosely packed greens, such as mesclun
Hot sauce, optional

Cook the bacon in a nonstick skillet over medium-high heat until crisp, about 12 minutes. Transfer to a plate lined with paper towels to drain. Reserve half of the bacon drippings in the skillet and measure out the other half into a ramekin. Set aside.

Reduce the heat to medium. Add the radishes and ramps and cook, stirring often, until just tender, about 3 minutes. Season with salt and pepper to taste. Using a slotted spoon, transfer to a plate lined with paper towels. Reserve any drippings in the skillet.

To make the eggs: Add the reserved bacon drippings from the ramekin back into the skillet and heat over medium-low heat until bubbling. Carefully crack the eggs into the skillet and cook for 30 seconds. Using a spatula, carefully flip the eggs over and cook until the whites are slightly soft and the yolks are runny, about 2 minutes. Season with salt and pepper to taste.

While the reserved bacon drippings for the eggs are heating, start warming the tortillas. Heat a clean, dry skillet over medium heat. Working in batches, add the tortillas and cook until warm and pliable, about 30 seconds on each side.

To assemble: Place the tortillas on a clean work surface. Divide the greens, eggs, radishes, and ramps evenly among the tortillas. Top with bacon and a drizzle of hot sauce, if desired. Serve at once.

Variation: You can substitute scallions for the ramps.

Recipe from Shadow Creek Farm
Photograph by Tristan Von Duntz

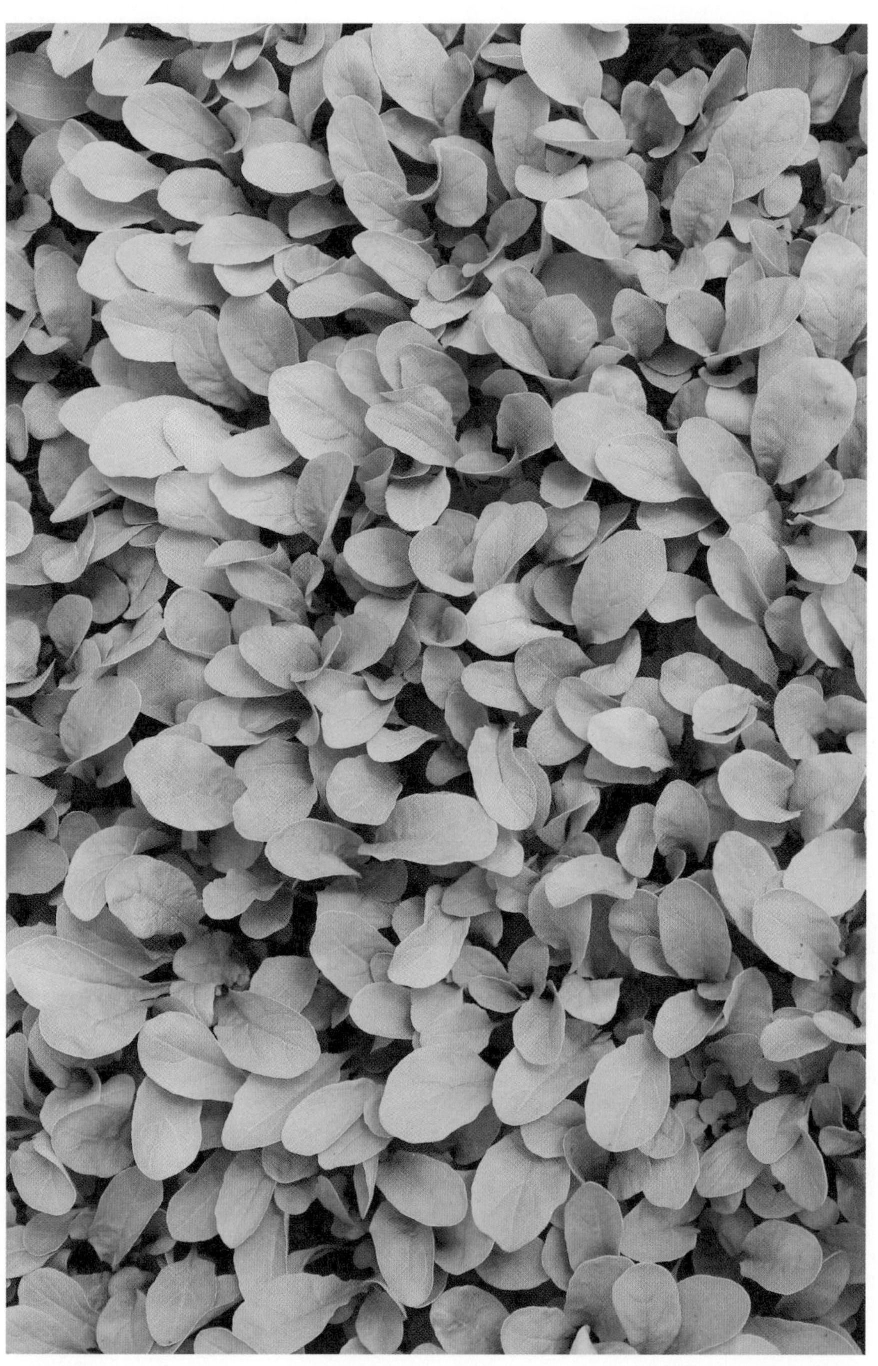

PROFILE

Jersey Girls Dairy & Farm Store

Lisa Kaiman wears two hats: one as a farmer, and the other as owner of Jersey Girls Dairy & Farm Store in Chester, Vermont. A love and respect for animals stimulates her desire to provide a better life for the creatures in her care, and in the process, offer nutritious, great tasting, wholesome food to the members of her community. She strongly believes that "we are all what we eat."

Her dairy farm is certified through Animal Welfare Approved and Buy Better Dairy. She says, "Every animal has the best possible life here, that is my responsibility as a farmer." The farm's cows are registered Jerseys, living an open space barn life with intensive rotational grazing. Because this is a grass-based dairy, animals are not fed fermented feed or silage, which can give dairy products an off flavor; all of Jersey Girls' products have a clean, distinct taste.

Milk is pasteurized and bottled on-site, and locals come to the dairy to buy raw milk. The processed milk is sold to area retailers, co-ops, restaurants, farmers' markets, and at the dairy's farm store. Jersey Girls' milk is high in butterfat, and some customers say the products remind them of how dairy used to taste. They also churn butter on the farm in small batches, then it's packed by hand.

Visitors are always welcome to stop by the farm store to buy comfort food that's ready to heat and eat. Items such as lasagna, macaroni and cheese, quiche, and pies are some of the mouthwatering offerings; all of them start with the freshest ingredients from the dairy. The store also sells quark, a fresh, soft, versatile cheese that is wonderful for making cheesecake, stuffed shells, or as a spread for toast or bagels. The eggs sold at the store come from the farm's free-range chickens, which are fed GMO-free feed and are very popular with visitors. There is also a large selection of the farm's meats, such as veal chops, cutlets, Jersey Boyz Vermont Veal Sausage and ground beef available.

Bull calves are raised for their rose veal, while heifer calves keep a balanced herd. The bull calves drink milk from free-feeders and eat hay. Once they weigh 400 pounds, around four months of age, they are taken to certified humane slaughterhouses, and the meat is sold to individual customers and chefs. Area chefs have come to realize that a calf raised on milk and in pasture in a stress-free environment is far superior to any meat they've had in the past. As veal produced in this way is considered a specialty item, it serves as a valuable source of farm income.

Lisa feels that there is a "veal renaissance" occurring in Vermont. With more and more foodies falling in love with the flavor of her rose-colored veal, it's no surprise that Jersey Girls veal products are appearing on the menus of high-end restaurants in Vermont as well as in New York. Other delicious farm items are available online with the option of overnight shipping. It's not surprising that the natural flavors of the farm's products shine through as they adhere to the farm's motto, Dairy Done Right, combined with Lisa's philosophy: Pure, Clean, and Simple.

Baked Frittata with Baby Spinach, Roasted Red Peppers, and Quark Cheese

Serves 6–8

Vermont quark cheese is the newest addition to Jersey Girls Dairy. Quark is a delicious, soft and mild fresh cheese made from pasteurized skimmed milk. It is a delicious substitute for ricotta, cream cheese, sour cream, or yogurt. This incredibly versatile cheese is handmade in small batches in the processing room at Jersey Girls Dairy, and then it's hand packed.

6 large eggs, lightly beaten
½ cup whole milk
Salt and freshly ground black pepper
½ cup packed baby spinach, cut into bite-size pieces
⅓ cup packed jarred organic roasted red peppers, drained and thinly sliced
½ cup fresh quark cheese at room temperature
½ teaspoon freshly minced basil
½ teaspoon freshly minced thyme
½ teaspoon freshly minced rosemary

Preheat the oven to 400 degrees Fahrenheit. Lightly grease a 9-inch pie pan with butter and set aside.

In a medium bowl, whisk together the eggs, milk, and salt and pepper to taste.

Spread the spinach and red peppers evenly over the bottom of the prepared pie pan. Pour the egg mixture over the vegetables. Arrange the cheese and herbs evenly over the top of the egg mixture.

Bake until the frittata is puffed and golden brown, about 20 minutes. Let rest for 10 minutes, then use a rubber spatula to loosen the frittata from the pie pan and carefully slide it onto a cutting board. Season with salt and pepper to taste. Slice into wedges using a serrated knife. Serve warm with fresh fruit or a tossed green salad.

Recipe from Jersey Girls Dairy & Farm Store

Organic Multicolored Beet Hash

Serves 4 as a main course with an egg; or 6 as a side dish

"This hearty, earthy dish is a local and staff favorite, especially during the colder months. Serve with your favorite style of eggs and a side of toast, if desired." —*Bonnie Paris Ott, manager, Freighthouse Market & Café*

- 3 large (about 2 pounds) assorted colored beets, scrubbed, tops and ends removed, diced into ½-inch pieces
- 1¾ teaspoons salt, divided
- 1 large (about 14 ounces) potato, such as Yukon Gold, peeled, and diced into ½-inch pieces
- ¼ cup extra virgin olive oil
- 1 large onion, peeled, and diced into ½-inch pieces
- 1 tablespoon garlic powder
- 1 tablespoon dried basil
- 1 teaspoon onion powder
- 1 teaspoon freshly ground black pepper
- 2 teaspoons finely grated lemon zest (preferably from an unwaxed lemon)
- Fresh minced parsley for garnish

Combine the beets and ½ teaspoon salt in a large pot of water and bring to a boil over medium-high heat. Reduce the heat to a simmer and cook until the beets are just fork tender, about 20 minutes. Drain the beets in a colander and transfer to a large bowl.

In a separate pot of water, combine the potatoes and ¼ teaspoon salt, and bring to a boil over medium-high heat. Reduce the heat to a simmer and cook until the potatoes are just fork tender, about 10 minutes. Drain the potatoes in a colander and transfer to the bowl with the beets.

Heat the oil in a large skillet over medium heat. Add the onions and cook, stirring occasionally, until light golden brown, about 10 minutes. Reduce the heat to medium-low. Add the beets and potatoes, garlic powder, basil, onion powder, the remaining 1 teaspoon salt, and 1 teaspoon pepper, and cook, stirring occasionally, until heated through, about 5 minutes. Adjust seasonings with salt and pepper to taste. Sprinkle with lemon zest and garnish with parsley.

Recipe from Freighthouse Market & Café
Photograph by Oliver Pairini

PROFILE

Sweet Simone's

Folks travel from near and far to sample the fabulous baked goods from Sweet Simone's Bakery in Richmond, Vermont. Owner Lisa Curtis specializes in cakes for all occasions, along with a variety of pastries, pies, bagels and muffins, cookies, and cupcakes complemented by an ever-changing selection of beautifully crafted treats.

Everything is made from scratch, including artisanal breads, using the best quality local and organic ingredients whenever possible. The bakery's consistent level of excellence makes each visit a mouthwatering adventure that keeps visitors coming back for more!

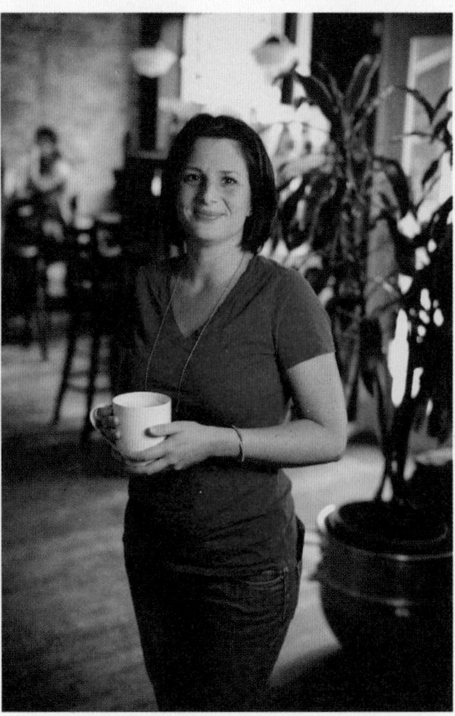

Photograph by Brent Harrewyn

Lemon Poppy Seed Muffins

Makes 24 muffins

"Our lemon poppy seed muffin is a favorite amongst children and adults. Its soft texture and tart flavor can be a perfect accompaniment to any breakfast or brunch, as well as stand on its own for an on-the-go snack. If you want to wow your guests, core the muffin and stuff it with lemon curd . . . you won't regret it!" *—Lisa Curtis, owner, Sweet Simone's*

2¾ cups all-purpose flour
2½ teaspoons aluminum-free baking powder
1¼ teaspoons baking soda
4¾ tablespoons poppy seeds
½ teaspoon salt
1¼ cups buttermilk
4 tablespoons finely grated lemon zest (preferably from unwaxed lemons)
¼ cup freshly squeezed lemon juice
2½ teaspoons pure vanilla extract
1 cup and 3 tablespoons unsalted butter, softened
1½ cups organic cane sugar
5 eggs, yolks and whites separated

Adjust the oven rack to the middle-lower part of the oven. Preheat the oven to 350 degrees Fahrenheit. Spray two 12-cup muffin tins generously with nonstick cooking spray or line with paper liners. Set aside.

In a large bowl, whisk together the flour, baking powder, baking soda, poppy seeds, and salt. Set aside.

In a medium bowl, combine the buttermilk, lemon zest and juice, and vanilla. Set aside.

In the bowl of a stand mixer, cream together the butter and sugar on medium speed until smooth. Add the egg yolks, scraping down the sides of the bowl as needed and beating just until smooth.

Add the dry ingredients alternately with the wet ingredients to the batter mixture, ending with the dry ingredients, and mix until smooth.

Using an electric mixer, beat the egg whites until soft peaks form. Fold the egg whites into the batter. Do not overmix. Fill the prepared muffin cups three-quarters full with batter.

Bake the muffins until the tops are golden brown and a toothpick inserted into the center of a muffin comes out clean, about 20 minutes. Allow the muffins to cool in the pan for 10 minutes before removing. Transfer the muffins to a cooling rack and allow them to cool until slightly warm.

Recipe from Sweet Simone's

Organic Pumpkin Seed Chipotle Crackers

Makes 2 large (about 10-inch x 12-inch) crackers

"I enjoy seeds! In crackers or cereal, on breads, and in cookies. These thin, crisp, crackers, reminiscent of lavash bread, are spicy, seedy, and yummy on their own or with toppings. Feel free to add or reduce the chipotle to your liking." —*Elizabeth Feinberg, owner, Vermont Amber Organic Toffee*

¾ cup organic raw green pumpkin seeds
4 tablespoons organic unsalted butter, cold and cut into small pieces
¾ teaspoon chipotle powder
¾ teaspoon smoked sea salt
1 cup organic whole wheat pastry or all-purpose flour
1 cup grated cheddar cheese or Monterey Jack cheese, or a combination
3 tablespoons water, or as needed

Preheat the oven to 375 degrees Fahrenheit.

To toast the pumpkin seeds: Place the seeds in a clean, dry 10-inch skillet and toast over medium heat, stirring often, until golden, about 5 minutes. Transfer to a bowl and allow them to cool. Transfer to a zipper lock bag, seal the bag, then lightly crush the seeds with a rolling pin. Set aside.

Place the butter, chipotle powder, and salt in a food processor and pulse for 1 minute. Add the flour, cheese, and water, then process until the dough starts to form, adding additional water as needed. Add the pumpkin seeds and process until the dough is fully combined.

Turn the dough out onto a clean, lightly floured work surface and form into two disks. Wrap the dough disks in plastic wrap and refrigerate for 1 hour.

Place a piece of parchment paper, large enough to fit on a half-sheet-size baking sheet, on a clean work surface. Turn the dough out onto the piece of the parchment paper. Top with another sheet of parchment paper and flatten the dough with your hands. Next, roll out the dough to ¼ inch thick, then carefully place the dough, along with the parchment paper, on a baking sheet. Repeat with the second dough disk. Carefully remove the top piece of parchment paper, leaving the bottom piece under the dough. Bake until the crackers are golden brown, about 12 minutes. Let cool completely, then break the crackers into desired sizes. Serve with chèvre or cheddar cheese, if desired.

Recipe from Vermont Amber Organic Toffee
Photograph by Oliver Parini

PROFILE

Buffalo Mountain Food Co-operative & Café

The Buffalo Mountain Food Co-operative stands firmly behind the non-GMO movement, mirroring this belief in their support of the local farms and farmers who utilize this practice. Opening its doors in 1975, the co-op moved several times before settling at its present location in the heart of downtown Hardwick, Vermont. The not-for-profit co-operative is member-owned. This membership entitles those folks who belong to the co-op shopping privileges at the facility with access to a large selection of locally grown foods and products. The folks at Buffalo Mountain like to say that the food they sell is grown, or made, "with the health and well-being of our planet and its inhabitants in mind."

To be able to offer items at the lowest prices possible, members are directly involved in the daily workings of the store, which helps to defray operating costs. Their mission is to offer "Food for People, not for Profit." To achieve this goal, every effort is made to make membership accessible to all interested parties that might benefit from this worthy venture.

The co-operative carries a variety of high-quality products that support local providers. These fairly priced items must be produced in an environmentally safe and socially conscious manner before they will even be considered as merchandise for the co-op. Preference is given to organic products that are grown locally or regionally. Organically grown means without genetically modified organisms, hormones, chemical additives, or artificial preservatives or flavorings. Items that are certified Fair Trade, or are produced by other cooperatives, move to the top of the list as well. The manner in which products are packaged is also taken into account, with close attention paid to whether an item's outer covering is recycled or recyclable in nature. The issue of humanely raised farm animals is always considered when purchasing meats, eggs, and dairy products.

Along with food products, a wide assortment of other items is also available. Debra Wilson is in charge of buying the co-op's wine and beer, focusing on Vermont and regional offerings. Members will find a home goods and wellness section, along with an area dedicated to pet supplies. Items are selected with health and safety factors in mind. Those searching for a gift will find something here; there are intriguing selections from local writers, crafters, and artists, with a variety of imports from Fair Trade providers.

Tucked away on the building's second floor is the co-op's café, managed by chef Miranda Hunt and Debra Wilson. They work with food produced by many of the same farmers who supply the co-op downstairs. Loving to cook for people, these able chefs explain, "Working in the café is a little like dinner parties all the time." With a wide spectrum of products available for purchase, and a comfortable café to satisfy one's hunger, the Buffalo Mountain Food Co-operative lends new meaning to the phrase "one-stop shopping."

Café Quiche

Serves 8

"As you can see, there are endless variations for our café quiche. Much is dependent upon what we have available and who is making the quiche. Our crust recipe is from a pie and pastry cookbook; however, feel free to make your own or use a high-quality, store-bought crust."
—Debra Wilson, manager, Buffalo Mountain Food Co-operative & Café

Crust
9-inch pie crust, homemade or high-quality store-bought in a disposable pie plate

Filling
2 medium leeks, white and light green parts only, trimmed and rinsed thoroughly
2 tablespoons butter, divided
½ pound shiitake mushrooms, cleaned, stems removed and thinly sliced
Salt and freshly ground black pepper
6 large organic eggs, lightly beaten
1½ cups organic heavy cream or milk
1 teaspoon fresh minced thyme
½ cup (2 ounces) shredded Gruyère cheese
1 4-ounce log fresh goat cheese, crumbled
8 multicolored cherry tomatoes, halved

Preheat the oven to 375 degrees Fahrenheit. If making a homemade pie crust, prepare according to recipe directions.

Using a mandoline slicer or sharp knife, cut the leeks into paper-thin slices.

Heat 1 tablespoon of butter in a large skillet over medium heat, add the leeks and cook, stirring occasionally, until tender, about 10 minutes. Transfer to a bowl and set aside. Heat the remaining 1 tablespoon of butter and add the mushrooms and cook, stirring occasionally, until soft and tender, about 5 minutes. Transfer to the bowl with the leeks and toss until well combined. Season with salt and pepper to taste.

In a large bowl, whisk together the eggs, cream, thyme, and salt and pepper to taste.

Spread ¼ cup of the Gruyère cheese over the bottom of the pie crust. Spread half of the leek mixture evenly over the crust. Carefully pour half of the egg mixture over the vegetables. Sprinkle with half of the goat cheese. Repeat with the remaining ingredients, ending with the goat cheese. Arrange the tomatoes evenly over the top. Place the quiche on a baking sheet and bake until the egg mixture is set in the center, about 50 minutes. Let cool for 15 minutes, then cut into wedges and serve.

Variations: You can vary the vegetables and herbs according to the season and what is in your refrigerator, such as onion, garlic, asparagus, broccoli or cauliflower florets, artichoke hearts, peppers, Swiss chard, and basil. Feel free to experiment with other cheeses, such as Parmigiano-Reggiano, blue cheese, Swiss cheese, and provolone cheese.

From Buffalo Mountain Food Co-operative & Café
Photograph by Oliver Parini

Farmco
STOLTZFUS

PROFILE

Meadows Bee Farm

Meadows Bee Farm in Windham, Vermont, is a sustainable homestead that embraces earth-friendly farming practices. Owner Leigh Merinoff is the creator of Leigh's Bees, an artisanal line of body creams and tinctures that are made using herbs long known to heal the skin and body. The herbs used in her products are grown on the farm.

The farm hosts a school-to-farm program that encourages local students to visit and learn farming and gardening techniques. The Young Farmers Badge Program teaches children how to raise livestock and grow food, awarding participants badges as they learn and master certain practices. An intern program invites folks from all over the world to live on the farm for anywhere from three weeks to a year as part of its agricultural community.

Housed on the property is an agricultural library that contains more than 2,000 books. These books contain subject matter on progressive agriculture, theory, science, and biodynamic research. The library is open to the public, and visitors can borrow any book that may be of interest.

Visitors are encouraged to take part in a small public arts program. A ceramic studio invites adults and children to join in learning hand-building and wheel techniques. There is a craft barn with an herb drying room, as well as space to create wool handicrafts, such as carding, spinning, and felting. A blacksmith shop offers insight into this uncommon occupation.

Leigh Merinoff is a diverse biodynamic farmer. The raw milk from her small dairy is a large part of what the farm produces. Hives and honey bees, heritage breed livestock, gardens, and orchards of heirloom apples and pears are all part of her earth-friendly community. It is Merinoff's belief that the programs and practices offered at Meadows Bee Farm will in some small way help to bring about ecological, social, and economic sustainability.

Farm Yogurt Cheese

Makes 6 logs

This cheese is delicious by itself, as a spread for crackers, a filling for lasagna or stuffed pasta shells, or for a great twist on an old classic—cheese-laced beef meatballs.

½ gallon raw milk
½ tablespoon yogurt culture
1 teaspoon salt
Freshly ground black pepper

Heat the raw milk in a large saucepan over medium heat until it reaches 110 degrees Fahrenheit. Add the yogurt culture, stirring to distribute it evenly through the milk, cover, and place immediately on a warm heating pad or seed starter mat. Wrap a thick, warm blanket around the saucepan and let it sit until the milk turns into yogurt, about 7 hours. **Note:** The side of the pot under the blanket will need to be checked often with a thermometer so an accurate temperature can be maintained. Since heating pads vary in their heat output, you may need to switch the temperature settings to maintain the temperature as close to 110 degrees Fahrenheit as possible.

Line a large strainer with a tea towel and place it over a large bowl. Carefully pour the newly made yogurt into the lined strainer. Tie the edges of the tea towel and suspend it from a sturdy kitchen faucet or a hook overnight to drain into a large bowl.

The next day, stir in the salt until well combined. Form into six 4-inch-long by 1-inch-wide logs. Put the pepper onto a small plate with a flat surface. Take a cheese log and roll it into the pepper, gently patting the spice into the log to coat. Repeat with the remaining cheese logs. Place the cheese logs on a large plate, cover with plastic wrap, and refrigerate.

Recipe from Meadows Bee Farm

Tip: Don't discard the reserve liquid in the bowl; you can freeze it and add it to soups or smoothies.

Note: There are two ways to make a yogurt culture: from a few tablespoons of high-quality, store-bought plain yogurt, such a Butterworks Farm organic plain yogurt, or with a yogurt starter powder.

Cheese Coating Variations: Try Herbes de Provence, red pepper flakes, paprika, or even a light dusting of cocoa powder.

CHAPTER 2

SANDWICHES, SPREADS, AND VINAIGRETTES

Oven-Roasted Organic Pulled Pork Sandwiches with Spicy Apple Cider Vinegar Slaw

Serves 6–8

The recipe makes more barbecue sauce than needed for the pork. Store any leftovers in an airtight container in the refrigerator for up to 2 weeks.

Dry Rub

1 garlic head (about 8 cloves), peeled and coarsely chopped
4 tablespoons ground cumin seeds
1½ teaspoons extra virgin olive oil, divided
1½ teaspoons freshly ground black pepper
2¼ teaspoons coarse salt
1½ teaspoons chili powder

1 bone-in organic pork roast (about 3½ pounds), preferably shoulder or Boston butt, at room temperature

Spicy Apple Cider Slaw

¾ cup mayonnaise, homemade or store-bought
2 tablespoons organic, unfiltered apple cider vinegar
2 tablespoons extra virgin olive oil
1 teaspoon coarse salt
Freshly ground black pepper
2 pounds cabbage, such as red, green, or Napa, shredded
½ small red onion, thinly sliced
1 large jalapeño, seeded and thinly sliced

Barbecue Sauce

1½ cups homemade or high-quality store-bought ketchup
¼ cup packed organic dark brown sugar
2 tablespoons molasses
2 medium garlic cloves, minced or finely grated
¼ cup organic, unfiltered apple cider vinegar
2 teaspoons sweet or hot paprika
1 teaspoon freshly ground black pepper
1 teaspoon dry mustard powder
⅛ teaspoon cayenne pepper, optional

8 buns, such as coriander buns or artisanal hamburger buns
Pickles, optional

To make the dry rub: Mince the garlic in a food processor. Add the cumin and 1 teaspoon olive oil and pulse until combined. Add the pepper, salt, chili powder, and the remaining ½ teaspoon of olive oil and pulse until a sticky paste forms, adding additional oil as needed. Place the pork in a 9-by-13-inch baking dish. Using your hands or a small spatula, evenly apply the rub on all sides of the roast; loosely cover with foil, making sure the foil does not touch the rub, and allow to marinate for 1 hour at room temperature.

To make the pulled pork: Preheat the oven to 250 degrees Fahrenheit. Roast the pork, covered loosely with foil, in the oven until the meat is fork tender and an instant-read thermometer inserted into the thickest part of the meat reads 185 degrees Fahrenheit, about 6½ hours.

While the meat is roasting, make the spicy apple cider slaw. In a small bowl, whisk together the mayonnaise, apple cider vinegar, olive oil, salt, and black pepper to taste. Place the cabbage, red onion, and jalapeño in a large bowl and toss with the dressing until well coated. Adjust seasonings with salt and pepper to taste. Cover and refrigerate for at least 1 hour before serving.

Once cooked, allow the meat to rest for 30 minutes. While the meat is resting, make the barbecue sauce. In a medium saucepan, combine the ketchup, brown sugar, molasses, garlic, vinegar, paprika, black pepper, dry mustard, and cayenne pepper, if using, until well combined. Bring to a simmer over medium-low heat and cook, stirring constantly, for about 10 minutes. Adjust seasoning with salt and pepper to taste.

While the meat is still warm but cool enough to handle, use your fingers or two forks to shred the meat into pieces, discarding any large pieces of fat or bones. Place the meat in a large bowl with two-thirds of the sauce, tossing until well combined, adding additional sauce as needed, to taste.

To assemble: Place some of the pork on the bottom of each bun, then spoon some of the slaw on top. Place the remaining buns on top and serve with pickles on the side, if desired, and additional barbecue sauce.

Recipe from Full Moon Farm, Inc.
Photograph by Olive Parini

The Village Roost Café & Marketplace

Isabelle and Rogger Alvarado are the owners of The Village Roost Café & Marketplace in Wilmington, Vermont. The couple raised their family in Connecticut, traveling to Vermont with their children every winter weekend to go skiing. As the years passed, the Alvarados saw that there was a need for a coffee shop in the Wilmington area. Wanting to fill this void in 2013, they purchased the building where The Village Roost is now located. Because of the serious flooding and water damage caused by Hurrican Irene in 2011, the structure required extensive repairs before they could open for business.

Their eldest daughter, Britny, and her husband Sam, who were living in New Zealand at that time, enthusiastically moved back to the United States to help with the project. Stripping the walls down to the studs and replacing the electricity and plumbing significantly altered the timeline for opening. The business opened its doors on April 3, 2015, and is now buzzing with satisfied patrons as Britny and her husband happily manage the venture.

Britny's degree in nutrition and food sciences and environmental studies from the University of Vermont, along with Sam's experience working at an organic grocery store, have helped to foster an enduring enthusiasm for healthy, pure foods. Their interest in flavors from around the world has inspired some of the café's culinary creations, such as its New Zealand meat pies. Both Britny and Sam demonstrate their passion for nourishing food by using organic, non-GMO, and sustainable products in the café's everyday offerings, always supporting their philosophy of eating fresh, local, and healthy.

The Village Roost is tucked away in the center of historic Wilmington. It offers a rotating menu that features soups, salads, and savory sandwiches, such as the Green Mountain—made with caramelized onions and maple balsamic dressing, it never seems to disappoint. The restaurant's organic coffee and espresso choices adds a warming touch to anyone's day. Everything is made by hand in small batches. The ingredients used are organic, as well as GMO-, antibiotic, and hormone-free. They never use preservatives. The couple buys locally sourced products, knowing that by doing so they are helping the local economy.

The café offers a choice of dining areas. The back porch with its brick fireplace allows guests to enjoy the pleasures of being outdoors. Inside, visitors find a comfy living room space with a welcoming sofa where they can relax and sip a variety of coffees and espresso. Those who opt for more conventional surroundings will enjoy the cozy café with its free Wi-Fi and board games.

The folks at The Village Roost are extremely grateful for all the support they have received from those in the community. As a new business, they realize that building positive relationships between chefs and farmers supports Vermont and its organic and non-GMO movement. It is their belief that by helping small organic farms to survive they are also enabling the organic movement to spread and flourish.

Green Mountain Sandwich with Maple Balsamic Vinaigrette

Makes 4 sandwiches

The earthy caramelized onions and maple balsamic vinaigrette add a subtle sweetness to the sandwich. The peppery flavor of the arugula provides the perfect balance alongside the tart apple slices and roast turkey. This dressing makes more than you will need for the sandwiches. Use the leftovers as a marinade for chicken or as a dressing for local greens.

Maple Balsamic Vinaigrette
Makes about 3 cups
⅔ cup high-quality balsamic vinegar
½ cup pure maple syrup
1 tablespoon Dijon mustard (equal parts grainy and smooth, combined)
1¼ cups sunflower oil, preferably non-GMO
Salt and freshly ground black pepper

Caramelized Onions
Makes about 1 cup
1 tablespoon unsalted butter
1 pound yellow or white onions, halved and sliced into ⅛-inch-thick half-rounds
Salt and freshly ground black pepper

Green Mountain Sandwich
4 slices of Vermont cheddar cheese
2½ ounces thinly sliced roasted turkey, for each sandwich, homemade or store-bought* **(see directions on page 233)**
1 Granny Smith apple, cored and cut into ⅛-inch slices
1¼ cups packed arugula
8 slices of bread, such as rye or multigrain, toasted

Pickles, optional

To make the dressing: Place the vinegar, maple syrup, and mustards in a blender and pulse until combined. While the machine is running, slowly add the oil until a creamy vinaigrette forms. Season with salt and pepper to taste. Set aside.

Note: If you are roasting the turkey yourself, caramelize the onions while the turkey is roasting in the oven.

To caramelize the onions: Melt the butter in a large skillet over medium heat. Add the onions and cook for 2 minutes, stirring frequently. Reduce the heat to low and continue to cook, stirring occasionally, until the onions are soft and caramelized, about 60 minutes. Season with salt and pepper to taste. Remove the onions from the heat and set aside.

To assemble the sandwich: Evenly divide the cheese on 4 slices of bread; top with turkey, apple slices, caramelized onions, and arugula. Drizzle each with the maple balsamic vinaigrette to taste. Season with salt and pepper to taste. Top with the remaining bread slices. Serve with a pickle on the side, if desired.

Variation:

Note: You will need to brine the turkey for 3 days before you intend to serve the sandwiches.

Brine

4 cups vegetable broth
½ cup kosher salt
½ cup organic cane sugar
¼ lemon, cut into thin slices
½ tablespoon molasses
1 pound local antibiotic- and hormone-free turkey breast

To brine the turkey breast: Combine the vegetable broth, salt, sugar, lemon slices, and molasses in a medium stockpot and bring to a boil over medium-high heat. Remove from the heat and let cool on the countertop for 30 minutes, then refrigerate until the brine is cold, about 30 minutes. Place the turkey breast in the brine, cover, and refrigerate for 3 days, turning the meat halfway through brining. Remove the turkey breast from the brine and pat dry with paper towels, discarding the remaining brine. Preheat the oven to 375 degrees Fahrenheit. Cook the meat until the internal temperature reaches 165 degrees Fahrenheit, about 70 minutes. Allow the turkey to rest for 15 minutes, then thinly slice the meat, as needed, for sandwiches.

Recipe from The Village Roost Café & Marketplace
Photograph iStockphoto.com

Footprint Farm, LLC

Nestled in a valley between the Hogback Mountains and Lewis Creek, surrounded by forested hillsides, lies Footprint Farm. The 10-acre parcel is located in Starksboro, Vermont, about 35 minutes south of Burlington. It is a diversified CSA farm owned by Taylor Hutchison and Jake Mendell.

The couple met at a little farm in California when they were working as outdoor educators. Jake grew up in Vermont and traveled to California after studying health and nutrition in college. Taylor, who's from central California, took undergraduate courses in public health and decided to go into food education after working at a public health organization in Boston for a year. While in California, they first taught children and milked goats before moving on to intern at a second educational farm in the state. During this internship, Taylor learned the CSA and vegetable production side of the farm, while Jake focused on animal husbandry skills. Both farms were certified organic, and the couple is very much in agreement with the movement's principles and methods.

When an amazing land opportunity became available in Vermont, the young couple decided to move east to follow their farming vision. Now they grow 2 acres of certified organic vegetables and flowers and raise pastured egg chickens. They also sell pork and a modest amount of maple syrup, both of which are not certified, although they are produced using the same organic principles. Along with providing vegetables, eggs, and meat to the CSA shareholders, some of the products are sold at local farmers' markets. The produce grown is most often determined by the team's own personal preferences. The heart of the farm is its diversified CSA program. Because of the variety of produce grown, there is an ability to be flexible if a certain crop doesn't do well during the growing season.

The animals help with mowing pastures. Chickens are rotated every four to seven days so they have access to fresh areas of grass and fertilize the fields evenly. The pigs are moved as often as the chickens, but at the edge of the fields so they can keep honeysuckle under control and clear out the brush from around trees. The pigs are fed leftover produce from the farmers' markets, or those offerings that weren't nice enough to sell. In the process, the pigs turn what they have eaten into fertilizer, which enriches the farm's soil. The porkers also eat organic grain.

Taylor and Jake make a good team; he manages the animals, monitors soil health and fertility plans, and keeps the farm's buildings and equipment in working order. She grows beautiful flowers and keeps track of finances and planting schedules. They both organize events for the Vermont Young Farmers' Coalition. This group helps identify and address barriers that young farmers face, such as land access and student loan forgiveness. The coalition hosts events and workshops for young farmers and works with organizations such as Rural Vermont, which addresses issues affecting farmers at the state level.

Jake and Taylor agree that their commitment to organic farming comes from a deep desire to contribute to the long-term health and viability of their farm's soil and the people for whom they grow the food. These two young farmers believe that going through the organic certification process lends a legitimacy to the organic farming movement, thereby giving it a voice on the national level. They realize that they have the ability to make a difference in the future of organic farming, and through this knowledge comes empowerment!

Meatball Banh Mi with Maple Sriracha Mayonnaise (Vietnamese Sandwich)

Makes 6 sandwiches

This recipe requires some advance planning; start the recipe 7 days before you intend to make the sandwich. The sweetness from the maple syrup balances the heat from the red jalapeños. The maple sriracha will keep for up to 6 months in an airtight container in the refrigerator.

Maple Sriracha

Makes 1 pint

1½ pounds fresh red jalapeño peppers, stems removed with tops intact

6 medium garlic cloves, peeled and coarsely chopped

3 tablespoons pure maple syrup, preferably dark robust

¾ tablespoon fish sauce, such as nam pla or nuoc nam

½ teaspoon salt

½ cup distilled white vinegar

Process the peppers and garlic in a food processor until minced. With the processor running, slowly add the maple syrup, fish sauce, and salt until combined. Adjust seasonings with maple syrup and salt, if desired. Pour mixture into a sanitized quart-size mason jar, cover, and let sit at room temperature.

Check jar daily for fermentation activity; little bubbles will start to form in the mixture, about 4 days. Once fermentation begins, stir daily until the mixture stops rising in volume, an additional 3 days.

Transfer the mixture to a blender. Add the vinegar and process until smooth. Place a fine-mesh strainer over a nonreactive bowl and carefully pour the mixture through the fine-mesh strainer, pushing all the liquid and as much pulp as possible through with the back of a spoon.

Transfer the sriracha to a small saucepan and bring to a boil, stirring frequently, over medium-high heat. Reduce the heat and simmer, stirring often until the sauce thickens enough to coat the back of a spoon, about 25 minutes. Allow the sriracha to cool, then transfer it to an airtight container and refrigerate until ready to use.

Creamy Maple Sriracha Mayonnaise

Makes ¾ cup

½ cup high-quality mayonnaise, homemade or store-bought
2 scallions or green onions, minced
1 tablespoon maple sriracha **(see recipe on page 37)**
2 teaspoons fresh lime juice
½ tablespoon finely grated lime zest (preferably from an unwaxed lime)
Salt

In a small bowl, whisk together the mayonnaise, scallions, maple sriracha, lime juice, and lime zest. Season with salt to taste. Adjust seasonings with additional lime juice and zest if desired. Cover and refrigerate, up to 1 day, until ready to use.

Pickled Vegetables

Makes about 4 cups

¼ cup rice vinegar
3 tablespoons white vinegar
1 tablespoon fresh lime juice
3 tablespoons organic cane sugar
1 teaspoon kosher salt
2 cups (2 large carrots) peeled and coarsely grated carrots
2 cups (about 6) peeled and coarsely grated daikon radish
¼ cup chopped fresh cilantro

In a medium bowl, whisk together the vinegars, lime juice, sugar, and salt. Add the carrots, radishes, and cilantro, tossing until well combined. Let stand at room temperature, stirring occasionally, for 1 hour.

Meatballs

Makes about 18 meatballs

1 pound ground pork
1 egg, lightly beaten
¼ cup minced fresh basil leaves
2 garlic cloves, minced
1 teaspoon finely grated ginger
3 scallions or green onions, finely chopped
1 tablespoon fish sauce, such as nam pla or nuoc nam
1 tablespoon maple sriracha **(see recipe on page 37)**
2 teaspoons organic tamari soy sauce
1 teaspoon freshly ground black pepper
Sesame oil

2 baguettes, cut into 6-inch lengths
Fresh sprigs of cilantro, to taste

Lightly grease 1 rimmed baking sheet. Set aside.

In a large bowl, combine the pork, egg, basil, garlic, ginger, scallions, fish sauce, maple sriracha, soy sauce, and pepper until just combined. Adjust seasonings with additional maple sriracha, if desired. Do not overmix.

Heat 1 tablespoon of the oil in a large skillet over medium-high heat until hot, but not smoking. Using a ⅛ cup measure, scoop and drop the meatballs, in batches, directly into the skillet and cook, turning carefully with a spatula, until browned on all sides and cooked through, about 7 minutes for each batch. With a slotted spoon, carefully transfer the meatballs onto the prepared baking sheet. Repeat with the remaining meatballs, adding oil as needed.

To assemble sandwiches: Cut each baguette piece horizontally in half, then pull out about half of the soft bread in the center of each piece, leaving approximately a ½-inch-thick shell. Spread some sriracha maple mayonnaise over each bread piece. Using a slotted spoon, divide the pickled vegetables between the sandwiches. Add 3 meatballs to each sandwich. Gently press on the sandwich tops and serve at once.

Note: If you can't find daikon radishes, red radishes can be used as a substitute.

Recipe from Footprint Farm, LLC
Photograph by Oliver Parini

Garlic Scape Kale Pesto

Makes approximately 1 cup

Pesto freezes well and will keep, frozen, for up to 3 months. Remember to omit the cheese if you are planning to freeze your pesto. After defrosting, fold in the cheese right before serving.

¼ cup coarsely chopped unsalted walnuts
½ cup coarsely chopped garlic scapes, firmly packed (approximately 3 garlic scapes)
½ cup coarsely chopped kale, stems and inner ribs removed and discarded, firmly packed
½ cup extra virgin olive oil
¼ cup grated Parmesan cheese, plus more for garnish
Salt and freshly ground black pepper to taste

Process the walnuts, garlic scapes, and kale in a food processor until well combined. While the processor is running, slowly add the oil in a steady stream until well blended, scraping down the sides of the bowl as needed. Add the cheese and blend until the desired texture is achieved. Season with salt and pepper to taste.

Recipe from Health Hero Farm
Photograph by Oliver Parini

Arugula Pesto with Marcona Almonds and Organic White Truffle Oil

Makes approximately 1½ cups

This peppery pesto is delicious brushed on chicken or fish, as a crostini topping, served as a garnish on top of tomato soup, or added as a spread for a decadent twist on the classic grilled cheese sandwich.

1 medium garlic clove, chopped
⅓ cup Marcona almonds, coarsely chopped
2 cups firmly packed arugula leaves, thick stems removed
¼ cup firmly packed basil leaves
½ cup extra virgin olive oil, or as needed
2 tablespoons organic truffle oil, plus extra for drizzling
Zest and juice of ½ lemon, preferably unwaxed
½ cup finely grated Parmigiano-Reggiano cheese, plus more for garnish
Kosher salt and freshly ground black pepper to taste

Process the garlic and almonds in a food processor until minced. Add the arugula, basil, oils, and lemon zest and juice, then continue to process until the desired texture is achieved, scraping down the sides of the bowl as needed.

Spoon the pesto into a decorative bowl and fold in the cheese. Season with salt and pepper to taste. Drizzle truffle oil over the top and sprinkle with cheese, if desired. Serve.

Recipe from Tracey Medeiros
Photograph by Tracey Medeiros

Arugula

This small-leaved plant is also known as salad rocket, roquette, Italian cress, and racola. It is a member of the Brassicaceae family, commonly known as the mustards. The group includes broccoli, Brussels sprouts, cabbage, mustard, radish, and collard greens. This versatile plant was brought to America by British colonists, but didn't gain popularity until the 1990s. Arugula is available year-round at grocery stores and may be found wrapped in bunches with the roots still attached, or in cellophane packaging labeled baby arugula. Look for smaller leaves, as they tend to be milder in flavor; those that are left on the plant for too long become bitter in taste. Arugula has a peppery flavor, with a trace of nuts and mustard, so if you are a mild iceberg lettuce fan it may give your taste buds a tangy surprise. I usually mix arugula with other salad greens to lend a hint of gusto to my leafy creations.

When shopping for arugula, avoid packaged products with flowers that are still attached to the stems; their leaves can be tough and bitter. The flowers, pods, and seeds are all edible. Before putting arugula into your refrigerator's vegetable bin, be sure to sort through the leaves, throwing out those that are yellow, wilted, or bruised. The vegetable bin should be set at high humidity. The greens are at their best if used within 3–4 days of purchase.

Wash your greens before using by placing the leaves in a container of cold water and swishing them back and forth to get rid of any dirt. If the roots are still attached, be certain to trim the stems. Drain well and gently pat dry.

Arugula is considered a vegetable when it is cooked, and an herb if used in small amounts to flavor salads, meats, or pasta sauce. The greens can be used to liven up soups, stews, casseroles, juices, salads, or just simply as a vegetable. Its pungent flavor makes this herb a delightful additive to raw pesto and sauces. For a flavorful alternative, slip some of the young leaves into BLT sandwiches, burgers, grilled cheese, or wraps, then be prepared for rave reviews. Arugula pairs well with citrus, roasted beets, pears, pine nuts, olives, tomatoes, and certain cheeses, such as goat, blue, and Parmigiano-Reggiano.

Arugula is easy to grow in containers, raised box gardens, and window boxes. It does well when space is limited. The plant grows 2–3 feet high and has creamy white four-petal flowers. Leaves are ready to harvest within 40 days of planting. Too much heat causes the leaves to have a bitter flavor, which makes spring and early fall the best time for growing milder tasting leaves. Arugula needs only 3 hours of sunshine a day. Remember to allow some of the flowers to go to seed to be used for your next planting cycle. Pick the leaves as needed, as the plants will continue to produce new ones.

Making more informed decisions about dietary choices has a trickle-down effect, which impacts both health and lifestyle. In the case of arugula, with its high-nutrient profile, the health benefits are impressive, proving that good things do indeed come in small packages. Healthy eating has never tasted so good!

Roasted Delicata Squash and Red Onion Hummus with Roasted Squash Seeds

Makes approximately 4 cups

This hummus recipe has a nice combination of sweet and savory. The roasted delicata squash and red onion adds a great dimension with an earthy sweetness and creamy texture combined with the woody pine flavor from the fresh rosemary leaves.

Hummus

2 delicata squash (about 1 pound each)
3½ tablespoons extra virgin olive oil, divided, plus extra
Salt and freshly ground black pepper
1 pound red onions, peeled, ends removed, and cut into halves
1 teaspoon pure Vermont maple syrup
1 medium garlic clove, peeled and coarsely chopped
1½ cups cooked chickpeas, drained (reserving the juice), and rinsed
2 tablespoons tahini, or as needed
¼ cup fresh lemon juice, or as needed
½ teaspoon fresh chopped rosemary leaves, plus extra for garnish

Roasted Delicata Squash Seeds

Delicata seeds
Extra virgin olive oil
Himalayan fine pink salt and freshly ground black pepper

To make the hummus: Preheat the oven to 450 degrees Fahrenheit. Lightly grease a baking sheet and set aside.

Cut the squash in half lengthwise, then scoop out the seeds and strings, reserving the seeds for later use. Drizzle with 1 tablespoon of the oil, making sure to evenly coat the squash. Place them, cut-side down, on the prepared baking sheet. Season with salt and pepper.

Place the onions in a bowl and toss with ½ tablespoon of the oil, maple syrup, and salt and pepper to taste. Place the onions, cut-side down, on the same baking sheet with the squash. Roast until the squash is fork tender and the onions are caramelized, about 35 minutes. Set aside to cool.

While the squash is cooling, start roasting the squash seeds. Reduce the oven temperature to 325 degrees Fahrenheit. Rinse the squash seeds to remove any stringy pulp. Drain in a colander. Pat the seeds dry with paper towels, then place them in a small bowl and toss with just enough olive oil to coat. Spread the seeds in an even layer on an ungreased baking sheet and season with Himalayan salt and pepper to taste. Bake, stirring occasionally, until the seeds are dry and crunchy, about 25 minutes. Set aside to cool. The seeds can be stored in an airtight container and will keep for up to 1 month .

When the squash is cool enough to handle, coarsely chop, leaving the skins on, or scoop out the flesh and discard the skins. Transfer to a food processor and add the onions, the remaining 2 tablespoons of oil, garlic, chickpeas, tahini, lemon juice, and rosemary. Process until smooth, adding the reserved chickpea juice as needed. Adjust seasonings with lemon juice, olive oil, and salt and pepper. Transfer to a bowl, drizzle with olive oil, and garnish with roasted seeds and rosemary. Serve with crusty bread, vegetables, or crackers.

Recipe from Tracey Medeiros
Photograph by Brent Harrewyn

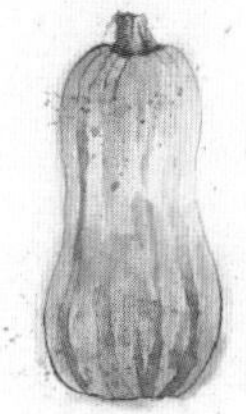

Delicata Squash

Delicata squash, or *Cucurbita pepo*, which includes cucumbers and zucchini, is an heirloom vegetable, meaning that it has been grown from seeds that have been passed down from generation to generation. Growers save the seeds from their best plants, which is why heirloom vegetables are known for their high quality and wonderful flavor.

Delicata was around as far back as the late 1800s, when it was in demand until it became evident that delicata was prone to certain diseases. The squash disappeared until a resurgence of interest in the late 1990s, when Cornell University developed a disease-resistant, high-yield variety called the Cornell Bush Delicata. Thanks to this discovery, delicata squash has returned to grocery stores, farmers' markets, and dining room tables. Other varieties include Sweet Dumpling, which is good, stuffed; Sugar Loaf, an oval-shaped variety; and the very sweet Honeyboat.

The average delicata is 5–6 inches long, 2–3 inches in diameter, and weighs 1–2 pounds. Its flesh is firm and fine-grained, with a color that ranges between yellow and orange. The flavor is much like that of a sweet potato—moist, sweet, and savory.

Delicata is the perfect beginner's squash; it can be baked, boiled, roasted, steamed, pureed, or sautéed. It has a sweet, nutty flavor and makes a delicious addition to soups, salads, and entrees. Baking preserves the nutrients and accentuates the delicata's sweet flavor.

The squash holds its shape well when baked, making it ideal for stuffing with meats, cheeses, fruits, vegetables, or simply a dusting of your favorite seasonings. Just slice the delicata in half lengthwise. (There is no need to peel delicata when baking, broiling, or roasting it.) Scoop out the seeds and membranes. Place the halves, skin side down, in a dish with ½ inch of water, then season or stuff as desired. Cover and bake for 30–45 minutes at 375 degrees Fahrenheit. Because delicata is smaller than other winter squash and has thinner skin, it also cooks faster.

For those who may be gluten intolerant and desire an alternative to wheat pasta, cut the delicata into ribbons or noodle-shaped slices, then top with your favorite tomato sauce or topping. Whether you decide to remove the skin will depend upon your personal preference. Gluten intolerant or not, this makes a wholesome mealtime option.

Nutritionally, delicata is an excellent source of vitamins A and C, fiber, and potassium. It is free of fat and saturated fats, cholesterol, and sodium. One cup of cooked squash contains approximately 100 calories and about 4 grams of sugar.

Fresh delicata squash is best from August to October. You can freeze cooked delicata to enjoy whenever you crave its flavor. Delectable delicata, a winter squash by any other name would not taste as sweet!

Helpful Hint: A grapefruit spoon works well for scooping out the seeds and stringy membranes.

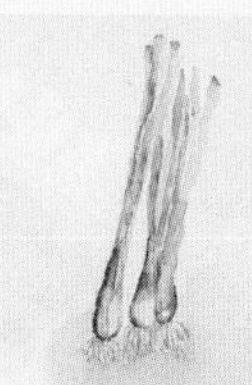

Ramps

A tiny harbinger of spring, the ramp, also known as a wild leek, pokes its leafy head out of the ground anytime from mid-March to early April, depending upon the region. Ramps are one of the first wild edibles to ripen every year. The ramp is native to North America, its name coming from the word "rams," or "ramson," an Elizabethan term meaning wild garlic.

Ramps resemble lily of the valley. They usually have two or three bright green leaves that give off the scent of garlic when cut or broken. A small white bulb, which grows below the surface of the soil, is attached to a stem with deep purple or burgundy tints. The entire plant is edible, with some folks opting to eat it raw. A word of advice: ramps have a pungent onion flavor, so you might want to avoid close contact with friends and family while snacking on these delights.

High in vitamins A and C, some people believe that ramps are effective in fighting colds and the flu. Ramps have the same capacity to reduce cholesterol as garlic. Mountain folk in Appalachia swear by their healing powers. Ramps are a member of the allium family, which includes onions, chives, and leeks.

Over the last twenty years, the demand for ramps has greatly increased, due in part to cooking shows and upscale foodie magazines, which have extolled the culinary delights of this plant. Chefs in big cities give this *Allium tricoccum* star status on their menus, increasing its popularity.

If you're interested in gathering your own ramps, here are a few helpful hints. Ramps like forested terrain that is shady and sandy, and they are often found near rivers and streams. They often grow on the north side of embankments in small clumps. Tear off a leaf and you will be sure to recognize the ramp by its distinctive onion, garlicky smell. Remember to always positively identify any wild edible before ingesting it.

After harvesting, use the ramps quickly. The leaves can be refrigerated and will last 3–4 days before they begin to wilt. They have a stronger flavor than the bulb. Ramps can be used in place of onions and garlic; just keep in mind that they are considerably stronger in taste so use a smaller amount when cooking. Add them raw to salads or sandwiches, or sauté them and use in soups, sauces, burgers, scrambled eggs, and omelets.

In the mountains of West Virginia there are festivals and events to celebrate their arrival in the spring. In Putney, Vermont, you can enjoy the Southern Vermont Wild Foods' Festival, where ramps are the focus of the festivities.

There is a concern that ramps are being overharvested, and some wonder about economics versus sustainability. It takes 6–18 months for ramp seeds to germinate, while the plant needs 5–7 years to produce seeds. In some areas, such as the Great Smoky Mountains National Park in North Carolina and Tennessee, ramp harvesting was banned in 2004, and in Quebec the sale of ramps has been banned since 1995. There the plant is labeled a "vulnerable" species.

Folks either like ramps or hate them, but whatever the case, we delight as the tips of its leaves poke through the sun-warmed soil announcing that spring has arrived at last!

Ramp and Pea Pesto

Makes approximately 2 cups

The sweetness from the Marcona almonds and peas nicely balances the pungent garlicky-onion flavor of the ramps. This pesto is delicious brushed on grilled corn on the cob, as a crostini topping, tossed with roasted vegetables, or evenly spread over pizza dough.

1 tablespoon plus ⅓ cup extra virgin olive oil, divided
2½ cups packed ramps, root ends trimmed, bulbs, slender stems, and leaves cut into ½-inch pieces
1 cup frozen peas, cooked according to package, or fresh peas, blanched briefly in boiling water
½ cup coarsely chopped Marcona almonds
2 tablespoons fresh lemon juice
½ cup freshly grated Parmigiano-Reggiano cheese
Sea salt and freshly ground black pepper

To make the ramps: Heat 1 tablespoon olive oil in a medium skillet over medium heat. Cook, stirring frequently, until wilted, about 2–3 minutes. Remove from the heat and set aside to cool.

To make the pesto: Process the ramps, peas, the remaining ⅓ cup oil, almonds, and lemon juice in a food processor until the desired texture is achieved. Spoon the pesto into a decorative bowl and fold in the cheese. Season with salt and pepper to taste. Adjust seasonings with additional oil and lemon juice, if desired.

Recipe from Tracey Medeiros
Photograph by Debra Somerville Photography

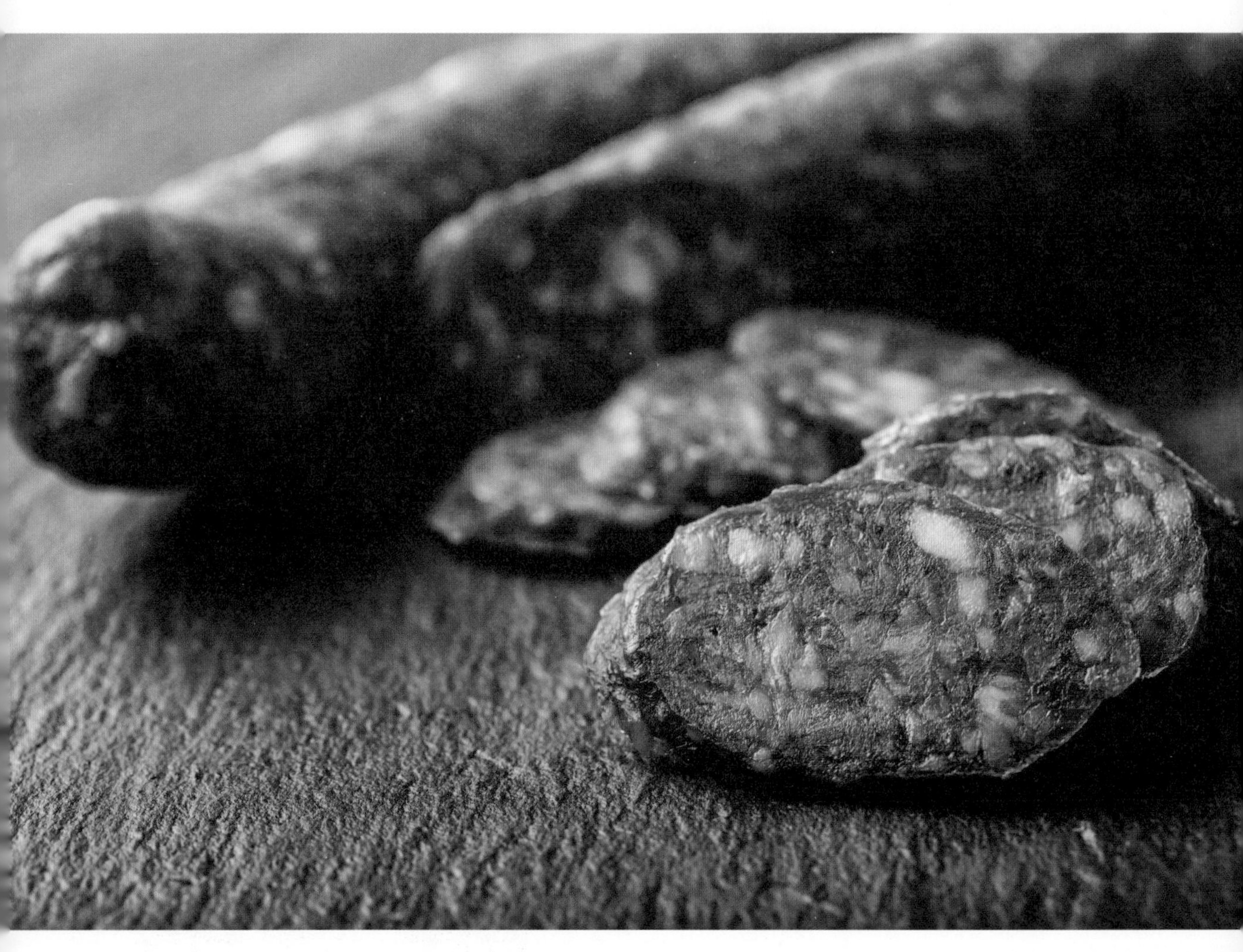

Queso Fundido with Chorizo

Serves 6

"Queso fresco is a traditional Mexican cheese and a quintessential part of Mexican cuisine. The name queso fresco means 'fresh cheese' in Spanish. In October 2011, we launched Organic Queso Fresco, a soft and mild part-skim cheese with fresh milk flavor and a little bit of acidity to give it some zing. Organic Queso Fresco shreds and melts nicely, making it a perfect topping for tacos, pizza, burritos, salads, or on any other dish that you may want to use with mozzarella and other fresh cheeses." —*Carleton Yoder, owner, Champlain Valley Creamery, Ltd.*

8 ounces Mexican chorizo-style sausage, casings removed
1 poblano pepper, seeded and finely chopped
1 tablespoon chopped cilantro, plus extra for garnish, optional
8 ounces queso fresco, cut in ½-inch chunks
Lime wedges, optional

Preheat the oven to 375 degrees Fahrenheit.

Sauté the chorizo in a medium skillet over medium heat, breaking up with a fork into small chunks. Stir until browned, about 5 minutes.

Using a slotted spoon, transfer the chorizo to a 9-inch pie pan. Reserving the sausage drippings in the skillet.

In the same skillet, sauté the poblano pepper over medium heat until tender and slightly browned, about 2 minutes.

Transfer the pepper to the pie pan with the chorizo, scattering it evenly over the top. If using, sprinkle the cilantro evenly over the chorizo layer.

Scatter the cheese evenly over the top, then bake until melted and bubbly, about 10 minutes. Garnish with cilantro, if desired. Serve as a dip with your favorite tortilla chips and lime wedges on the side.

Recipe from Champlain Valley Creamery, Ltd.

PROFILE

V Smiley Preserves

V Smiley was born on her parents' farm in New Haven, Vermont. Food was the center of life back then, and young V discovered early on that she was very comfortable in the kitchen. As she grew older, her admiration for the creativeness involved in the process of food crafting increased. After moving to the West Coast, she worked in the food industry and gained the skills needed for the art of preserve making. In 2015, she returned to her childhood home with her partner, Amy. Being back at her mother's 150-acre farm gave V the opportunity to implement systems and procure supplies that will help her grow the company.

She lives on the farm, which has been playfully named, Lil To Do Farm, using one of the buildings on the property as her office. The cooking and preparation of the preserves is done in a space on Main Street in Bristol, Vermont.

V Smiley Preserves are exclusively sweetened with local honey. The company's honey-sweetened jams, marmalades, and conserves are made with fresh strawberries, blueberries, rhubarb, gooseberries, oranges, and a myriad of other delicious fruits. Amy is in charge of the aromatics and all of the tomatoes used in the preserves.

Whenever possible, fruits are sourced from local organic providers, with the farm growing organic fruits as well. V makes anywhere from 40 to 50 flavors a year, an exceedingly time-intensive process. Loving the creative framework that cooking seasonally creates, this capable businesswoman appreciates the challenges.

Additional pectin is never added to V Smiley Preserves, allowing the nature of each fruit to shine through. Feeling that every fruit behaves differently when it goes through the preserving process, V believes that the use of pectin lessens the fruit's individuality, texture, and temperament.

At V Smiley Preserves, the philosophy is honesty, simplicity, idealism, whimsy, and respect for ingredients and farmers. The whimsy is exemplified by the bevy of buzzing bees that adorn each jar, while the ingredients speak for themselves. The preserves are available for purchase online as well as in the states of: Vermont, New York, New Jersey, California, and Massachusetts, as well as Seattle, Washington.

Bosc Pear Vanilla Lime Marmalade

Makes approximately 7 half-pint jars

"This recipe makes a lovely condiment for cheese. The marmalade is sweet but interspersed with zips and zaps of bitter from the rind. I think it's that sweetness from the honey and vanilla that makes it so magical with aged goat cheeses, Pecorino Romano or Parmigiano-Reggiano cheese. If you are canning the marmalade, follow the jar manufacturer's instructions. If you want to eat your marmalade right away, simply extract the vanilla bean from the mixture and place in glass jars and let cool. Store marmalade in the refrigerator if you aren't canning it. You can eat the marmalade immediately, but I recommend waiting a couple weeks. The flavors continue to develop and will be in full display several weeks after you make the marmalade." —*V Smiley, owner, V Smiley Preserves*

2 pounds 14 ounces very ripe Bosc pears, cut into ⅛-inch-thick slices
1 pound 1 ounce limes, ripened to a nice gold-green color, at room temperature
1 vanilla bean pod
2 pounds 8 ounces Vermont honey
5 ounces lemon juice, strained

To make the pear juice: Place the pear pieces in a nonreactive pot and cover with water so it is 1 inch above the fruit. The pear slices should float freely in the water. Bring to a boil over medium-high heat, then reduce the heat to a simmer, cover, and let simmer for 3 hours. Check the fruit occasionally, adding additional water if the fruit is no longer floating freely in the water. Once the liquid has become slightly viscous, remove the pot from the heat. Place a fine-mesh strainer over a nonreactive bowl and carefully pour the pears and water through the strainer. Cover the straining fruit with a lid or plastic wrap and allow to drip for 12 hours.

While the pears are simmering, prepare the limes. Working lengthwise, as though you were making lime wedges, cut the limes into quarters. Working widthwise, cut each quarter into thin slices. The pieces should look like tiny pie slices. Place the sliced limes in a nonreactive cooking pot and cover with water. Bring to a boil over medium-high heat, then reduce the heat to a simmer for 5 minutes. Strain the limes in a colander, discarding the cooking water. Return the lime slices to the same nonreactive pot and cover with water so it is 1 inch above the limes and bring to a boil over medium-high heat. Reduce the heat to a simmer, cover, and let simmer until the fruit is very tender, about 35 minutes. Remove the pot from the heat and allow the limes to rest in the cooking liquid for 12 hours. "To this day, during this step of the cooking process, I still pull these lime pieces out and check with my mouth to see if the peels are done. I'm looking for an almost melt-in-your-mouth type of texture from the rinds, otherwise you will end up with chewy lime rinds," notes V Smiley.

The next day, place the vanilla bean on a work surface and split it in half lengthwise using a paring knife. Scrape the seeds along with the vanilla pod into an 11-quart nonreactive pan, such as an enameled Dutch oven, or divide the mixture in half and cook in two large stockpots. Add the pear juice, lime slices along with the cooking liquid, honey, and lemon juice. Bring the mixture to a full boil over high heat. Do not stir the mixture until it reaches a boil to avoid slowing down the cooking process.

During the final cooking stage, when the bubbles have gotten very small and the top of the cooking mixture has a fizzy, ballooning, glossy look to it, use a silicone spatula to feel along the bottom of the pan, making sure there is no sticking. You may need to slightly reduce the heat to prevent the mixture from boiling over onto the stovetop.

To test the doness of the marmalade: Remove the pan from the stovetop. While the marmalade is resting, place a small plate in the freezer. Once the plate has chilled, remove from the freezer and place 1 teaspoon of the mixture onto the plate and allow it to sit for 30 seconds. Carefully tilt the plate. If the marmalade is ready, the mixture will be a soft gel that moves slightly. If the mixture is thin and runs down the plate easily, it is not done, and the mixture needs to continue to boil until set. **Tip:** A skin will form on the surface of the marmalade when it is done. You will see the skin begin to form when the marmalade is resting during the freezer test.

Recipe from V Smiley Preserves

Tips from V Smiley

- You want to cook the marmalade at the highest temperature possible throughout the entire cooking process—this is critical in order to keep the flavors fresh and the color light. In order to achieve this, the cooking time must be short.
- If you're cooking in a copper pan, you'll want to mix all the ingredients together before pouring it into the copper pan. Copper pans are unlined, making them highly reactive to acidic foods. Honey makes the recipe okay to cook in copper.

Strawberry Ginger Butter

Makes about 1 pint

This recipe makes more than you will need for the Coconut Banana French Toast **(see page 2)**. Use the leftover butter as a spread on toast, waffles, or muffins.

2 cups organic Earth Balance or another nondairy butter, at room temperature
3–4 fresh strawberries, hulled and coarsely chopped
1 tablespoon organic ginger powder
1 tablespoon organic confectioners' sugar
1 teaspoon organic cinnamon powder
1 teaspoon finely grated orange zest

Place all the ingredients in a food processor and pulse until smooth, scraping down the sides of the bowl as needed. Transfer the butter to a sheet of plastic wrap and roll into a log. Chill in the refrigerate for 1–2 hours.

Recipe from Pingala Café & Eatery
Photograph by Oliver Parini

Williamsville Eatery

The Richardson family's connection to the Williamsville, Vermont, food community began soon after they moved to the area, in the late 1980s. Their new neighbors taught them about fruit trees, bees, sugaring, chickens, gardening, and so much more. In the early years, Lauri, the family matriarch, studied permaculture, which launched new ideas about growing food sustainably.

As a child, son Dylan would wait for the school bus in front of the historic Williamsville General Store. His connection to the store continued as he grew older and worked there part-time. One of the longest continually run general stores in Vermont, it was a time-honored presence in the town until its closing in 2007.

Several years later, the owner of the building approached Dylan with an invitation to lease it and open a restaurant. Dylan and his father, Glenn, discussed a partnership, evaluating their options before deciding to develop a business plan and embarking on this bold venture. They were thrilled at the prospect of working together and serving their community.

It took a year of designing, planning, and renovating before the Williamsville Eatery opened its doors in July of 2014. Lauri runs the dining room and makes the delicious desserts. Glenn and Dylan are in charge of the kitchen, handling the cooking and business side of things.

They support the small, family-owned farms in the area, purchasing as much of the restaurant's produce, grains, meats, and beverages as possible from them, choosing those that practice sustainable and natural farming.

The menu draws from Vermont-grown and milled organic flour, wild mushrooms that the Richardsons collect, and some not-so-common vegetables that are used as garnishes. Pizza is the restaurant's signature dish, its handmade crust created from organic Vermont wheat. These delectable pies are cooked in an 800-degree wood-burning oven. There's a variety of "small plate" options to choose from, including house-made meatballs made with local, grass-fed beef and pork, fresh-baked focaccia bread, and roasted organic beets with tarragon freshly picked from Lauri's garden. Also offered are an assortment of entrées and appetizers, all of which pair well with the eatery's selection of craft beer and cider, and small producer wines. With an availability of vegetarian dishes, the restaurant's diverse seasonally driven menu has something that is sure to please even the most discerning of palates.

The eatery has received the coveted Snail of Approval Award from Slow Food Vermont. This recognition is given to restaurants that have been deemed outstanding among their peers by contributing to the quality, authenticity, and sustainability of Vermont's food supply. Because of Williamsville Eatery's commitment to the local food movement, they have also been accepted as a member of the Vermont Fresh Network, earning the title of Golden Barn Honoree.

The restaurant serves dinner each week from Thursday to Sunday. On those nights, visitors will find the Richardson family hard at work serving wholesome, delicious food to the community they love. As Glenn happily shares, "To see familiar faces walk in the front door night after night is truly heartwarming, it motivates us to make each plate as perfect as possible." Dylan concurs, adding, "We're doing what we love in a space that we like to be in!" What more could anyone possibly ask for?

Springtime Japanese Knotweed Chutney

Makes about 2½ cups with Japanese knotweed shoots and 3 cups with fresh rhubarb stalks

Japanese knotweed is a wild edible. It is both tart and sweet tasting—like rhubarb. The stems are juicy, hollow, tubes with a fibrous texture, similar to bamboo in structure. "Knotweed chutney is a great addition to dessert cheese plates or savory dishes. Japanese knotweed is an invasive species growing in disturbed areas, like at the roadside. We are careful about where we collect this perennial plant given possible roadside contaminates. But with the invasion of the plant, we are inspired by the old adage: *If you're given lemons, make lemonade! — Lauri Richardson, Williamsville Eatery*

1¼ cups organic brown sugar
1 cup organic unfiltered apple cider vinegar
1 pound (6 cups) Japanese knotweed shoots, using only the juicy, lower part of the stems, or 1 pound, 2 ounces (4 cups) fresh thick rhubarb stalks, trimmed and cut into ½-inch pieces
½ cup golden raisins, coarsely chopped
2 tablespoons chopped crystalized ginger
2 small shallots, peeled and minced (about ⅓ cup)
1 medium garlic clove, peeled and minced
2 teaspoons finely grated ginger root
Zest and juice of 1 small orange
1½ teaspoons mustard seeds
1 teaspoon cumin seeds
½ teaspoon salt

In a large heavy-bottom pot, combine the sugar and vinegar and bring to a simmer over medium-high heat, stirring constantly, until the sugar dissolves, about 4 minutes.

Add the knotweed, raisins, crystalized ginger, shallots, garlic, ginger root, orange zest and juice, mustard seeds, cumin, and salt, and bring to a boil. Reduce the heat to a simmer and cook uncovered, stirring occasionally, until the knotweed has softened and the mixture has thickened and turns a dark brown color, about 2 hours if using knotweed shoots and 1½ hours if using rhubarb stalks. **Note:** The pieces should start to fall apart and be very soft when gently pressed under a spoon. Adjust seasonings with additional orange juice, if desired, and salt to taste.

Let cool completely and store in the refrigerator for up to 2 weeks or process using safe canning procedures to keep for up to 1 year.

Recipe from Williamsville Eatery

PROFILE

Pangea Farm, LLC

Jonathan Namanworth grew up in Manhattan and graduated from Cornell University with a background in plant science and research. A love of Vermont's natural beauty and an appreciation for its locally produced goods drew him to the state in 2015. He now leases 30 acres in Shoreham, Vermont, farming 2 acres with an additional 2 acres newly plowed and tilled, ready to be planted in the spring. This pastoral setting is surrounded by hundreds of acres of beautiful orchards with a breathtaking view of the Adirondack Mountains of New York. His decision to become an organic farmer was based on a desire to help preserve and increase the availability of naturally grown products.

The farm is named after the super continent of Pangea that existed 200 million years ago, when Eurasia and North America were joined as one. Jonathan chose this unique name to symbolize the gathering together of the diverse origins of the foods we eat today.

Because of his background in plant research, Jonathan feels the need to experiment and try new things. He believes that knowing the physiological capabilities of a crop makes it possible to manipulate environmental conditions when cultivating, mimicking the plant's natural requirements. If a crop can be grown in Vermont with a reasonable amount of effort, he sees no reason not to try to do so, especially when the process can create a wider range in the diversity of fresh, locally grown goods. It is his intention to continue experimenting with domesticating nonnative crops in his region of Vermont, some of which are peanuts, sugarcane, quinoa, and cotton.

This innovative farmer tries his best to allow the farm to run under natural conditions. He only intervenes when there is a threat to the crop, such as a lack of rain or need for weeding and insect cover on susceptible produce. Jonathan feels that providing a natural growing environment allows plants to do what they do best: grow and produce the finest natural product possible. Although Pangea is just one small farm in a patchwork landscape of producers, its owner is doing his part to contribute to the organic effort in Vermont and keep the movement strong.

Fresh Pico de Gallo

Makes 3 cups

This recipe is a great way to showcase locally grown tomatoes. For a spicier salsa, use some of the seeds and membranes from the jalapeño pepper. Pico de gallo can be stored for up to 2 days in an airtight container in the refrigerator.

1½ pounds ripe tomatoes, preferably Roma, seeded and diced
½ small red onion, minced
2 medium garlic cloves, peeled and minced
½ jalapeño pepper, seeded and minced
½ cup chopped fresh cilantro leaves, plus more for garnish
½ teaspoon finely grated lime zest
1 tablespoon fresh lime juice
¼ teaspoon salt

Mix all of the ingredients together in a medium bowl, gently stirring until well combined. Cover and refrigerate for 1 hour. Adjust seasonings with additional lime juice, cilantro, and salt to taste. Garnish with additional cilantro and serve with your favorite tortilla chips.

Recipe from Pangea Farm, LLC

Full Sun Company

When Full Sun Company's cofounders Nataka White and David McManus met in Vermont in 2011, they put their heads together and came up with the idea of creating a company that would not only produce a new food product, but also support the growth of small, diversified family farms in Vermont and the surrounding region. There was no denying that the pair had the skill set for the venture. David had experience working in the processed food industry, helping to launch the well-known Applegate organic meat company. Nataka was cofounder and an executive at Vermont Biofuels Associates, Acorn Renewable Energy Co-op, and bio-energy program director of the Vermont Sustainable Job Fund.

Their company, Full Sun, uses a novel business model, contracting with farmers to grow sunflower and canola seeds, then providing them with seed stock that is best suited for growing in Vermont's climate and soil to produce oil. Currently, only 2–3 percent of Full Sun's sunflower and canola seeds are grown in Vermont, but Nataka and David are recruiting local growers. They are in the process of contracting approximately 30 percent of their non-GMO canola and 20 percent of the sunflower crop from family farms in Vermont, New York, and Maine. The balance of the canola will come from a farmer in Ontario, Canada, and the sunflowers from several farms in that same region. The farmers who grow the seeds must adhere to non-GMO or organic farming standards.

The business operates out of an oilseed mill in Middlebury, Vermont. Approximately 3,000 pounds of seed pass through a single mechanical expeller press each day, producing 100 gallons of unfiltered oil and a coproduct (the organic material that is left after the pressing) of 1 ton of meal. Full Sun bags and sells the high-fat meal to area farmers as feed for chickens and hogs, or as fertilizer. The partners chose this cold-press method because it yields more flavorful oils than those that are heavily refined and mass produced. Cold-pressed means that no chemicals are used in the procedure, which is exceptionally clean. All parts of the crop are utilized, so nothing goes to waste.

Full Sun's oils are obtained from the first pressing of the seeds, giving them the distinction of being extra virgin seed oils. This method helps to retain the flavor, golden color, and nutty aroma of the seeds. The oils are perfect for low heat sautéing, drizzles, sauces, dressings, marinades, and finishing oil. The product is sold throughout the Northeast at natural grocery stores, food co-ops, farm stores, CSAs, and health and wellness centers.

The company's sunflower oil is low in saturated fat and rich in heart-healthy oleic acid and monounsaturated fats, as well as omega 3, 6, and 9. It is an excellent source of vitamin E. The canola oil is also low in saturated fat and contains omega 3 and 6 and fatty acids. Both are certified non-GMO products.

Netaka and David plan to grow many more acres of sunflowers and canola in Vermont. Eventually, Vermonters may see sunflowers popping up alongside hay and cornfields. In the meantime, the owners of Full Sun are carefully tending to each batch of oil, "from seed to bottle," looking to establish their product as a leader in the category of small batch culinary craft oils.

Tahini Garlic Vinaigrette

Makes approximately 2 cups

This tangy, creamy vinaigrette pairs perfectly with Brussels sprouts, roasted cauliflower, and broccoli.

3 tablespoons organic, unfiltered apple cider vinegar
3 tablespoons fresh lemon juice
1 tablespoon sesame tahini
1 teaspoon tamari
1 teaspoon pure maple syrup
3 medium garlic cloves, minced
½ cup canola oil
½ cup sunflower oil
¼ cup olive oil
Kosher salt and freshly ground black pepper

In a medium bowl, whisk together the vinegar, lemon juice, tahini, tamari, maple syrup, and garlic. Slowly whisk in the oils until emulsified. Season with salt and pepper to taste. Store in the refrigerator for up to 1 week.

Recipe from Full Sun Company

Ginger Sesame Vinaigrette

Makes approximately 1½ cups

This simple recipe is delicious poured over soba noodles or drizzled over salad greens.

3 tablespoons organic, unfiltered apple cider vinegar
3 tablespoons fresh lemon juice
2 tablespoons tamari
2 teaspoons pure maple syrup
1 teaspoon toasted sesame oil
2 medium garlic cloves, peeled and minced
2 tablespoons finely grated ginger
½ cup canola oil
½ cup sunflower oil
Kosher salt and freshly ground black pepper

In a medium bowl, whisk together the vinegar, lemon juice, tamari, maple syrup, sesame oil, garlic, and ginger. Slowly whisk in the oils until emulsified. Season with salt and pepper to taste. Vinaigrette will keep in the refrigerator for up to 1 week.

Recipe from Full Sun Company

CHAPTER 3

SAVORY SOUPS

Soup's On!

The advent of winter, with its falling snow and bone-chilling temperatures, seems to elicit a desire to fill our tummies with something warm and comforting. For me, one of winter's fondest childhood memories is coming in from the biting cold to be greeted by a steaming bowl of delectable soup. Watching the tendrils of steam gently rise and curl made my mouth water in happy anticipation of the first delicious spoonful. Soup warmed my innards back then and still does today. Whether you are cold, feeling sick, or just plain hungry, a bowl of savory soup is a magic elixir that just seems to make life a little bit brighter and warmer.

In today's world, the old standards of canned tomato, vegetable, and chicken noodle soup have been joined by those freshly made with seasonal offerings such as apple-butternut squash, creamy braising greens, or maple-roasted beet soup with fresh goat cheese and pistachios. Many folks now have a strong commitment to eating healthy, driven by a desire to know where their food comes from and how it is grown and prepared. Consumers are more food savvy, loyally supporting their local food community and the products that it produces.

Those who study the history of food tell us that soup goes back to the early beginnings of cooking. Because it was so easy to make, soup was the perfect choice for traveling cultures and those who remained in one place, as well as the rich and poor, healthy and sick. "Portable" soups were eaten by soldiers, explorers, and travelers for hundreds of years. These were made by boiling seasoned meat until a thick syrup-like substance was left that could be dried and stored for months. Our dry soups of today, which were introduced in the 1930s, are descended from these.

The evolution of different varieties of soup was determined by local ingredients and tastes. Good examples of these are: New England clam chowder, Spanish gazpacho, Russian borscht, Italian minestrone, French onion, Chinese wonton soup, and Portuguese kale.

The modern word soup is derived from "sop" or "sup," meaning the slice of bread on which the broth was poured. In the Middle Ages, soup consisted of a piece of bread soaked in a liquid, or over which the liquid had been poured. Bread was a necessary part of the dish because it sopped up the liquid, taking the place of spoons.

Commercially made soups became popular with the invention of canning in the nineteenth century. Doctor John T. Dorrance, a chemist who worked for the Campbell Soup Company, invented condensed soup in 1897.

Soup has found a lasting place in our culture, both in our kitchens and language. For example:

Alphabet Soup—meaning a large number of acronyms used by administration

In the Soup—being in a bad situation

Soup Kitchen—a place that prepares food for those in need

Stone Soup—a popular children's book written by Marcia Brown

Soup to Nuts—meaning from beginning to end

Using a wide variety of locally grown produce, we are drawing our families back to the table with an exciting array of delicious, healthy soups, making the dinner table a gathering place once more.

Northern Lake Fish Chowder

Serves 6

The sweet, crisp flavors of the hard apple cider provide the perfect counterpoint to the smoky flavor of the lake fish and smooth, velvety texture from the cream and fish stock.

¼ pound thick-cut bacon, diced into small pieces
1 ounce butter
½ pound carrots, peeled, trimmed and diced into medium pieces
½ pound leeks, cleaned, trimmed, and thinly sliced
½ pound celery root, peeled, trimmed and diced into medium pieces
1 tablespoon chopped garlic
1 tablespoon fresh assorted herbs, such as parley, tarragon, thyme, sage, or rosemary, minced, plus extra for garnish
½ cup hard apple cider
1½ quarts fish stock, warmed
½ pound potatoes, such as Yukon Gold, peeled and cut into ½-inch pieces
1 cup organic heavy cream, warmed
1¼ pounds applewood smoked lake fish, such as walleye, trout, or salmon, pin bones removed and cut into 2-inch pieces
1¼ cups fresh or frozen corn kernels
Salt and freshly ground black pepper to taste
Baby red sorrel, for garnish, optional

In a large, heavy-bottom stockpot, cook the bacon over medium heat, stirring occasionally, until crisp, about 8 minutes. Remove the bacon from the pot with a slotted spoon and drain on paper towels, reserving the drippings in the pot.

Melt the butter in the same stockpot with the reserved bacon drippings over medium heat. Add the carrots, leeks, and celery root. Cook, stirring often, until the leeks are very tender, about 8 minutes. Add the garlic and herbs and cook, stirring often, until fragrant, about 1 minute. Increase the heat to medium-high and add the hard apple cider. Cook until reduced by half, stirring frequently, about 3 minutes.

Add the stock and potatoes and reduce the heat to a simmer. Cook until the potatoes are fork tender, about 15 minutes.

Slowly add the warm cream, fish, and corn. Simmer until the fish is heated through and the corn is tender, about 10 minutes. Season with salt and pepper to taste.

Garnish with reserved bacon, herbs, and baby red Swiss chard, if desired.

Recipe from Chef Doug Pain of Juniper Bar & Restaurant, Hotel Vermont
Photograph (page 62) by Oliver Parini

Spring Broth with Green Garlic, Dandelion, and Mustard Greens

Serves 4

"This soup makes a light early summer meal that takes advantage of the flavorful and healthy greens that come on as May turns to June. The base of the broth is slivered green garlic, the mellow, verdant spring allium, homemade chicken broth (you can substitute vegetable broth if you prefer), and tamari. Wilted dandelion and mustard greens add just enough bite and a hint of bitterness." *—Alison Baker, former kitchen manager and chef, Cedar Circle Farm & Education Center*

2 tablespoons extra virgin olive oil
2 bulbs green garlic, white and green parts, trimmed, bottom of bulb and paper layers removed, cut into ½-inch pieces on the bias
8 cups (2 quarts) homemade or store-bought low-sodium chicken stock
1 tablespoon organic wheat-free tamari
3 cups loosely packed dandelion greens, stems removed, cut into thin strips
3 cups loosely packed mustard greens, stems removed, cut into thin strips
8 large fresh ravioli
Kosher salt and freshly ground black pepper
¼ cup shaved Parmigiano-Reggiano cheese
1½ tablespoons chopped fresh parsley

Heat the oil in a medium Dutch oven or stockpot over medium heat. Add the green garlic and cook, stirring frequently, until soft, about 5 minutes. Slowly whisk in the chicken stock. Increase the heat to medium-high and bring to a boil. Reduce the heat to a simmer and cook for an additional 10 minutes. Add the tamari, stirring until well combined.

Add the greens and continue to simmer, stirring occasionally, for another 2 minutes.

Turn the heat off and add the ravioli to the soup. Allow the ravioli to sit in the soup until cooked through and just tender, about 4 minutes. Adjust seasonings with salt and pepper to taste.

To serve, place some of the Parmigiano-Reggiano into shallow soup bowls, sprinkle with chopped parsley, and ladle some broth and pasta into each bowl. Serve with crusty bread and a tossed green salad.

Recipe from Cedar Circle Farm & Education Center

Variations: Watercress, escarole, baby spinach, or arugula can be substituted for dandelion greens. Alternatives for mustard greens would be Swiss chard, kale, spinach, or escarole.

Maple-Roasted Beet Soup with Fresh Goat Cheese and Pistachios

Serves 6 to 8

This soup has a delicious combination of sweet and earthy. It has a creamy tang from the goat cheese and a sweet earthiness from the roasted beets, onions, and garlic. The orange juice and zest adds a brightness and punch of flavor, while the crushed pistachios give the dish a nice crunchy texture.

Soup

3 pounds red beets, scrubbed
1½ tablespoons pure maple syrup, plus extra as needed
1½ tablespoons extra virgin olive oil, divided
Salt and pepper to taste
1 medium onion, peeled, trimmed, and quartered
6 medium garlic cloves, unpeeled
1 quart low-sodium chicken stock
2 cups orange juice, preferably fresh
1½ teaspoons fresh thyme leaves
1 tablespoon pistachio oil, plus more for drizzling

Garnishes

6–8 thin baguette slices, toasted
1 4-ounce log fresh goat cheese, crumbled
2 teaspoons finely grated orange zest
¼ cup (1 ounce) salted shelled roasted pistachios, crushed

To make the roasted beets: Preheat the oven to 400 degrees Fahrenheit. Remove the beet greens, reserving them for another purpose. Transfer the beets to a large bowl and toss with the maple syrup and 1 tablespoon olive oil. Season with salt and pepper. Wrap the beets loosely in foil, then transfer to a baking sheet. Roast until fork tender, about 60 minutes, depending on the size of the beets. When the beets are cool enough to handle, wrap one beet at a time in a paper towel and rub the skin away, discarding the skins, then coarsely chop.

To make the roasted onion and garlic: Place the onion and garlic cloves in a medium bowl and toss with the remaining ½ tablespoon olive oil. Season with salt and pepper. Add the onion and garlic cloves to the baking sheet with the beets for the last 30 minutes of cooking time. When the garlic is cool enough to handle, peel off the skins and discard. Coarsely chop the onion.

Working in batches, puree the soup ingredients in a blender or food processor until smooth. Place the soup in a medium stockpot and cook until heated through. Adjust seasonings with maple syrup, if desired, and salt and pepper to taste.

Ladle the soup into bowls. Carefully, place 1 baguette slice on top of soup. Garnish with goat cheese, ¼ teaspoon orange zest, and crushed pistachios. Drizzle with pistachio oil and serve.

Recipe from Tracey Medeiros
Photograph by Brent Harrewyn

Note: If you are roasting really big beets, place the onions and garlic in a small baking dish or oven-safe skillet so you can pull them out separately and allow the beets to keep roasting on their own as needed.

Variation: Spread the goat cheese directly onto the baguette slices instead of scattered over the soup.

Tip: Enjoy the reserved beet greens raw in a salad or sautéed with garlic and olive oil as an easy side dish.

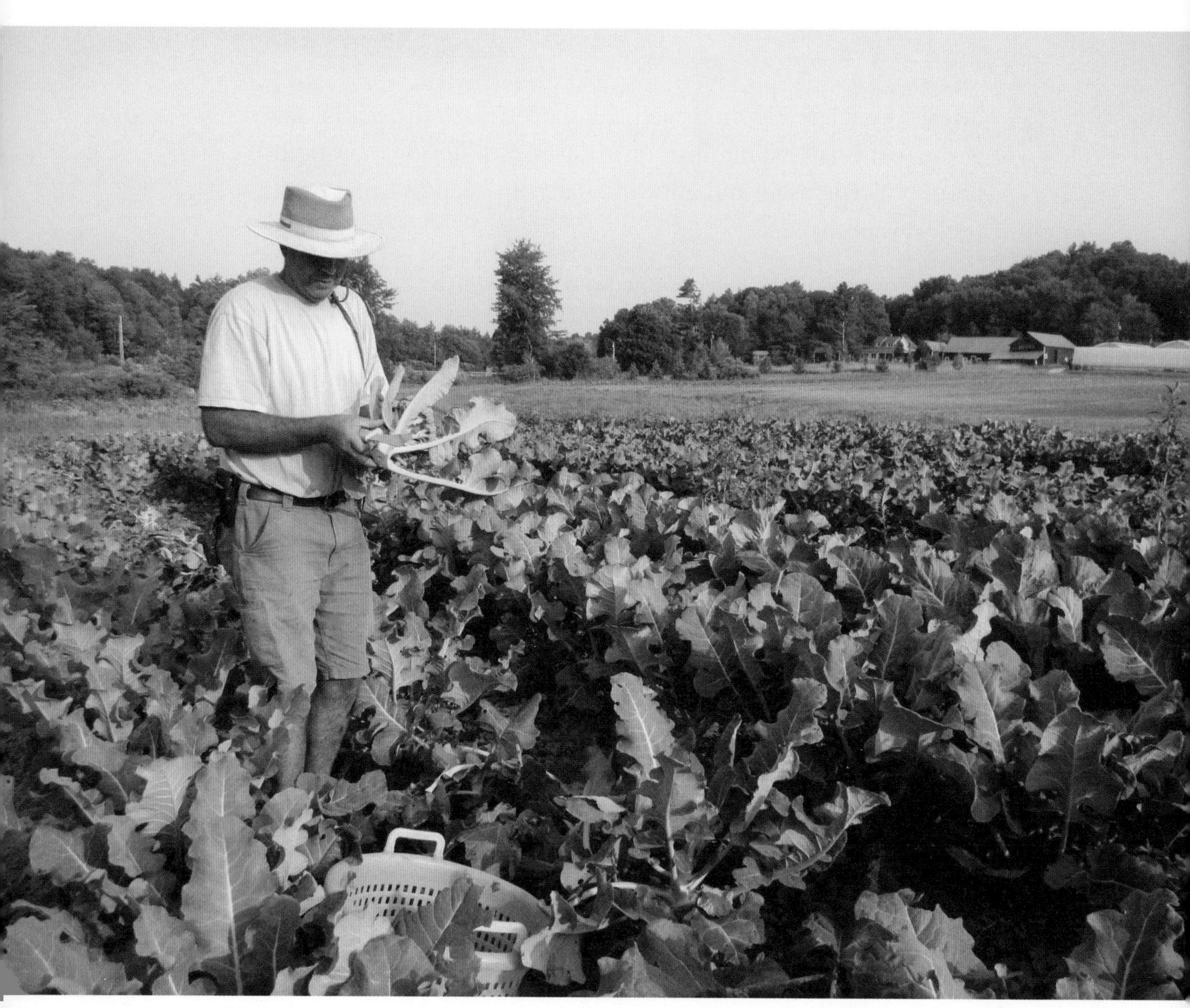

Wood's Market Garden

PROFILE

Wood's Market Garden had been in the Wood family since 1890, with the farm stand established in the 1920s. The business has been a well-known and valued part of the Brandon, Vermont, scene for as far back as people can remember. The farm stand, with its lovely hanging plants and colorful assortment of annuals and perennials, is a popular spot to shop for freshly picked produce and flowers.

Its current owner, Jon Satz, started his farming career working for a biodynamic farmer in Hatfield, Massachusetts. As biodynamic farming was a precursor to organic and sustainable practices, Jon learned the basics early on. This was when he first mastered how to grow vegetables and became truly immersed in the process of growing food. When the time was right, Jon began looking for land to farm and a place to call home. The search eventually lead him to Wood's Market Garden and its owners, Sally and Bob Wood. The Woods soon came to realize that Jon's deep passion for farming and use of sustainable practices aligned with their own agricultural philosophies. With their support, and a great deal of help from the Vermont Land Trust, Jon and Courtney Satz bought the property in 2000, becoming the first non-Wood family members to call the farm home.

On the 150-acre property they grow more than 50 different kinds of organic produce on 70 acres of cultivated land. There are seven greenhouses, which are used for early tomatoes and flowers. Fields of pick-your-own strawberries draw many visitors who love to go home with containers full of juicy, flavorful berries. During the growing season, the farm stand overflows with fresh, delicious produce along with artisanal cheese, organic milk, local dairy products, locally produced meats and poultry, fresh baked goods, maple syrup, raw honey, homemade pickles, jams, and much more. A popular CSA welcomes its members to the farm each week to pick up their bountiful shares.

Jon, Courtney, and their two sons are continuing the legacy the Wood family started generations ago. The fields that have been producing fresh food for the Brandon community for more than 100 years continue to do so. Folks still line up at the farm stand appreciating the mouthwatering results of Jon's hard work. For him, organic farming just seems fundamental. He said, "I simply want to grow healthy food while growing healthy soil." The bounty from the property's fields clearly shows that this farmer has made his dream come true.

Photograph courtesy of Wood's Market Garden

Heirloom Tomato Gazpacho Soup

Serves 4–6

A no-cook gazpacho is a great make-ahead dish. Serrano chile peppers have a wonderful bright yet biting flavor, which adds delicious layers to the soup. Cutting back on the number of serrano chile seeds can reduce the spiciness to your preferred level. Letting this refreshing soup sit overnight in the refrigerator will allow all of its flavors to meld together.

3 pounds (about 6 medium) ripe heirloom tomatoes, assorted colors, cored and cut into chunks
1½ cups (1 heirloom) pickling cucumber, such as Bushy, coarsely chopped
½ sweet bell pepper, such as yellow or orange, cored, seeded, and coarsely chopped
1 small serrano chile pepper, stemmed, halved lengthwise, and seeded, optional
1 large garlic clove, peeled and quartered
2 large fresh basil leaves
2 teaspoons organic, unfiltered apple cider vinegar, plus extra for serving
⅓ cup extra virgin olive oil, plus more for drizzling
Kosher salt and freshly ground black pepper

Garnishes
Diced avocado
Homemade or high-quality store-bought croutons

Working in batches, if necessary, puree the tomatoes, cucumber, bell pepper, serrano chile pepper, if using, garlic, and basil in a blender or food processor until smooth.

While the motor is running, add the vinegar. Slowly add the olive oil and pulse until well combined.

Transfer the soup to a large glass bowl or pitcher, cover, and refrigerate until the soup is very cold, at least 2 hours and up to overnight.

Before serving, adjust the seasonings with vinegar and salt and pepper to taste. Ladle the soup into bowls and drizzle with olive oil, if desired. Top with diced avocado and croutons.

Recipe from Wood's Market Garden
Photograph courtesy of Wood's Market Garden

Heirloom Tomatoes

Nothing speaks more of summer's bounty than a humble farm stand's display of red, succulent tomatoes, the sight of which prompts our taste buds to hum a happy tune. Often, we are drawn to those that are symmetrically shaped and blemish-free. Next to this handsome group you can frequently find the heirloom, which, because of its irregular shape, may be easily dismissed as a less-than-acceptable option. Don't let appearances deceive you—heirlooms are indeed one of summer's most mouthwatering delights.

Heirloom tomatoes are grown from seeds that have been passed down from generation to generation. Ordinarily, these seeds are at least 50 years old, having been hand-selected by farmers for a special trait. They are open-pollinated, meaning by insects or wind, not human hands. In the late 1980s, and early 1990s, the advent of the farm-to-table movement brought heirlooms to the attention of consumers and food writers. Their popularity has increased in recent years because shoppers have discovered that they have a greater flavor than hybrids.

Worldwide there are more than 3,000 varieties of heirloom tomatoes being actively cultivated. Intriguing names such as Yellow Brandywine, Cherokee Purple, Ruby Gold, Green Zebra, and Brown Derby are well known to gardeners. Heirlooms range in size from the Mexico Midget tomato, which is said to be the smallest and about the size of a blueberry, to the Mortgage Lifter, weighing in at 2 pounds or more. For the home gardener, there are many options to choose from.

Heirloom tomatoes offer a diversity of flavor and color. Interestingly, there is no correlation between a tomato's color and its flavor; each variety may have its own unique taste. The best way to verify a tomato's ripeness is to give it a gentle squeeze; it should feel soft to the touch, but not squishy. Surprisingly, heirlooms sold at grocery stores are not always locally grown. Remember that the farther your tomatoes have to travel, the less flavorful they will be. Visit a local farm stand or farmers' market to find just-picked flavor.

Don't be deterred by a tomato with cracked skin, as long as your choice is not leaking juice it is perfectly fine and just as tasty as its unblemished partners. Choose tomatoes that feel heavy for their size. Take a whiff; a ripe heirloom should give off an earthy odor, but avoid those that have a musty aroma. Treat your heirlooms with kid gloves—randomly piling tomatoes on top of each other when bagging may squash those that are softer. If you're the lucky recipient of green tomatoes from a neighbor, be sure to keep them stem side down in a paper bag or cardboard box arranged in a single layer. Always store your tomatoes in a cool place away from sunlight. There are conflicting opinions concerning refrigerating tomatoes; I keep mine at room temperature, as it seems to preserve the flavor.

Heirloom tomatoes cost a bit more than their hybrid relatives, but they are well worth the little bit extra in cost. In recent years, they have actually become more economically accessible to a wider range of consumers. Heirloom tomatoes are all about flavor, color, and texture. I love slicing into one of these delicious treasures and reveling in its sweet, rich flavor—truly a taste of summer!

Creamy Jerusalem Artichoke Soup with Vermont Maple Smoked Cheddar Cheese

Makes 6 servings

Vermont maple smoked cheddar cheese has a delicate balance of smoky and nuttiness that complements the earthy and slight nutty-sweet flavor of the Jerusalem artichokes. The soup is irresistibly creamy with a rich flavor that's perfect for autumn. Serve this rustic soup with a tossed green salad and a nice crusty baguette.

- 2 slices thick-cut bacon, diced
- 2 tablespoons unsalted butter
- 1¼ pounds Jerusalem artichokes, scrubbed, peeled and cut into ½-inch cubes
- 1 medium yellow onion, peeled and diced
- 1 small red beet, trimmed, scrubbed, and cut into ½-inch cubes
- 1 large carrot, peeled and cut into ½-inch cubes
- ½ pound sausage, preferably linguica or chourico, diced
- 2 teaspoons fresh minced rosemary leaves, plus extra for garnish
- ⅛ teaspoon toasted ground caraway seeds, optional
- 2 medium garlic cloves, peeled and minced
- ⅓ cup all-purpose flour, preferably King Arthur organic
- ½ pound Yukon Gold potatoes, scrubbed, peeled and cut into ½-inch cubes
- 1 bay leaf
- 1½ quarts chicken stock, warmed
- 1½ teaspoons finely grated lemon zest (preferably from an unwaxed lemon)
- 1 tablespoon fresh lemon juice
- 1 cup shredded Vermont maple smoked cheddar cheese
- ¼ cup heavy cream
- Kosher salt and freshly ground black pepper

Cook the bacon in a large pot or Dutch oven over medium-high heat, stirring frequently, until crisp, about 4 minutes. Using a slotted spoon, transfer the bacon to paper towels to drain and set aside. Leave the bacon drippings in the pot.

In the same pot with the bacon drippings, melt the butter over medium heat. Add the Jerusalem artichokes, onion, beet, and carrot to the pot and cook, stirring occasionally, over medium heat until the onion is soft and translucent, about 5 minutes. Add the sausage, rosemary, and caraway seeds and continue to cook, stirring frequently, until the sausage is lightly browned, about 6 minutes. Add the garlic and cook until fragrant, about 1 minute. Reduce the heat to medium-low. Add the flour and cook, stirring often, for 5 minutes. Add the potatoes and bay leaf, then slowly whisk in the stock. Bring to a simmer over medium heat, whisking frequently. Continue to simmer, uncovered, stirring occasionally, until the potatoes are fork tender, about 15 minutes. Remove the bay leaf. Add the lemon zest and juice.

Transfer half of the soup to a food processor or blender and puree until smooth. Return the pureed soup to the stockpot.

Stir in the cheese ¼ cup at a time, stirring frequently, until completely melted. Slowly whisk in the cream. Season with salt and pepper to taste.

Ladle into soup bowls and garnish with the reserved bacon and rosemary. Serve at once.

Recipe from Tracey Medeiros
Photograph by Brent Harrewyn

Note: Linguica and chourico are Portuguese-style pork sausages that can be found in many supermarkets. Chourico is spicier than linguica, so choose the one that best suits your taste.

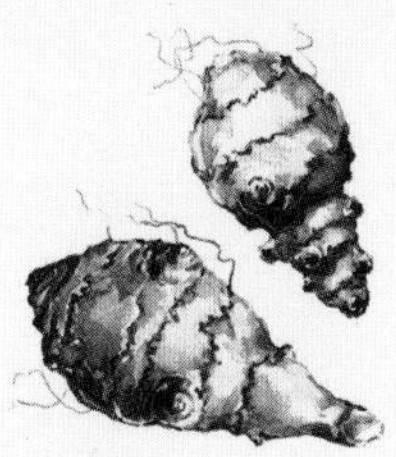

Jerusalem Artichokes

Don't let the name deceive you, Jerusalem artichokes are artichokes in name only. Although the two vegetables are distantly related members of the daisy family, the similarities end there. The name came from the Italian settlers in the United States who called the plant "girasole," meaning sunflower, for its resemblance to the garden sunflower. Girasole was often mispronounced, hence the name Jerusalem, while artichoke came from the fact that the plant tastes much like its namesake.

The Jerusalem artichoke, also called sunchoke, sunroot, earth apple, or topinambour, is found from eastern Canada, west to North Dakota, and south to northern Florida and Texas. Native Americans cultivated the plant as a food source, and when Europeans arrived they sent the tubers back to Europe, where it became a popular crop. It fell into relative obscurity in North America, but resurfaced in the late 1900s and early 2000s.

The plant, cultivated for its tuber, is easy to grow. Even a small piece of tuber will grow if left in the ground, so the Jerusalem artichoke can ruin gardens by smothering nearby plants and taking over large areas. Farmers who grow them and wish to rotate their fields have, at times, had to use weed killer to stop their spread. Each root can make an additional 75–200 tubers in a year.

Tubers store their carbohydrates as inulin rather than starch. Because it is not digested naturally, inulin is known to have a laxative effect on some people's digestive systems. Inulin may cause gas and bloating in certain folks, so it's best to start out with a small sampling of the vegetable. Many people have no problem at all, but those with genetic fructose problems should be wary.

Jerusalem artichokes are usually available year-round in supermarkets. Peak seasons are fall and early spring. Since they are not in high demand, examine the package carefully to make sure your selection is fresh. Select those that are firm to the touch and free of black spots and blemishes. Look for those with fewer knobs to avoid waste when peeling. Stored in the produce drawer, the tubers should last 2–3 weeks. Once refrigerated, the plant's inulin is converted to fructose, causing the tubers to develop a sweeter taste.

Sunchokes can be used as a substitute for potatoes because they have a similar texture, but a sweeter nuttier flavor. Raw and thinly sliced they are ideal in salads, with a crispness like water chestnuts. They can be sliced and roasted like potatoes, sautéed, or made into a gratin. The French are famous for their creamy sunchoke soup, but the root vegetable is also good pureed (make sure to peel first) and mixed with cream and butter.

Sunchokes oxidize when exposed to air, just like apples, so toss with a little lemon juice before cooking. When making a puree or soup, add a pinch of tartar or lemon juice to the cooking water to prevent your tubers from turning gray, an issue caused by the vegetable's high iron content.

The knobby tubers are high in fiber, have negligible amounts of fat, and zero cholesterol. They contain more potassium than most vegetables and are a good source of iron and copper. With 2 percent protein, no oil, and a lack of starch, the Jerusalem artichoke adds a healthy, flavorful touch to any dish.

Three Crows Farm

PROFILE

Born and raised in the upper valley of Vermont, Angus Baldwin has lived most of his life in the Green Mountain State. After eight years of working on truck farms, which produced crops that were sold wholesale, he decided to use this experience to start a small, efficient farm of his own. As he had always worked with plants rather than animal production, Angus thought that making a living using a smaller-scale wholesale model investment was a more practical way to go.

Farming on rented land in Jefferson, Vermont, his first priority is soil health, maximizing soil efficiency and vitality. To accomplish this goal, he avoids tillage as much as possible and carefully manages nutrients, soil structure, and the number of different species of plants he grows. The hardworking farmer never stops working to improve soil quality, thereby providing his plants with the ability to be more resistant to disease and pests. This process allows him to produce certified organic, higher-quality crops at a lower price.

Angus grows only as much as he can sell and states, “A farmer should reject waste. If quality were the incentive instead of quantity, this would go a long way toward remediating the myriad of problems that arise in the field of agriculture.”

Sales to local restaurants make up half of the farm’s business. Angus realizes that location is important, as city prices are vastly different from costs in rural areas. He keeps up with his competitors and what they have to offer, constantly communicating with customers to see what products are of value to them. A good example is the farm’s signature vegetable, tomatillos, which means little tomatoes in Spanish. These small green tomatoes are delicious in sauces and very popular with chain stores. Their high productivity and ease of care has afforded the farm a level of profitability that has prompted Angus to call them “survival food.”

Due to the large turnover in the restaurant industry, the farm business can be very unpredictable. Angus knows that his customers must appreciate the products he has to offer; the farm’s produce must stand out from the run-of-the-mill items that his chefs would normally buy from food service companies. He always keeps in mind that the restaurant business is no easier than farming, continually appreciating how hard his customers are working, and grateful for the fact that they are taking the time to collaborate with him. The owner of Three Crows Farm has learned through experience that good communication is paramount to all successful business relationships.

White Bean Soup with Winter Greens and Sausage

Serves 4–6

"This is a very old recipe that belongs to my grandmother. The soup was created in Italy during World War II, because there was not much food available. The ingredients found in this recipe were the only things that locals could forage and, yet the soup was absolutely delicious." —*Chef Tony Devito, Trattoria La Festa, a Three Crows Farm customer*

2 tablespoons olive oil, divided
½ pound Italian sweet sausage, casings removed
1 medium onion, thinly sliced
1 large bunch of winter greens, such as kale or dandelion greens, trimmed and cut into 2-inch-thick ribbons, or 1 large head young puntarelle, trimmed, outer leaves removed
3 medium garlic cloves, peeled and minced
2 quarts low-sodium chicken broth, homemade or store-bought, warmed
1 15-ounce can white beans, such as cannellini or Great Northern, drained and rinsed
1 teaspoon finely grated lemon zest (preferably from an unwaxed lemon)
½ teaspoon fresh lemon juice
Salt and freshly ground black pepper
Crème fraiche
Fresh basil leaves, minced
Sourdough bread, optional

Heat 1 tablespoon olive oil in a large Dutch oven over medium heat. Add the sausage and cook, breaking up the meat with a fork, until it begins to brown, about 10 minutes. Using a slotted spoon, transfer the sausage to a bowl, reserving the drippings in the pot.

Add the remaining 1 tablespoon olive oil and onion slices to the pot with the reserved drippings. Cook, stirring often, over medium heat for 5 minutes. Add the greens and garlic, cover, and cook, stirring occasionally, over medium-low heat, just until the greens are tender, about 5 minutes. Stir in the chicken broth and bring to a simmer over medium heat.

Using a potato masher or the back of a fork, slightly mash half of the beans. Add all of the beans, lemon zest and juice to the Dutch oven and simmer until the greens are tender and the flavors have melded, about 25 minutes. Add the sausage and continue to simmer until heated through. Adjust seasonings with lemon juice, salt, and pepper to taste. Garnish with a dollop of crème fraiche and basil. Serve with sourdough bread, if desired.

Recipe from Tony Devito, owner of Trattoria La Festa, for Three Crow Farm
Photograph by Oliver Parini

Note: Puntarelle or catalogna is an Italian green that belongs to the chicory family. It has a slightly bittersweet quality. Save the outer leaves for stir-fry or a braise.

How to prepare puntarelle: Prepare a large ice bath. Set aside. Tear the dark leafy parts into bite-size pieces. Using a knife, remove the hollow stalks from the inner core of the puntarelle and reserve for another use, such as a salad. Cut the inner core into thin strips lengthwise. Place the strips in the prepared ice bath for 1 hour. Drain and pat dry with paper towels. Store in the refrigerator until ready to use.

MKT: Grafton

The 200-year-old MKT: Grafton general store reopened in 2015 with new owners, Ali Hartman and June Lupiani, at the helm. For first-time visitors, the store's unusual name may be a topic of conversation, with some folks quickly catching on that the initials stand for market, while others continue to puzzle over its meaning. The store offers specialty foods, with an emphasis on regional and artisanal products, and Grafton cheese is a perfect example.

MKT: Grafton's owners want their business to be a part of the twenty-first century, yet still offer outstanding personal service, consistently good products, and prices that please. To achieve this goal, they carry a selection of items that showcase the state of Vermont and the surrounding region. With the help of the MKT: Grafton team and their wide range of skills, experience, and knowledge, visitors are expanding their food repertoire to learn about and try the best Vermont has to offer.

The two-story brick general store has high ceilings and white walls, conveying a sense of orderliness and open space in a New Age, eclectic sort of way. Ali and June have built strong relationships with local producers and purveyors, and they are proud members of the Vermont Fresh Network, NOFA Vermont and Slow Food Vermont. They are constantly working to expand their network of local and organic providers.

Open seven days a week, the store's café uses fresh local ingredients to surprise diners with a variety of daily specials and a menu that changes quarterly. June, a registered dietician and restaurant-trained chef, is in charge of the kitchen. Almost everything is prepared from scratch, using real ingredients that make each dish shine. The in-house baker creates a delicious array of goodies that have visitors wishing they had left room for just one more bite.

The owners of MKT: Grafton focus on food that is aligned with community values of quality and sustainability. To do so they provide their patrons with daily provisions, grocery items, local produce, meat, dairy, wine, craft beer, and local cider. Ali and June want folks to know that "Everything on our shelves and in our cases has been lovingly made by producers that we have personally selected." They work to create experiences that "honor products, partners, and patrons."

Warming Harvest Soup

Makes 3½ quarts; serves 7–9

"This soup, starring roasted squash and crisp apples, is earthy and bright. The addition of ginger and turmeric make it warming and perfect for sipping through the fall and winter. The Vermont maple syrup makes it familiar, while the coconut milk takes us somewhere far away." *—Ali Hartman, owner, MKT: Grafton*

Soup

1 large butternut squash (about 2½ pounds), peeled and cut into ½-inch pieces
1 tablespoon extra virgin olive oil, or as needed
Kosher salt and freshly ground black pepper
1 stick organic butter
1 sprig fresh rosemary
1 large onion, peeled and chopped
2 medium carrots, peeled and chopped
1½ cups chopped celery
4 medium organic apples, cored, peeled and chopped (about 2 cups)
4 tablespoons fresh minced ginger (about a 4-inch piece)
5 cups water or vegetable broth
2 13.6-ounce cans organic unsweetened coconut milk, plus extra for drizzling
⅓ cup pure Vermont maple syrup
1 teaspoon turmeric
¼ teaspoon ground cinnamon
⅛ teaspoon freshly grated nutmeg

Roasted Butternut Seeds

Reserved butternut squash seeds
1 teaspoon extra virgin olive oil, or as needed
Salt and pepper to taste

Crème fraiche

Preheat the oven to 375 degrees Fahrenheit. Lightly grease a baking sheet. Set aside.

Cut the squash in half lengthwise. Scoop out the seeds and strings, reserving the seeds. Peel and cut the squash into 1-inch pieces. Place the squash in a large bowl and drizzle with oil, making sure it is evenly coated. Season with salt and pepper. Place the squash on the prepared baking sheet and roast, stirring occasionally, until fork tender, about 40 minutes.

Melt the butter in a large stockpot over medium heat. When the butter has melted, reduce the heat to medium-low and allow the butter to bubble. Continue to cook until the butter browns, about 4–5 minutes, gently swirling the pan every minute or so. Add the rosemary, onion, carrots, and celery, and cook, stirring occasionally, for 10 minutes.

Add the apples and ginger and continue to cook, stirring occasionally, for 10 minutes. Add the roasted squash, broth, coconut milk, maple syrup, turmeric, cinnamon, and nutmeg. Bring to a simmer over medium heat and cook for 30 minutes.

While the soup is cooking, make the roasted squash seeds. Preheat the oven to 325 degrees Fahrenheit. Rinse the squash seeds to remove any stringy pulp. Drain in a colander. Pat the seeds dry with paper towels. Place them in a small bowl and toss with just enough olive oil to coat. Spread the seeds in an even layer on an ungreased baking sheet and season with salt and pepper to taste. Bake, stirring occasionally, until the seeds are dry and crunchy, about 25 minutes. Set aside to cool.

Remove the soup from the heat and let cool slightly. Remove and discard the woody rosemary stem. Working in batches, puree the soup in a food processor, blender, or with an emulsion blender. Return the soup to the pot and adjust seasonings with salt and pepper to taste, then cook until heated through.

Ladle the soup into bowls and drizzle with coconut milk, a dollop of crème fraiche, and sprinkles of squash seeds.

Recipe from MKT: Grafton

Tip: For a bit of a kick, garnish soup with curried cashews and a sprinkle of minced garlic or chili flakes.

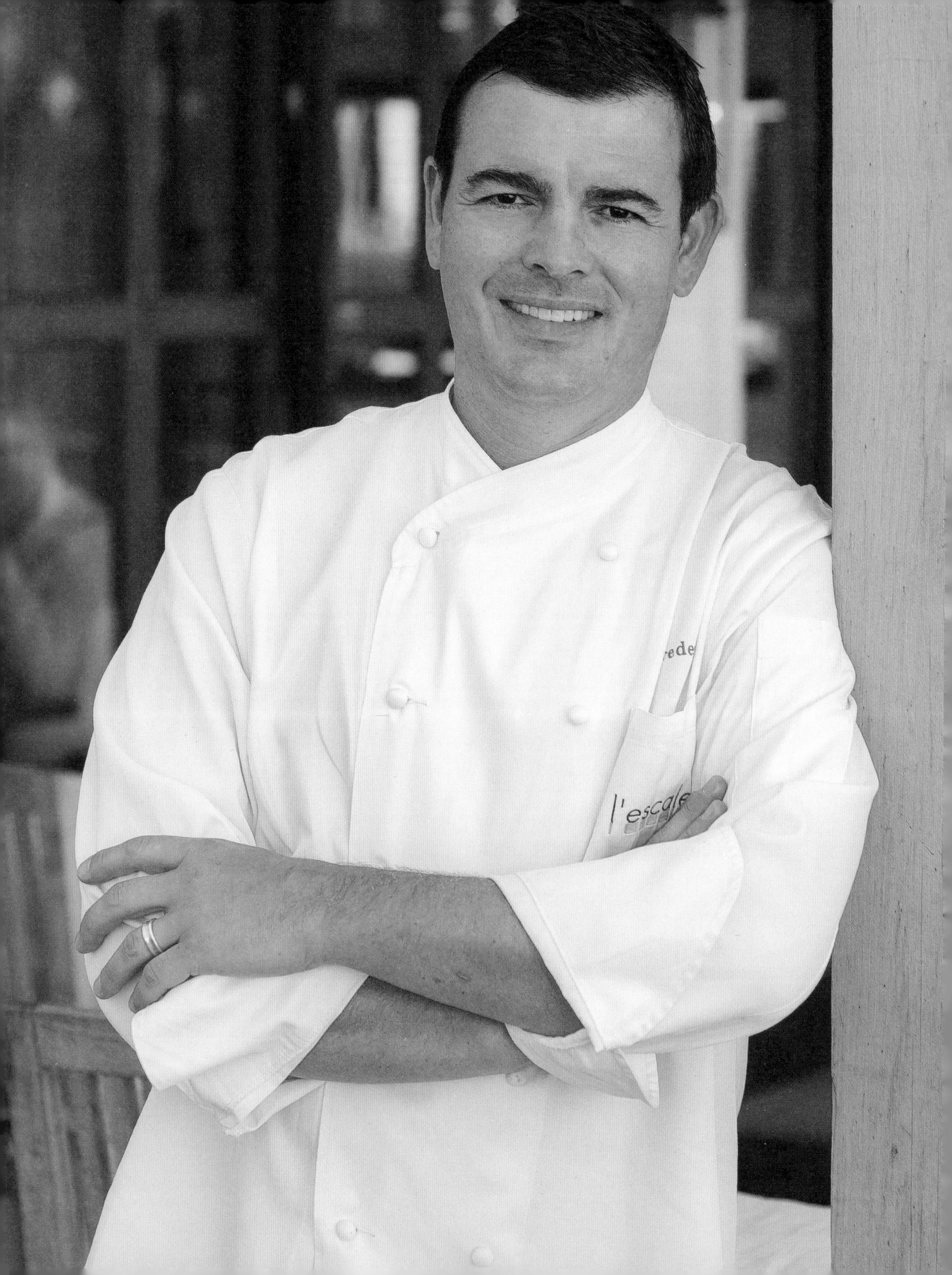
l'escale

Executive Chef Frederic Kieffer

Artisan Restaurant Tavern & Garden at Four Columns Inn

Growing up in the countryside west of Paris, Frederic Kieffer spent his summers working in local restaurants, where he discovered a true passion for cooking. Following his calling, Kieffer enrolled into the well-known L'Ecole Superieure de Cuisine Française, Ferrandi in Montparnasse, Paris, where he was classically trained in French cuisine.

Upon graduation, a series of apprenticeships in Paris led him through the kitchens of such renowned restaurants as Taillevent, Le Chiberta, and the Hôtel Lutetia. Back in the states, he began his career in the kitchen of Tentation Caterers in New York City and as the chef at the Museum of Natural History in Manhattan. In addition, Kieffer was instrumental in the opening of the Los Angeles Music Center in California.

As Chef Kieffer's culinary reputation grew, he was given the opportunity to reopen Windows on the World, one of the most iconic venues in the world, with famed restaurateur Joseph Baum, then owner of the Rainbow Room. Kieffer considers this to be one of the greatest honors of his career and will always have a special place in his heart, especially after 9/11.

After working at Water's Edge restaurant on Long Island and being the opening chef of the celebrity-owned Man Ray Restaurant, Chef Kieffer opened l'Escale at the Delamar Greenwich Harbor Hotel. "Through some introductions and living in Westchester, New York, the l'Escale opportunity was an exciting project, big enough to rival those in New York City, with an exquisite hotel on the water, and it gave me the opportunity to return to my French roots," Kieffer shares.

The well-established chef opened Gaia, also located in Greenwich, Connecticut. Gaia is the goddess who cares for the earth, according to Greek mythology, and that was at the heart of the concept. This is where Kieffer's dedication to farm-to-table was solidified and became his cooking philosophy. Valuing the source of products and quality before it became trendy has long since become a part of Kieffer's legacy. Under his guidance, both l'Escale and Gaia received an "Excellent" rating from *The New York Times*.

As executive chef and partner of Artisan Restaurant at Delamar Southport, Connecticut, his farm-to-table menu received a "Don't Miss" rating by *The New York Times* and Three Stars from *Connecticut Magazine*, in addition to countless other awards and accolades.

Currently, Chef Kieffer is also involved at Four Columns in Newfane, Vermont, the first farm-to-table restaurant in the country, which originally opened in 1965. As it celebrated its grand reopening in August 2015 with an Artisan Restaurant & Tavern, a garden, and a complete renovation of the inn, Executive Chef Kieffer is thrilled to carry on its rich heritage, adding his farm-conscious flair guiding and mentoring the culinary team of Artisan Newfane. Part of an Artisan trilogy, the third Artisan was scheduled to open in mid-2017 at the new Delamar West Hartford Hotel in Connecticut.

Photograph by Kelly Fletcher

Navy Beans and Swiss Chard Minestrone Soup with Poached Farm Egg

Serves 10

"This soup is a perfect winter mood lifter, with its rich, flavorful smoky and tangy notes. The different layers always makes you come back for more: creamy beans, crunchy beet tops, and an unctuous farm egg. Best of all, it is a very healthy soup." —*Executive Chef Frederic Kieffer, Artisan Restaurant Tavern & Garden at Four Columns Inn*

Navy Beans

1 pound organic navy beans, washed, picked over, and soaked overnight

Soup

2 ounces extra virgin olive oil
6 ounces Vermont uncured smoked bacon, cut into ¼-inch pieces
1½ cups (about 1 large) onion, peeled, trimmed, and cut into ⅓-inch cubes
1 cup (about 2 medium) carrots, washed, peeled, and cut into ⅓-inch cubes
½ cup (½ organic rib) celery, trimmed and cut into ⅓-inch cubes
8 large tomatoes, washed, cored, and cut into ½-inch cubes
6 medium garlic cloves, peeled, trimmed, and crushed with a garlic press
2 quarts vegetable stock or water
¼ cup sherry vinegar or red wine vinegar
2 teaspoons kosher salt
1 bunch organic rainbow Swiss chard, trimmed, stems removed, and cut into ½-inch strips (about 4 cups loosely packed)

Poached Eggs

10 local farm chicken eggs
Freshly grated Parmigiano-Reggiano cheese, for garnish

Drain the beans and set aside.

Heat the olive oil in a large heavy-bottomed stockpot over medium heat. Add the bacon and cook for 2 minutes. Add the onion, carrots, and celery and continue to cook, stirring occasionally, for 4 minutes. Add the beans, tomatoes, garlic, stock, and vinegar, and 2 teaspoons salt. Bring to a simmer, stirring occasionally, for 45 minutes. Season with salt to taste and continue to simmer until the beans are tender, about 25 minutes. Add the Swiss chard and continue to simmer until the Swiss chard is tender, about 10 minutes. Adjust seasonings with salt to taste.

While the Swiss chard is cooking, start poaching the eggs. Bring 3 inches of water in a large saucepan to a simmer. Crack the eggs into individual small bowls or ramekins. Carefully slide the eggs into the water, making sure they do not touch. Turn off the heat, cover, and cook for 4 minutes. Using a slotted spoon, carefully remove the eggs from the saucepan.

To serve, ladle the soup into bowls and top with a poached egg in the center of each bowl. Garnish with cheese. Serve at once.

Recipe from Artisan Restaurant Tavern & Garden at Four Columns Inn
Photograph by Stephanie Challis

> **Variation:** Deep fry the eggs. When poaching or deep frying the eggs, make sure to keep the yolks runny. Poaching the eggs is healthier, but frying them adds a great crunchiness to the dish.

CHAPTER 4

ORGANIC AND HEIRLOOM VEGETABLES FROM FIELD TO FORK

Roasted Beets Candied and Pickled With Multicolored Pickled Green Beans and Micro Herbs

Serves 8–10

The pickled green beans are tangy and crunchy while the candied beets are sweet and tender. This recipe makes more pickled green beans than needed for the recipe. The extra pickled green beans are delicious as a garnish, or as a substitute for a pickle when eating a sandwich, or added to a tossed green salad.

Roasted Beets

Note: *The roasted beets will be used and divided equally in both the candied beets and pickled beets recipes.*

4 pounds red beets, scrubbed and divided
2 tablespoons extra virgin olive oil
Kosher salt and freshly ground black pepper

Candied Beets

Note: *You will need to marinate the beets at least 2 days before you intend to serve them.*

2 pounds roasted beets
2½ cups unfiltered apple cider vinegar
1 cup organic brown sugar
1 cinnamon stick
¾ tablespoon salt
½ tablespoon whole cloves
½ dried chili pepper or ¾ teaspoon chili flakes
1½ cups ice

Pickled Beets

Note: *You will need to pickle the beets at least 2 days before you intend to serve them.*

2 pounds roasted beets
2½ cups unfiltered apple cider vinegar
2 tablespoons organic brown sugar
½ cinnamon stick
1 tablespoon salt
3 whole cloves
1 large garlic clove, peeled and crushed
1 tablespoon mustard seeds
1 tablespoon coriander seeds
½ dried chili pepper or ¾ teaspoon chili flakes
2 bay leaves
1½ cups ice

Pickled Green Beans

Note: *You will need to pickle the beans at least 1 day before you intend to serve them.*

1 pound multicolored green beans, trimmed and cleaned
2 tablespoons olive oil
2 cups apple cider vinegar
1 tablespoon salt
2 tablespoons minced fresh dill
1 tablespoon organic cane sugar

Brown Butter
¼ pound (4 ounces) unsalted butter

Sour Cream
1 cup (½ pint) sour cream
¾ teaspoon lemon juice or white wine
Salt and freshly ground black pepper

Garnishes
1 cup shaved fresh fennel
⅓ cup micro herbs
⅓ cup basil leaves, thinly sliced
Extra virgin olive oil, for drizzling

To make the roasted beets: Preheat the oven to 400 degrees Fahrenheit. Remove the beet greens, reserving them for another purpose. Transfer the beets to a large bowl and toss with the olive oil. Season with salt and pepper. Wrap the beets loosely in foil, then transfer to a baking sheet. Roast until fork tender, about 50–60 minutes, depending on the size of the beets. When the beets are cool enough to handle, wrap one beet at a time in paper towels and rub the skin away. Continue until the skin has been removed from all the beets. Divide the roasted beets equally for the candied beets and pickled beets recipes.

To make the candied beets: Place 2 pounds of the roasted beets in a medium glass or nonreactive bowl and set aside. Combine the vinegar, brown sugar, cinnamon stick, salt, cloves, and chili pepper in a saucepan and bring to a boil, stirring often, over medium-high heat. Pour this marinade over the beets, then cover with the ice. Let cool to room temperature, cover with plastic wrap, then refrigerate for at least 48 hours.

To make the pickled beets: Place the remaining 2 pounds of roasted beets in a medium bowl and set aside. Combine the vinegar, brown sugar, cinnamon stick, salt, cloves, garlic, mustard seeds, coriander seeds, dried chili pepper, and bay leaves in a saucepan and bring to a boil, stirring often, over medium-high heat. Pour the brine over the beets, then cover with the ice. Let cool to room temperature, cover with plastic wrap, then refrigerate for at least 48 hours.

To make the pickled green beans: Toss the beans with the olive oil and place the beans in a 1-quart jar with a tight lid. Combine the vinegar, water, salt, dill, and sugar in a saucepan and bring to a boil, stirring often, over medium-high heat. Pour the brine over the green beans and seal the jar. Let cool to room temperature, then refrigerate overnight.

To make the brown butter: In a small saucepan, melt the butter over medium heat. Stirring occasionally, cook until the butter turns a toasty brown color, about 11 minutes. Remove from the heat and allow to cool until just warm. Strain the butter through a fine-mesh strainer or cheesecloth to remove all the solids. Transfer to a small saucepan and keep warm until ready to use in the sour cream.

To make the brown butter sour cream: Whisk together the reserved brown butter, sour cream, lemon juice, and salt and pepper to taste. Set aside until ready to use.

To assemble: Slice the beets ⅛-inch thick. Transfer the beets to individual plates. Divide evenly half of the pickled beans (about 2 cups) and a scattering of shaved fennel. Top the beets and green beans with dollops of the brown butter sour cream and season with salt and pepper to taste. Top with micro herbs (mini herbs that are harvested when they are quite young) and basil leaves. Drizzle with olive oil, if desired. Serve at room temperature.

Note: Enjoy the reserved beet greens as a pizza topping. Wash them, remove the stems, then slice them crosswise into thin ribbons, and scatter on top of pizza.

Recipes from Kismet, LLC
Photograph (page 92) by Oliver Parini

Grilled Bread Salad with Broccoli Rabe, Cherry Tomatoes, and Parmigiano-Reggiano Cheese

Serves 4

This easy-to-prepare salad has lots of flavors, from the slightly bitter tasting broccoli rabe to the mildly sweet tomatoes, as well as bright citrus notes from the lemon juice. The assortment of colored tomatoes makes a striking contrast with the green broccoli rabe.

1 pint multicolored heirloom cherry tomatoes
2 bunches broccoli rabe, thick ends trimmed
4 tablespoons extra virgin olive oil, or as needed, divided, plus extra for the grill grate
Sea salt and freshly ground black pepper
2 whole lemons, tops and bottoms trimmed, cut lengthwise in half, seeds removed
½ tablespoon organic cane sugar
4 bread slices (½ inch thick), such as country-style
1 tablespoon thinly sliced fresh purple or green basil leaves
2 medium garlic cloves, peeled and mashed into a paste
4 tablespoons freshly grated Parmigiano-Reggiano cheese

Skewers

Presoak the bamboo skewers for 30 minutes or have metal skewers ready. Slide the tomatoes onto the skewers. Set aside.

Heat a gas or electric grill to medium heat and generously brush the cooking grate with oil.

Place the broccoli rabe in a colander and wash well under cold running water. Run a knife down the center of any thick stalks, more than ½ inch thick, leaving the stems intact at the top. Drizzle with 2 tablespoons olive oil and season with salt and pepper to taste. Set aside.

Brush the lemons with ½ tablespoon olive oil and season with salt and pepper to taste. Place the sugar on a small plate and dip each of the lemon halves, cut side down, into the sugar. Grill the lemons, cut side down, until golden brown at the edges, about 5 minutes. Using tongs, carefully flip the lemons over and grill for 2 more minutes. Remove from the grill and set aside. When cool enough to handle, squeeze the lemon juice into a small bowl.

Generously brush both sides of the bread slices with 1 tablespoon olive oil and season with salt and pepper to taste. Grill the bread, flipping once until crisp and golden brown on both sides, about 2 minutes per side. Transfer to a plate and allow to cool.

Meanwhile, arrange the broccoli rabe in a single layer across the grill grate. Grill, turning often, for about 4 minutes. Transfer to a large bowl.

Brush the tomatoes with the remaining ½ tablespoon of olive oil and season with salt and pepper to taste. Arrange the tomato skewers evenly across the grill grate. Grill until nicely blistered in spots, about 5 minutes. When cool enough to handle, carefully remove the tomatoes from the skewers into the bowl with the broccoli rabe.

Cut the bread slices into ½-inch cubes and add to the bowl with the vegetables. Add the basil, garlic, and 3 tablespoons of lemon juice and toss until well combined. Arrange on a decorative platter. Drizzle with additional olive oil and lemon juice, if desired. Top with cheese. Adjust seasonings with salt and pepper to taste. Serve at room temperature.

Recipe from Tracey Medeiros
Photograph by Brent Harrewyn

Broccoli Rabe

This green cruciferous vegetable is known by a variety of names, just a few of which are rapini, rapa, rapine, Chinese broccoli, and turnip broccoli. Here in the United States it is commonly known as broccoli raab, or broccoli rabe, which is pronounced "rob." Do not be misled by the fact that broccoli is part of its name; this vegetable is closely related to the turnip, not broccoli, and is thought to have originated in China or the Mediterranean. Part of this confusion may lay in the fact that the top of the plant consists of clusters of broccoli-like buds, which have a softer look than those of the broccoli plant.

When making your selection at the store or farmers' market, be sure that the florets are tightly closed and dark green in color. Look for stems that are small, firm, and green; avoid plants that have wilted, yellowing leaves. Plants with smaller leaves are younger, more tender, and milder in taste. If your selection smells like cabbage, it has been around too long, so choose another. Since broccoli rabe can have a strong rather bitter flavor, which is similar to mustard greens, the above advice will hold you in good stead. Remember, it may take a while to acquire a taste for broccoli rabe, but once you do you will sing its praises for life.

You can happily feel guilt-free when you sit down for a serving of broccoli rabe. One cup has only 9 calories, and a 3½-ounce portion provides more than half the daily requirements for vitamins A and C. It is a good source of folate (a B vitamin), vitamin K, potassium, calcium, and iron. Broccoli rabe is fat-free and cholesterol-free, as well as low in sodium. Seconds anyone?

This vegetable must be stored in the refrigerator. When doing so be sure to remove the twist tie and store in a plastic bag, washing when ready to use. Broccoli rabe will keep in the refrigerator for 4–5 days.

When preparing your broccoli rabe, clean it as you would other greens, removing ¼ inch from the bottom of the stems. Blanch before cooking to make it less bitter. To blanch, give the broccoli rabe a brief dunk in salted (optional) boiling water and follow with a dip in ice water. This will reduce the vegetable's bite. You can broil, stir-fry, steam, or sauté the leaves, stems, and florets. It is often steamed with lemon and garlic. When you sauté, use a little olive oil with as much garlic as suits your taste. You can remove the stems up to where the leaves begin, sautéing them first before adding the leaves. Sauté for 3–5 minutes, or until tender. Broccoli rabe can be used in salads, on pizza, or in sandwiches and soups. It makes a nice addition when combined with pasta, rice, or Italian and Asian dishes. Unleash your creativity, the sky's the limit!

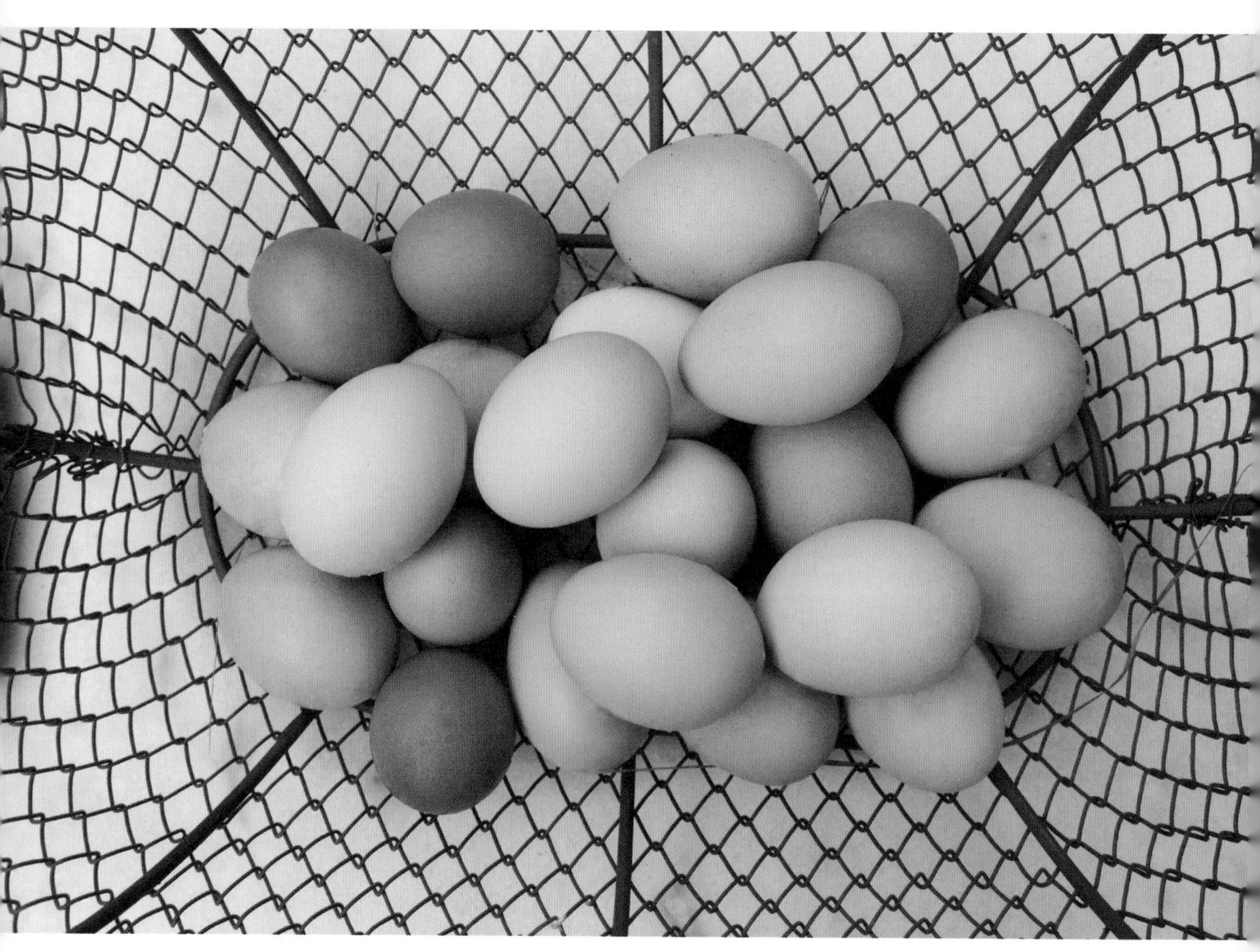

PROFILE

Bear Roots Farm

Jon Wagner and Karin Bellemare met in 2006 when they were both students at Green Mountain College in Poultney, Vermont. Jon took courses in agriculture, while Karin was motivated to work with food and soil by a friend who worked at the on-campus farm. They both agree that farming just crept up on them. After graduation, the couple started farming on the east end of Long Island, but found that the soil and pace of life was not what they were looking for. Their love for Vermont gave them a desire to return to the Green Mountain State, so they began the search for a place there they could call home. When the Watt Farm in South Barre, Vermont, came up for sale, the couple was overjoyed to find out that their proposal had been accepted. With the assistance of the Vermont Land Trust's Farm Access Program, the 87-acre former dairy farm was now theirs. They decided to name their new home Bear Roots Farm.

The hardworking team knew they had their work cut out for them, but they were committed to becoming organic farmers. This interest really happened by accident—they explain, "We started by growing our own organic food, and it slowly turned into a small business." The property is a mix of pasture, tillable land, and woods. Seven of the farm's 87 acres are utilized to grow diversified vegetables. Bear Roots is a year-round, certified organic vegetable farm that grows everything from earthy root vegetables to sweet fruit, all of which are distributed locally. Chickens and ducks are raised for eggs, and there are no plans to get into meat production. Jon and Karin tell their customers, "It is our mission to nurture our soil to produce a highly nutritious vegetable, ensuring that you, our customers, are happy and healthy, too!"

The barn that the cows previously called home now houses several walk-in coolers, a wash shed and farm stand. Karin is office manager, harvester, and CSA coordinator. When not working, she loves exploring the woods with her dog, riding horses, playing soccer, and just enjoying the mountain air. Jon, on the other hand, is a jack-of-all-trades—a vegetable grower who is passionate about soil, plant health, and poultry. If he is not farming, you can find him on the soccer field, in the kitchen cooking, or brainstorming some new invention.

The couple has set out to connect the community to their food, produce high-quality vegetables, and maintain the beauty of the landscape. They are doing this through a year-round CSA that sells vegetables to various restaurants in the surrounding area, as well as the Burlington Summer and Winter Farmers' Markets, and the Capital City Winter Market. By following strict guidelines for food production, without the use of pesticides and herbicides, the farm has been certified by NOFA-VT. Both Jon and Karin are in agreement, they have indeed found their dream farm!

Roasted Rainbow Potatoes with Mixed Herb Pesto

Serves 6

This versatile pesto is the perfect way to use leftover herbs. It is delicious added to egg dishes or tossed into bread dough for a subtle herbal note. Himalayan salt, known for its rose color, is a premium salt, widely touted for its mineral content.

Pesto

Makes about ½ cup

1 cup tightly packed fresh flat-leafed parsley leaves
1 tablespoon coarsely chopped fresh thyme leaves
1 tablespoon coarsely chopped fresh rosemary leaves
1 tablespoon coarsely chopped fresh sage leaves
1 tablespoon coarsely chopped fresh basil leaves
2 medium cloves garlic, peeled and cut in half
¼ cup (1 ounce) freshly grated Parmigiano-Reggiano cheese, plus extra for serving
2 teaspoons freshly grated lemon zest, plus extra for serving (preferably from unwaxed lemon)
½ cup extra virgin olive oil
Salt

Potatoes

2 pounds potatoes, assorted colors, such as purple, red bliss, and sweet, cut into 1-inch cubes
Himalayan pink salt
Freshly ground black pepper

Preheat the broiler to the highest temperature. Lightly oil a 9-by-13-inch baking dish and set aside.

To make the pesto: Process the parsley, thyme, rosemary, sage, basil, garlic, cheese, and lemon zest in a food processor. While the motor is running, slowly add the olive oil, scraping down the sides of the bowl as needed, until well combined. Season with salt to taste. Set aside.

To make the potatoes: Place the potatoes in a medium stockpot and cover with water. Bring to a simmer over medium-high heat and cook until the potatoes are just tender, about 5 minutes. Drain. Transfer the potatoes to the prepared baking dish. Add ¼ cup of the pesto to the vegetables and toss to combine, making sure to coat all the vegetables well. Season with salt and pepper to taste.

Broil, stirring every 5 minutes, until the potatoes are fork tender and golden brown, about 10 minutes.

Toss with additional pesto, if desired. Season with salt and pepper to taste. Adjust seasonings with additional cheese and lemon zest, if desired. Serve the potatoes with roasted chicken or fish and a fresh green vegetable.

Recipe from Bear Roots Farm

Charred Corn Salad with Cherry Tomatoes, Cilantro, and Cotija Cheese

Serves 4–6 as a side dish

"During the height of summer, this is one of Woodbelly Pizza's most popular side salads. The simple combination of sweet corn and cherry tomatoes, laced with fresh herbs and lime juice, is a great side dish for braised or roasted meats. Woodbelly buys fresh corn by the bushel from local farms." *–Suzanne Podhaizer for Woodbelly Pizza*

4 tablespoons butter
3 cups fresh corn kernels (cut from 4 medium ears of corn)
½ teaspoon salt
¼ teaspoon freshly ground black pepper
1 tablespoon fresh lime juice from 1 large lime
1 pint cherry tomatoes, halved
½ cup finely sliced scallions, white and green parts
½ cup (loosely packed) fresh cilantro leaves, minced
2 ounces cotija cheese, finely crumbled, plus more for sprinkling

Melt the butter in a large skillet over medium heat. Just as the butter begins to brown, add the corn, salt, and pepper, stirring often, until char marks appear all over, about 6 minutes. When the corn kernels start to jump around in the skillet, that is a good indication that the corn is done.

Transfer to a large bowl. Add the lime juice, tomatoes, scallions, cilantro, and cheese, tossing until well combined. Adjust seasonings with additional lime juice, if desired, and salt and pepper to taste. Garnish with additional cheese. Serve at once.

Recipe from Suzanne Podhaizer for Woodbelly Pizza
Photograph by Oliver Parini

Note: Cotija cheese is crumbly and salty, similar to feta cheese. It is also delicious when crumbled or grated over pizza and pasta dishes.

Variation: Add minced jalapeño, fresh basil, or mint to the mixture.

Tonewood Maple

Growing up on a farm in Canada, Dori Ross discovered early on the importance of maple trees and the products derived from them. As she explains, "Maple is iconic to Canadians, it's on our flag and in our blood!" This maple lover worked in Canada for the Gillette Company for five years before being transferred to the Boston area. That's when her family purchased a ski condo in Vermont's Mad River Valley. Dori worked in marketing for fifteen years before the decision was made to move the family to a farm in the Mad River Valley. It seemed like the perfect place to raise three children—lots of open space peppered with a mix of maple trees that could be tapped for personal use.

Tonewood Maple became a reality in March of 2012. Dori collaborates and works with two of the Mad River Valley's longstanding sugar bush maple farms, and their sugar makers, who supply her with rich maple syrup. Other producers around the state furnish the company with the solid forms of maple it needs. Solid forms of maple are created by the naturally occurring crystallization process that occurs when maple syrup is heated and stirred. Tonewood's solid forms include: maple cubes, maple flakes, maple cream, maple granules, and maple wafers. These forms of maple are made from just one ingredient—100 percent pure maple syrup. Her business is committed to preserving the maple farming industry and its multigenerational, sugar making families. She emphasizes, "My company is part food, part mission. Its goal is to share the culture and history of Vermont's maple industry."

The packaging and shipping of Tonewood's products are done in a garage on her property. This is where Dori and her small team—which increases during the busy holiday season—package maple syrup in the company's signature bottles, which feature a modern design. Solid maple cubes, delicate wafer candies, plus maple cream, flakes, and seasoning are packed in Tonewood's unique containers, which mirror the square shape of its maple cube—clean and sleek. The company logo, which depicts a mosaic droplet, represents the maple syrup grades and color tones: Golden Delicate, Amber Rich, and Dark Robust.

Dori Ross is most proud of Tonewood Maple's innovative tree adoption program, one of the first of its kind. Participants who adopt a maple tree receive a picture of their tree, an adoption certificate, and three bottles of its bounty, along with other maple goodies, during the course of the year. Roughly 300 maple trees have been adopted since the program has been in effect.

The company also seeks to protect maple production by limiting the effects of climate change by donating to the Proctor Maple Research Center at the University of Vermont. The center's focus is on climate change research, improving harvesting technology, and understanding maple tree physiology and health. Dori hopes that with her support, maple production in New England will be ensured for future generations. She says, "Our local Mad River Valley sugar makers are incredible forest stewards, working to ensure that their trees grow for hundreds of years."

As an active member of the Mad River Valley Network, Dori works with sugar makers, farmers, and chefs to create exceptional maple-inspired recipes. She clarifies, "Everything we do works within the boundaries of our local food movement to promote our terroir, or taste of place." Through the funding of climate change research, local farming efforts, and sustainable forest stewardship Dori is doing her part to preserve maple farming and production in Vermont—after all, maple is in her blood!

Maple Kale Salad with Toasted Almonds, Parmigiano-Reggiano Cheese, and Rustic Croutons

Serves 8

This simple salad is light, with subtle layers of flavors. The delicate sweetness from the maple syrup and maple shavings collaborates with the slight citrus notes from the lemon juice, as well as hints of nuttiness from the almonds and Parmigiano-Reggiano cheese. The croutons can be made ahead and stored in an airtight container for up to two days.

Croutons

1 tablespoon extra virgin olive oil
1 cup ¼-inch pieces country bread
Kosher salt and freshly ground black pepper

Toasted Almonds

1 cup sliced almonds

Maple Dijon Vinaigrette

Makes scant ½ cup dressing

4 tablespoons sunflower oil
2 tablespoons organic unfiltered apple cider vinegar
2 teaspoons Dijon mustard
4 teaspoons pure Vermont maple syrup
1 teaspoon minced garlic
Salt and freshly ground black pepper

Salad

14 ounces kale leaves, large stems removed, sliced into thin ribbons (about 8 cups)
¾ cup freshly shaved Parmigiano-Reggiano cheese
1 tablespoon fresh lemon juice, optional
Freshly shaved maple cube or maple flakes for garnish

To make the croutons: In a large skillet, heat the olive oil over medium heat until hot but not smoking. Add the bread pieces and cook, stirring often, until golden brown and crisp, about 4 minutes. Drain on a paper towel-lined plate. Season with salt and pepper to taste.

To make the toasted almonds: Place the almonds in a dry medium nonstick skillet and toast over medium heat, stirring often, until light golden brown, about 4 minutes. Remove from the skillet and set aside.

To make the vinaigrette: In a small bowl, whisk together the oil, vinegar, mustard, maple syrup, and garlic. Season with salt and pepper to taste. Set aside.

To make the salad: In a large bowl, combine the kale with 4½ tablespoons of the dressing. Using a pair of tongs, toss the kale until it slightly softens, about 4 minutes, adding more dressing to taste. Season with salt and pepper to taste. Top with almonds and cheese, tossing until well combined. Drizzle with fresh lemon juice, if desired. Garnish with maple shavings. Serve.

Recipe from Tonewood Maple
Photograph by Brent Harrewyn

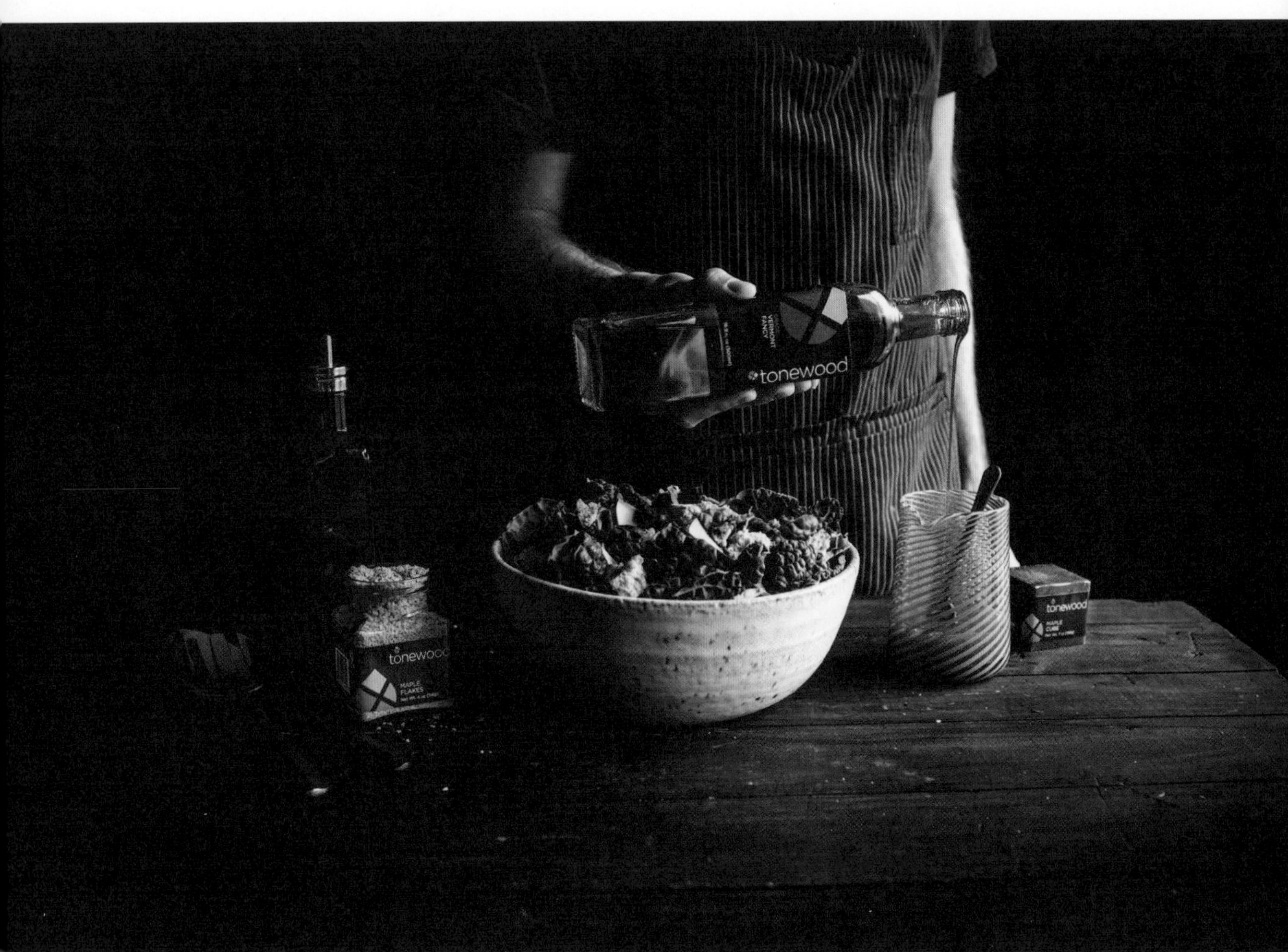

PROFILE

Marigold Kitchen Pizza

Making truly delicious, yet healthy pizza is a culinary art form that many have attempted, but few have successfully mastered. Not so for Marigold Kitchen, a small pizzeria tucked away in the village of North Bennington, in southwest Vermont. This treasure opened in 2008 as a venture between friends who wanted a great pizza shop in their neighborhood. To guarantee satisfaction, Marigold has made a promise to those who come through its doors: "If you do not enjoy your meal, the next one is on us." They really enjoy and are proud of what they do.

The restaurant has also pledged to use only the finest local organic produce, honoring the promise by partnering with many nearby farmers. This strong farm-to-restaurant connection enables Marigold Kitchen to use the freshest seasonal vegetables that are grown and harvested right there in southern Vermont.

Customers can choose from two original hand-tossed crust options, mixed wheat or whole wheat, both of which are prepared daily from dough using Vermont-grown organic flour. They also provide a made-in-Vermont gluten-free crust, thus being able to cater to all pizza lovers. Knowing that the pizza-making process must be perfect from start to finish, Marigold always begins with organic virgin olive oil and ends with locally sourced farm fresh cheeses. Marigold Kitchen has at least a dozen different types of cheeses in the shop, and most of them come from small Vermont farms.

This artisan pizzeria offers dietary options for those who require a vegetarian or vegan meal, including a vegan cheese. Marigold Kitchen Pizza is a member of the Vermont Fresh Network, an organization that supports the farmers and chefs who partner with each other to bring the freshest locally grown food to Vermonters and those who visit the Green Mountain State.

Marigold Kitchen is a BYOB pizzeria, but unlike many other restaurants, does not charge a corking fee, encouraging regulars to bring their favorite beer and wine.

With simply delicious pizzas, brick oven baked breads, and great salads, Marigold Kitchen Pizza is one of southern Vermont's best dining experiences. While they are open every day for dinner and open weekends for lunch and dinner, be sure to remember that this friendly neighborhood eatery does close during the winter, leaving its loyal patrons counting down the days until spring!

Rosie Pizza

Serves 4; 2 pieces each

"One of our local and staff favorites is our Rosie pizza. Our pizza dough uses a mixture of two organic flours: organic white flour from Champlain Valley Milling and organic whole wheat flour from Gleason Grains. It should be noted that our exact pizza dough recipe is a secret." —*Marigold Kitchen Pizza*

Caramelized Onions

2 tablespoons unsalted butter
1 large white or yellow onion, halved and sliced into ⅛-inch-thick half rounds
Kosher salt and pepper to taste

Pizza Dough

Coarse cornmeal
1 pound pizza dough, homemade or store-bought
1 tablespoon extra virgin olive oil, plus extra for drizzling
⅓ cup freshly shredded Parmigiano-Reggiano cheese, plus extra for sprinkling

Pizza Topping

⅔ cup organic crushed tomato pizza sauce
⅔ cup thinly sliced button or cremini mushrooms
4 ounces fresh mozzarella cheese, sliced ¼ inch thick, preferably Maplebrook Farm
4 ounces smoked mozzarella cheese, sliced ¼ inch thick, preferably Maplebrook Farm
8 very thin slices Prosciutto di Parma, coarsely chopped
½ teaspoon dried oregano

For Assembly

Extra virgin olive oil, for drizzling
1 cup packed baby arugula

At least 45 minutes before baking, set a pizza stone on the lowest rack of a cold oven and preheat to 450 degrees Fahrenheit.

To make the caramelized onions: Melt the butter in a large skillet over medium heat. Add the onions and cook for 2 minutes, stirring frequently. Reduce the heat to low, cover, and continue to cook, stirring occasionally, until the onions are soft and caramelized, about 50 minutes. Remove the onions from the heat and set aside.

To assemble: Sprinkle the cornmeal onto a pizza peel and place the dough on the peel. Gently deflate the dough. Using your hands, stretch out the dough into a 14-inch round pizza or 14-by-16-inch rectangle. Lightly brush the dough with olive oil. Sprinkle the Parmigiano-Reggiano cheese evenly over the crust. Slide the pizza crust onto the baking stone and bake for 5 minutes.

Leaving the crust on the baking stone, carefully spread the pizza sauce evenly over the dough, leaving a 1-inch border. Scatter the onions and mushrooms evenly over the dough, leaving a 1-inch border. Lay the mozzarella slices evenly over the dough, leaving a 1-inch border. Arrange the prosciutto evenly over the dough, leaving a 1-inch border. Sprinkle with oregano.

Bake until the edge of the crust is lightly crisp and the cheese is lightly browned, about 15 minutes.

Using the pizza peel, transfer the pizza to a large platter. Arrange the arugula in the center of the pizza. Sprinkle the top with Parmigiano-Reggiano cheese and drizzles of olive oil, if desired. Cut and serve.

Recipe from Marigold Kitchen Pizza

Note: If you don't own a pizza stone, you can use a flat (or upside down rimmed) baking sheet or a pizza pan.

Golden Well Farm & Apiaries

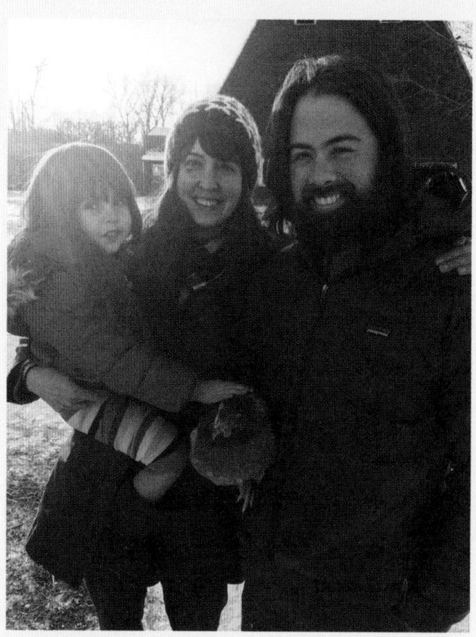

Ryan Miller and Nicole Burke first met in New Mexico, where a mutual love of honeybees brought them together. They moved back east to Vermont to be closer to Nicole's family, pursue their love of bees, start a farm, and start a family.

In 2012, the couple cofounded Golden Well Farm & Apiaries, a diversified vegetable farm located in New Haven, Vermont, along the New Haven River. The farm's vegetables are certified organic, its owners doing their part to ensure healthy soils, waterways, and ecosystems. The farm's CSA shares offer produce that is harvested and distributed to members within hours—fresh from farm to table.

Golden Well Farm & Apiaries offers "Bed and Breakfast Farm Stays" and also hosts retreats and community events. Their new "Farm to Pizza" night, featuring wood-fired pies and salads made with vegetables fresh from the fields and their farm-made APIS Honey Kombucha, is growing in popularity. Also located on the farm is 2 Wolves Center, which offers wellness classes, such as yoga and martial arts, along with community workshops and agricultural education events. Ryan and Nicole feel a strong sense of community involvement, which is demonstrated by their ever-growing relationships with local restaurants and their chefs, who buy the farm's produce and honey. They also sell at nearby farmers' markets and donate to the local food shelf.

The couple readily acknowledges, "The bees are our first love. They are amazing and intelligent beings that color our earth and give us so much of what we eat."

Photograph by Brian Crumley

Moroccan Spiced Rainbow Carrot Salad

Serves 4; 1 cup each

"This salad was inspired by an old Moroccan recipe that was passed down by my family and taught to me by my mother. This salad can be made the day before, just be sure to toss the salad a few times a day to meld the flavors." —*Nicole Burke, owner, Golden Well Farm & Apiaries*

4 cups (about 1½ pounds without tops) rainbow organic carrots, peeled and sliced into ⅛-inch rounds
5 tablespoons olive oil
3 tablespoons lemon juice, from 1 lemon
2 medium garlic cloves, crushed garlic
1½ teaspoons ground cumin
1 teaspoon paprika
½ teaspoon salt
½ teaspoon freshly ground black pepper
⅛ teaspoon cinnamon
⅛ teaspoon cayenne pepper
2 teaspoons raw honey
1 cup coarsely chopped cilantro leaves

Bring a pot of water, big enough to hold a steamer basket, to a boil over medium-high heat. Place the carrots in a steamer basket and steam over medium-high heat just until fork tender, about 5 minutes.

While the carrots are steaming, fill a large bowl with ice water. Set aside.

Drain the carrots, transfer to the bowl with ice water, and let cool completely, about 10 minutes. Drain and set aside.

In a large bowl, whisk together the oil, lemon juice, garlic, cumin, paprika, salt, pepper, cinnamon, cayenne pepper, and honey until well combined. Add the carrots and cilantro, tossing until well combined. Allow salad to cool in the refrigerator for at least 1 hour. Adjust seasonings with salt and pepper to taste. Serve.

Recipe from Golden Well Farm & Apiaries

Note: Plunging the cooked carrots in ice water stops the cooking process and helps to keep the carrots crisp and tender.

1000 Stone Farm

Kyle Doda moved to Vermont in 2012 to be closer to his extended family. His love of backpacking, skiing, and mountain biking drew him to the rocky, rolling hills of Brookfield, Vermont. After working on various farms for more than six years, he wanted to be part of a community that believed in, and supported, sustainability and clean water.

In 2012, after leasing land from family members, Kyle started a small four-season homestead farm on 3 acres of farmland. It was named after its location at 1000 Stone Road and the fact that folks jokingly say that the farm has the uncanny ability to grow beautiful rocks on its boulder-laden slopes.

The produce grown is certified organic, with a focus on companion planting, mechanical barriers, and crop rotation. This is done with the help of a greenhouse and five new hoop houses. The hoop houses are unheated, but allow for a large amount of greens to be produced during the colder months. The farm offers CSA shares, which include a delicious variety of produce, 45 weeks of the year. Offerings include: salad greens, kale, broccoli, cauliflower, Brussels sprouts, bok choi, tatsoi, chard, beets, carrots, onions, garlic, scallions, ramps, cherry and heirloom tomatoes, hot and sweet peppers, eggplant, and husk cherries, as well as other flavor-filled seasonal offerings. Kyle can be found at the Burlington Farmers' Market and Uncommon Market in Montpelier. His produce is also featured on the menus of a few local restaurants, where he has created relationships that not only work for the farmer, but the restaurant as well.

The farm's newest venture is oyster mushroom cultivation. The mushrooms are grown in reusable buckets on shredded straw that is inoculated with the proper mushroom spawn, which is determined by the time of year. Those involved with this project are excitedly waiting for the first harvest. Kyle readily admits that great things cannot be done alone and is extremely grateful to the wonderful folks who have offered to lend a hand.

Photographs by Tristan Von Duntz

Beet Salad with Red Onions and Baby Spinach

Serves 4

This colorful salad offers a balance of tangy, earthy, and mildly sweet!

3 cups (about 1 pound 5 ounces) assorted colored beets, washed, trimmed, peeled, and cut into 1-inch chunks
3 tablespoons extra virgin olive oil
Salt and pepper to taste
1 cup (half of a large onion) thinly sliced red onion
1 4-ounce log fresh goat cheese, crumbled
2 tablespoons fresh lemon juice
4 cups packed baby spinach
Fresh thyme leaves, for garnish

Preheat the oven to 400 degrees Fahrenheit. Lightly oil a quarter-sheet pan and set aside.

Place the beets in a large bowl. Drizzle the oil over the beets, season with salt and pepper to taste, and toss to combine, making sure to coat the beets well.

Spread the beets on the prepared sheet pan. Roast, stirring every 15 minutes, until the beets are fork tender, about 45 minutes. Allow the beets to slightly cool, about 20 minutes, reserving any leftover oil.

In a large bowl, combine the beets, reserved oil, onions, goat cheese, lemon juice, and spinach, tossing until well combined. Adjust seasonings with salt and pepper to taste. Garnish with fresh thyme and serve at once.

Recipe from 1000 Stone Farm
Photograph by Oliver Parini

Pingala Café & Eatery

Pingala Café and Eatery can be found on the first floor of the Chace Mill building, located alongside the winding Winooski River. In Sanskrit, the word Pingala means "sun energy and life force," which is the feeling the café hopes to convey with its large, sunny windows overlooking the river and downtown Winooski. The eatery's weathered wood floors, brick walls, and high ceilings exude a rustic charm. The mural on the walls reflects the Vermont landscape, complete with mountains, gardens, trees, and a food truck. Unlike outdoor food trucks however, guests are guaranteed a cozy, bright, and comfortable place to sit and enjoy their food.

The moment Trevor Sullivan set foot in Vermont, he knew he was home. Since he opened his eatery, he's cultivated relationships with a number of local organic farmers who support and follow the tenets of the non-GMO movement.

Inspired by his mother's cooking, Trevor strives to make food fun, delicious, and approachable. The menu at Pingala is 100 percent plant-based, with the ingredients coming from local farms, and many of the menu options are gluten-free.

Trevor admits that his café is a labor of love. He hopes to put vegan fare on the map in Burlington and beyond by letting the fresh organic produce speak for itself. Simplicity and diversity are the core values around which this dedicated chef has built his business, supported by a commitment to the well-being of our planet and its inhabitants.

Photograph by Oliver Parini

Charred Broccolini with Cashew Alfredo Sauce

Serves 6 as a main dish

For a smooth and creamy Alfredo sauce, it is important to presoak the cashews so they become tender and softened. If you don't have time to soak the cashews overnight, place them in a heat-resistant bowl, then fill the bowl with boiling water until the nuts are completely submerged and allow to soak for 30–40 minutes.

Cashew Alfredo Sauce
Makes 3¼ cups
2 cups raw cashew pieces
1½ cups water
1 tablespoon nutritional yeast
2 teaspoons fine sea salt
1 teaspoon garlic powder
½ teaspoon dried oregano
½ teaspoon dried basil

Pasta
1 pound fettuccine noodles

Brocolini
3 tablespoons extra virgin olive oil, plus extra for the grill
1 tablespoon tamari
1 tablespoon Dijon mustard
1 tablespoon tomato paste
2 medium garlic cloves, peeled and finely grated
1 teaspoon freshly ground black pepper
1–2 bunches broccolini, trimmed and cut into 3-inch-long pieces

Finely grated lemon zest, for garnish (preferably from unwaxed lemon)
½ cup homemade or high-quality store-bought croutons, lightly crushed, for garnish
Micro greens, for garnish

To make the cashew alfredo sauce: Place the cashews in a medium bowl. Fill the bowl with water, making sure the cashews are completely submerged. Soak the cashews overnight. Drain and rinse. Place the soaked cashews and the remaining ingredients for the Alfredo Sauce in a blender or food processor and process until smooth and creamy. Adjust seasonings with salt to taste.

Preheat a gas or electric grill to medium-high and generously brush the cooking grate with oil.

To make the fettuccine noodles: Bring a large pot of salted water to a boil, add the pasta, then cook until al dente. Drain and transfer to a large bowl.

While the pasta is boiling, make the broccolini. In a large bowl, whisk together the olive oil, tamari, mustard, tomato paste, garlic, and pepper. Adjust seasonings with salt to taste. Add the broccolini and toss until well combined. Remove the broccolini from the oil mixture and grill, covered, without flipping, until charred, about 8–12 minutes. Using tongs, transfer the broccolini to a platter and set aside.

To assemble: Add 2 cups of the sauce to the pasta and toss to coat well, adding more sauce as desired. Top each mound of pasta with a few stalks of broccolini. Adjust seasonings with salt and pepper to taste. Garnish with lemon zest, if desired, croutons, and micro greens. Serve at once.

Recipe from Pingala Café & Eatery
Photograph by Oliver Parini

Note: The Alfredo sauce makes more than you will need for this recipe. Serve the extra sauce over meatballs.

Sweet and Sour Beets

Serves 4–5 as a side dish

"People are often intrigued with the smoked maple syrup but don't always know how to use it. This is a beautiful beet recipe that highlights how perfectly the maple with a hint of smoke can go with vegetables. Orange juice complements the sweetness, while a dose of cider vinegar gives a little edge. Chopped chives balance the dish with a bit of onion and gorgeous green contrast."
—*Laura Sorkin, owner, Runamok Maple*

Beets

3 large beets (about 1 pound 6 ounces), peeled and sliced ¼ inch thick

Sweet and Sour Sauce

½ cup orange juice
2 medium garlic cloves, peeled and minced
3 tablespoons smoked maple syrup, plus more for drizzling
2 tablespoons organic, unfiltered apple cider vinegar
1 whole star anise
Salt and freshly ground black pepper
1 tablespoon butter
2 tablespoons fresh chopped chives

Place the beets, orange juice, garlic, maple syrup, vinegar, and star anise in a large skillet. Season with salt and pepper to taste. Bring to a boil over medium-high heat; then reduce to a simmer, cover, and cook until fork tender, about 50 minutes, turning the beets every so often to coat with the liquid. Using a slotted spoon, transfer the beets to a serving plate.

Bring the sauce to a simmer over medium heat. Whisk in the butter and continue to cook until the sauce thickens and coats the back of a spoon, about 4 minutes. Season with salt and pepper to taste. Drizzle the sauce over the beets. Garnish the beets with chives and drizzles of smoked maple syrup, if desired.

Recipe from Runamok Maple
Photograph by Oliver Parini

PROFILE

Mighty Food Farm

Mighty Food Farm is a certified organic mixed vegetable, strawberry, herb, bedding plant, and flower operation. Lisa MacDougall is the proud owner of the farm's 154 charming acres, 20 of which are used to grow a diverse assortment of vegetables and fruit. In July 2016, she purchased the beautiful property in Shaftsbury, Vermont, which offers prime loam, good water, and a spectacular view—the perfect place to call home.

This dedicated farmer takes no time off from May thru October, working 17-hour days. Lisa readily admits that during peak season she sees her customers more often than her family. She grows more than 40 different kinds of vegetables, "in quantities that could feed a village for a very long time," she says. Her patrons know that they might pay less for produce at the supermarket, but have found that locally grown food tastes better and offers them an opportunity to eat different varieties of fruits and vegetables. A good example being the farm's delicious Lillian's Heirloom Tomatoes and Magic Molly Purple Fingerling Potatoes, which are rarely found in grocery stores.

Lisa explains why she chose certified organic farming: "I have a deep belief in producing healthy food and know that if people eat better they will feel better, improving both our health and the environment. Farming organically and being certified is one way to help our country's food system."

The farm's CSA runs from June through March of the following year, offering subscribers ten months of pickups. Unlike other CSA programs, it is a free choice CSA, so members are able to pick and choose from a wide variety of produce.

Growing high-quality produce with respect for the environment is what Mighty Food Farm is all about!

Photograph by Tristan Von Duntz

Carrot and Spinach Slaw

Serves 8

This vibrant, festive slaw is fresh and aromatic, with a nice earthy and nutty flavor from the cumin seeds. The golden turmeric powder gives it a subtle warm color and a mild peppery flavor.

Vinaigrette
Makes about 1 cup
⅓ cup organic unfiltered apple cider vinegar
2 tablespoons sesame seed oil
2 tablespoons pure maple syrup
1 tablespoon low-sodium soy sauce
1 teaspoon cumin seeds
1 teaspoon turmeric powder
Salt and freshly ground black pepper

Carrot and Spinach Slaw
2 pounds carrots, peeled and shredded
1 cup packed fresh large-leafed spinach leaves, cut crosswise into ¼-inch-thick strips
1 medium shallot bulb, peeled and minced (about ¼ cup)
¼ cup toasted almond slivers, optional

To make the vinaigrette: Whisk together the vinegar, oil, maple syrup, soy sauce, cumin seeds, and turmeric in a small bowl. Season with salt and pepper to taste.

To make the carrot and spinach slaw: Combine the carrots, spinach, and shallots in a medium bowl. Add half of the vinaigrette, tossing until evenly coated, then add more to taste. Season with salt and pepper to taste. Cover and refrigerate for 2–3 hours before serving. Garnish with toasted almond slivers.

Recipe from Mighty Food Farm

PROFILE

Kettle Song Farm

Kettle Song Farm is situated on 65 sprawling acres nestled at the foot of Worcester Mountain in a tiny Vermont town of the same name. Although countrified, it is approximately 15 minutes from Montpelier, the state's capitol. Owner Jaiel Pulskamp grows organic vegetables on 4 acres of land, concentrating on soil health and microbes to produce robust plants. Her goal is to bring nutrient-dense foods to the surrounding community, believing that there is a direct correlation between the condition of the soil and the well-being of the people who share its bounty.

Jaiel does not like to use any type of pesticide, trusting that focusing on the integrity of the soil will enable crops to build a natural immunity along with an ability to defend themselves from pests. She understands that the healthier the soil is, the more nutrients crops will have to sustain and nourish our bodies.

She fell in love with organic practices, believing that we desperately need to change the way that food is grown. Since Kettle Song's owner feels strongly that chemical agriculture is harming our health and environment, the farm is doing everything possible to produce wholesome greens, squash, herbs, potatoes, garlic, and salad mix. The plan is to diversify into medicinal herbs and berries over the next few years. Dedicated to changing how and what people eat, Jaiel is working to educate chefs and customers about holistic food systems, stressing the hazards of products with genetically engineered ingredients.

Jaiel and her husband are both musicians. Because of their love of music, they often hear melody in life's most simple tasks. Each morning, the kettle's whistling tune brings a comforting predictability to the beginning of their busy day. This connecting of music to food helped the couple to create the perfect name for their farm, Kettle Song. Hopefully through Jaiel's unwavering commitment to organic practices and responsible land stewardship, Kettle Song's message will play on and on.

Brussels Sprouts with a Creamy Sriracha Dipping Sauce

Serves 4 as a side dish

This dipping sauce is smooth and creamy with a tangy heat and a hint of sweetness that pairs perfectly with the earthy Brussels sprouts.

Brussels Sprouts

1 pound Brussel sprouts, trimmed and halved lengthwise
3 medium garlic cloves, minced
2 tablespoons virgin coconut oil, melted
Salt and freshly ground black pepper

Creamy Sriracha Dipping Sauce

Makes about ½ cup

¼ cup sour cream
¼ cup mayonnaise
½ teaspoon prepared horseradish
½ teaspoon sriracha sauce
½ teaspoon garlic powder
¼ teaspoon cayenne pepper or chili powder

To make the Brussels sprouts: Preheat the oven to 400 degrees Fahrenheit. Lightly oil a rimmed baking sheet and set aside.

In a medium bowl, combine the Brussels sprouts, garlic, and oil until well combined. Place the Brussels sprouts on the prepared baking sheet in a single layer, cut side down. Season with salt and pepper to taste. Bake in the oven, stirring occasionally, until crispy and golden brown, about 20 minutes. Adjust seasonings with salt and pepper to taste.

While the Brussels sprouts are roasting, make the dipping sauce: In a small bowl, stir together the sour cream, mayonnaise, horseradish, sriracha sauce, garlic powder, and cayenne pepper, until well combined. Season with salt and pepper to taste.

Serve the Brussels sprouts at once with the creamy sriracha dipping sauce on the side.

Recipe from Kettle Song Farm
Photograph by Oliver Parini

Autumn Salad

Serves 4–5

This recipe has a wide variation of textures and flavors—the crispy, bitter Belgian endive leaves, mild sweetness from the delicata squash and Honeycrisp apple, and the tangy flavor and creamy texture of the blue cheese—that make this dish a nice departure from traditional salads.

Roast Squash

1 (about 1½ pounds) delicata squash
3 tablespoons organic brown sugar
2 tablespoons extra virgin olive oil
2 teaspoons fresh minced thyme
1 teaspoon Aleppo pepper
Salt and freshly ground black pepper

Dressing

Makes about 1 cup

2½ tablespoons rendered pancetta fat, divided (about one 4-ounce piece of pancetta)
3 tablespoons smooth Dijon mustard
3 tablespoons sherry vinegar
1 tablespoon pure maple syrup
½ cup extra virgin olive oil
Kosher salt and pepper

Salad

1 pound Belgian endive, trimmed, sliced crosswise into ribbons, about ½ inch thick
½ cup packed baby arugula
¼ cup assorted fresh herbs, such as chervil, tarragon, parsley, or chives, coarsely chopped
½ of a medium apple, such Honeycrisp, cored and cut into ⅛-inch-thick slices
½ cup walnuts, coarsely chopped
½ cup crumbled blue cheese, plus more for garnish

Preheat the oven to 450 degrees Fahrenheit. Lightly grease a baking sheet and set aside.

To make the squash: Cut the squash in half lengthwise and scoop out the seeds and strings. Cut the squash into half-moon slices, about ½ inch thick. In a medium bowl, combine the brown sugar, olive oil, thyme, and Aleppo pepper. Add the squash and toss until well combined. Season with salt and pepper to taste. Place the squash in a single layer on the prepared baking sheet. Roast until the squash is fork tender, tossing occasionally in the glaze, about 20 minutes. Set aside to cool to room temperature. Discard the skins, if desired.

While the squash is roasting, render the pancetta. Cut the pancetta into 1-inch pieces. Cook the pancetta in a medium skillet over low heat, turning the pieces occasionally, until the fat has melted away and the pancetta is crispy, about 35 minutes. Using a slotted spoon, remove the pancetta bits and reserve for garnish. Skim the rendered fat with a spoon and set aside.

To make the dressing: In a small bowl, whisk together 1½ tablespoons of the rendered fat, mustard, vinegar, and maple syrup. Slowly add the oil until well combined. Adjust seasonings with additional rendered fat, if desired, and salt and pepper to taste.

To assemble the salad: In a large bowl, combine the squash, endive, arugula, herbs, apple, walnuts, and blue cheese, tossing until well combined. Add ⅓ cup of the dressing, tossing until evenly coated, adding more to taste. Season with salt and pepper to taste. Garnish with reserved pancetta bits and cheese. Serve at once.

Recipe from JJ Hapgood General Store and Eatery

Baked Delicata Squash Seeds

To bake delicata squash seeds: Wash the seeds well and pat dry, then place on a cookie sheet in a single layer to dry. If you let the seeds dry completely, they will crisp up nicely when baked. Using 1 teaspoon of olive oil per squash, toss the dried seeds until coated with the oil, then place them on a cookie sheet. Season with sea salt and bake in an oven that's been preheated to 325 degrees Fahrenheit. Turn every 10 minutes until the seeds are golden brown. In about 20 minutes you have a healthy, delicious snack.

PROFILE

Elmer Farm

It was love that brought Jennifer and Spencer Blackwell together, a love of farming that is! The couple first met at the Intervale Center in Burlington, Vermont, a 350-acre complex comprised of a farmstead, greenhouse, barn, and various other enterprises and programs. Spencer was employed by the center, fixing equipment, working on building infrastructure, and managing the fields that were not being used by the farm program. Jennifer toiled on a large organic farm with a 450-member CSA program.

As a very young girl, Jennifer had spent many summers on her grandmother's farm learning about the art of growing food and its valuable connection to the community. Spencer started farming in college as a summer job, continuing to work at various farms after graduation, always dreaming of owning a place of his own. These experiences influenced the direction each of their lives would take, shaping their future together.

Thanks to the help and support of the Vermont Land Trust, the young couple was able to purchase Elmer Farm in 2006. The land access program provides qualified diversified farmers with access to good agricultural land and assists with the start-up. The farm had belonged to the Elmer family since the early 1800s; the Blackwells were the first non-Elmer family members to live there. The conserved 90-acre farm is located at the eastern edge of Vermont's Champlain Valley, just outside the village of East Middlebury. Receding glaciers have gifted the land with a mix of fertile soils that are excellent for growing vegetables. The couple explains, "We see the soil not as a medium to stand crops in, but as a living, breathing ecosystem."

With a combined 20 years of experience in growing vegetables, Jennifer and Spencer decided to plant a mix of organic vegetables and flowers. Elmer Farm is now a conserved and certified organic vegetable farm that serves the folks of Addison County, selling high-quality produce at farmers' markets, retail outlets, and through a CSA.

They grow 35 different vegetables, a beautiful assortment of flowers, and culinary herbs on 35 fertile acres. Many delicious heirloom varieties are included in these offerings. The owners are grateful for their five-member farm crew, knowing that they couldn't possibly do what they do without their hard work and dedication.

CSA members pick up their vegetables at the farm each week, selecting and creating their own weekly share from the available produce. This community-farm connection establishes a vital bond between local consumers and the hardworking folks who grow their food. Members can also harvest their own herbs and cut flowers once a week. Elmer Farm offers small, medium, and large shares to meet each customer's needs, striving to make farm shares affordable for all members of the community.

The Blackwell family, which now includes 10-year-old Angus, 7-year-old Ida, and 3-year-old Mabel, is involved with a number of farm-to-school efforts that give students an opportunity to learn about food production and good nutrition. It is their mission to assist local food agencies so that all members of the community can have access to nutritious produce. For this dedicated couple, farming is not a job, it is a lifestyle—one that they both truly love.

Elmer Farm's Napa and Red Cabbage Slaw

Makes about 4 quarts

This bright and lively slaw can be enjoyed on its own or served as a delicious topping for tacos or pulled pork sandwiches. This dish also makes a great side dish to bring to a barbecue, potluck, or picnic.

Dressing
Makes 1½ cups
½ cup extra virgin olive oil
¼ cup organic unfiltered apple cider vinegar
4 tablespoons freshly squeezed lime juice
¼ cup Dijon mustard
2 tablespoons honey or pure maple syrup
½ teaspoon salt
¼ teaspoon freshly ground black pepper

Cabbage Slaw
1 medium (2 pounds) head Napa cabbage, shredded
½ head (about 1 pound) red cabbage, shredded
1 bunch scallions, white and green parts trimmed and sliced thin (about 1 cup loosely packed)
3 medium carrots, peeled and grated
1 medium red pepper, cored, seeded, and minced
1 medium radish, trimmed and finely grated
½ cup fresh chopped cilantro leaves

In a small bowl, whisk together the olive oil, vinegar, lime juice, mustard, honey, salt, and pepper.

Place the cabbages, scallions, carrots, red pepper, and radishes in a large bowl and toss with the dressing until well coated. Adjust seasonings with salt and pepper to taste. Cover and refrigerate for at least 1 hour. Fold in cilantro and season with salt and pepper to taste right before serving.

Recipe from Elmer Farm
Photograph by Oliver Parini

The Inn at Round Barn Farm

The number of round barns in Vermont has decreased over the years, but one of these unique buildings is prominently featured at The Inn at Round Barn Farm. It has been said that the unusual design originated with the Shakers, who constructed their barns in this peculiar fashion "to prevent the devil from catching you in the corners." The round barn is constructed with twelve exterior walls, creating an intriguing venue for weddings, art exhibits, cultural, and other community events. The barn was registered in the National Registry of Historic Places in 1988.

The picturesque inn, which operates as a bed and breakfast, is located in Waitsfield, Vermont. It is situated on 240 acres of grassy meadowlands that are sprinkled with sparkling ponds and breathtaking mountain vistas. Each of the inn's twelve rooms offers beautiful views of the surrounding countryside and charming gardens. The ambience is one of peaceful solitude.

Kim and Jim Donahue are the proud owners of the charming bed and breakfast. Executive Chef Charlie Menard, a native Vermonter, oversees the culinary side of the business, which includes breakfast, snacks, and afternoon treats, as well as the food served for special events. A graduate of the New England Culinary Institute, he has traveled the world, always knowing that he would one day return to Vermont. His culinary philosophy does not center on creating a specific food style, but rather on serving the "most responsibly sourced, wholesome food possible."

The grounds at the inn host a 5-acre organic garden located not far from the round barn. In charge of this area is David Hartshorn, a local organic farmer whose own farm is located a short distance down the road. David has worked with Chef Charlie for many years and was instrumental in gaining the garden's organic certification. He decides which fruits, vegetables, and herbs are best suited for planting. He confers daily with Chef Charlie about the needs and expectations for each day's menu. After years of working together, the two have developed a system that works well. When the busy chef requests a particular food item, David always seems to know the amount that's needed. At day's end, Chef Charlie often drops by the Hartshorn farm stand to place an order for the next day and visit for a while.

Before his day begins, the enthusiastic chef may stop by the garden to see what's ready to harvest. Master Gardener Carol Charles oversees the many herb and edible flower beds scattered throughout the grounds. The products from these gardens also find their way to the busy kitchen.

Guests are treated to a two- or three-course breakfast each morning. The day's offerings could be blueberries and lemon curd, sweet breads, scones, or cheddar chive biscuits followed by buttermilk pancakes or croque madame, with braised greens and heirloom potatoes. The menu changes daily, always featuring fresh, organic options, some of which are supplied by David and other local organic farmers.

Chef Charlie occasionally offers private cooking classes for the inn's guests. Whether making tantalizing hors d' oeuvres, comfort food, or hand-rolled pasta, the chef's creativity makes each class a memorable, fun-filled experience. A man of many talents, his latest project is "The Canteen Creemee Company," a farm-to-counter snack bar and creemee (soft-serve ice cream) stand located in the Waitsfield village square.

Buttercup Squash and Feta Cheese Soufflé

Makes seven 8-ounce ramekins or a 2-quart soufflé

"This recipe uses the buttercup squash—the underappreciated sibling of the butternut squash. After being persuaded by both my father and my mother to try this squash, I was immediately smitten, and my butternut soup is now buttercup soup. I also began to seek new uses for the squash, such as this soufflé. Don't be afraid; this recipe is really very easy and unique. It makes a wonderful, unexpected side dish to any meal." —*Chef Charlie Menard, The Inn at Round Barn Farm*

1 medium buttercup squash (about 2 pounds)
4 tablespoons unsalted butter, plus more for greasing
¼ cup all-purpose flour, plus more for dusting
1½ cups milk, warmed
¼ cup freshly grated Parmigiano-Reggiano cheese
¼ cup crumbled feta cheese
6 large eggs, separated
1 teaspoon salt
⅛ teaspoon freshly ground black pepper
¼ teaspoon hot sauce
Fresh minced rosemary or thyme for garnish
Cranberry relish or pickled cranberries, for accompaniment
Crackers

Position an oven rack in the center of the oven. Preheat the oven to 350 degrees Fahrenheit. Coat seven 8-ounce ramekins with butter. Lightly flour each ramekin, discarding any excess flour, and set aside. Lightly grease a 9-by-13-inch baking dish for the squash. Set aside.

Cut the squash in half lengthwise, then remove and discard the seeds and strings. Place the squash, cut-side down, in the prepared baking dish. Roast until fork tender, about 1 hour. Set aside to cool. When the squash is cool enough to handle, scoop out the flesh, transfer to a food processor, and process until smooth. You should have approximately 1½ cups of pureed squash.

Melt the butter in a 2-quart saucepan over medium heat. Whisk in the flour and cook, whisking often, until light golden brown, about 4 minutes. Slowly add the milk and cook, whisking often, until the sauce is thick and bubbling. Add the cheeses and mix until the they have melted. Remove from the heat and let cool to warm temperature.

In the meantime, using a stand mixer, beat the egg whites until stiff peaks form.

In a large bowl, whisk together the egg yolks, salt, pepper, and hot sauce. Whisking continuously, slowly add half of the cheese mixture into the egg yolks. Then add the egg mixture back into the remaining cheese mixture in saucepan. Add the squash and stir until well combined. Using a rubber spatula, gently fold half of the egg whites into the cheese mixture until just blended. Fold in the remaining egg whites until just blended.

Ladle the mixture into the prepared ramekins right under the rim. Place on a baking sheet. Bake the soufflés, uncovered, until puffed, lightly browned, and firm to the touch, approximately 30 minutes.

Garnish with rosemary. Serve at once with cranberry relish or pickled cranberries and crackers.

Recipe from Chef Charlie Menard, The Inn at Round Barn Farm

PROFILE

Valentine Farm

In 2001, Mark Cannella followed a friend, who would later become his wife, to the beautiful state of Vermont. Looking for a chance to become involved with agriculture, he apprenticed with a certified organic market gardener and found the job to be a perfect fit. Organic production met his goals for land stewardship and his desire to grow high-quality produce from a small-scale operation.

After farming on various rental properties for several years, he and his wife, Megan, broke ground for a new farm in East Montpelier, Vermont, in 2013. The farm's name stems from Mark's grandfather, Willis Valentine Miller, a man who had a lifelong love for growing things. On this small farm they grow specialty potatoes on ½ acre, with plans to expand the potato business and add a few more crops in the future.

Mark is focused on plant health and field dynamics, which made the resolution to grow organic produce a pretty simple decision. Because Valentine Farm is a part-time operation, its owners can be patient when it comes to crop rotation. As heavy cultivation would be too time consuming, fields and crops are rotated to suppress weeds. A variety of organic crop protectants are used to prevent disease and ensure a quality product, with minerals and amendments applied to balance the soil.

The farm's Vermont Certified Organic potatoes are cured and stored to maintain quality through the following spring. By targeting a few varieties, the farm can offer chefs a consistent product that they can count on through the winter months. Valentine Farm is a team effort, with Mark and Megan, along with their daughters, all helping with the planting and harvesting and of their delicious potatoes.

Cheesy Baked Potatoes with Broccoli, Caramelized Onions, and Bacon

Serves 6

These stuffed spuds are delicious as a main dish all on their own. Serve the potatoes with a green salad and a crusty bread.

Baked Potatoes

6 large (10 to 12 ounces each) baking potatoes, such as russet, scrubbed and dried
Extra virgin olive oil
Salt and freshly ground black pepper

Caramelized Onions

1 tablespoon unsalted butter
1 pound yellow or white onion, halved and sliced into ⅛-inch-thick half-rounds
Salt and freshly ground black pepper

Topping

4 bacon slices, diced
1½ cups broccoli florets, steamed until tender and chopped into bite-size pieces

Cheddar Cheese Sauce

Makes about 3 cups

2 cups whole milk
¼ cup butter
¼ cup all-purpose flour
2 cups coarsely grated sharp cheddar cheese
1 teaspoon ground mustard
Salt and freshly ground black pepper to taste
1¼ tablespoons thinly sliced fresh chives

To bake the potatoes: Preheat the oven to 425 degrees Fahrenheit. Line a baking sheet with foil. Set aside. Rub the potatoes with oil. Place the potatoes on the prepared baking sheet. Season with salt and pepper to taste. Using the tines of a fork, pierce the potatoes 6–8 times. Bake until the potatoes are fork tender, about 50 minutes, depending on the size of the potatoes. Let the potatoes rest for 10 minutes.

While the potatoes are baking, caramelize the onions. Melt the butter in a large skillet over medium heat. Add the onions and cook for 2 minutes, stirring frequently. Reduce the heat to low and continue to cook, stirring occasionally, until the onions are soft and caramelized, about 55 minutes. Season with salt and pepper to taste. Remove the onions from the heat and set aside.

While the onions are caramelizing, start cooking the bacon. Sauté the bacon in a medium sauté pan over medium heat, stirring occasionally, until crisp, about 12 minutes. Using a slotted spoon, transfer the bacon to a paper towel-lined plate to drain and set aside.

While the potatoes are resting, start the cheese sauce. Heat the milk in a saucepan over medium heat until it just begins to simmer.

In a separate medium saucepan, melt the butter over medium heat. Add the flour and cook, whisking often, until light golden brown, about 3 minutes. Whisking continuously, slowly add the milk, until the sauce is thick and bubbling. Add the cheese and mustard and continue to whisk until the cheese has completely melted. Adjust seasonings with salt and pepper.

To assemble: Slice the potatoes down the middle. Top with broccoli and caramelized onions. Drizzle with the cheese sauce. Garnish with bacon and chives. Serve at once.

Recipe from Valentine Farm
Photograph by Tristan Von Duntz

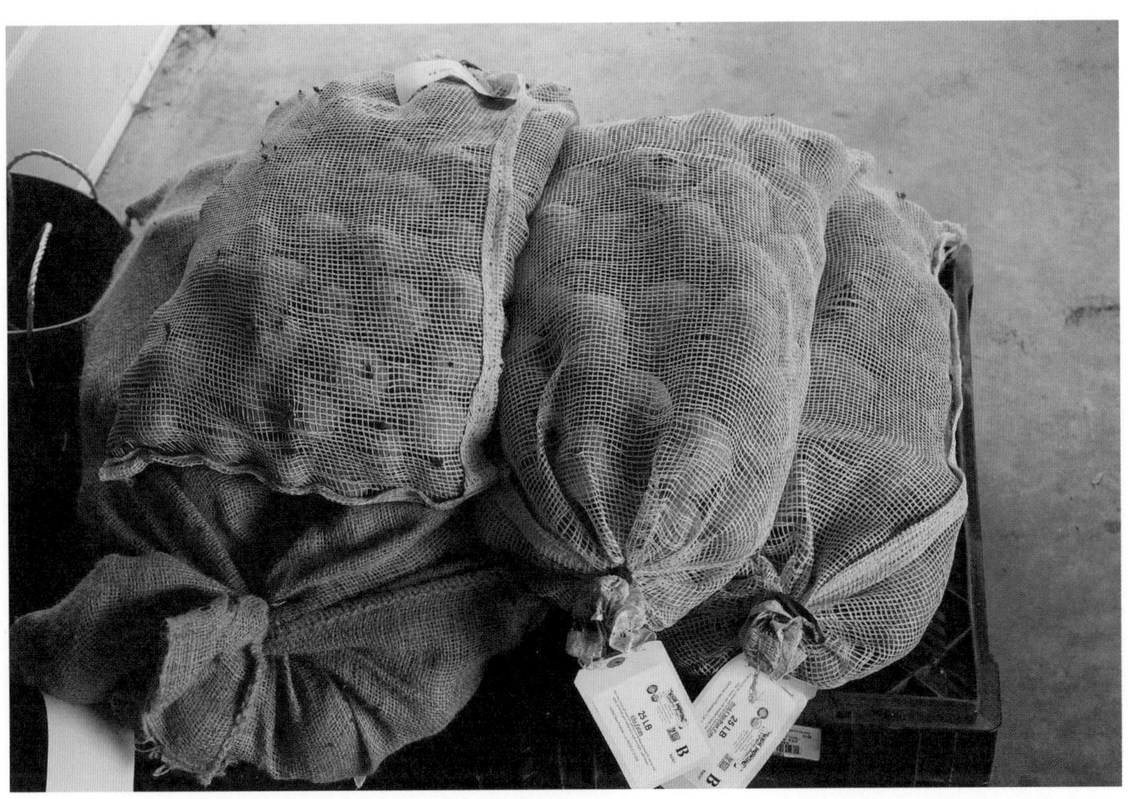

PROFILE

Benito's Hot Sauce

Back in 2004, Benito Maniscalco worked as a waiter in a Mexican restaurant in New Jersey. He loved their hot sauce, but always felt that there was one very important element missing from the product: heat. At that time, the backyard vegetable garden he tended behind his rented house was full of organic cayenne, habanero, and jalapeño peppers that he planned to preserve. Thinking that hot sauce would be the perfect means of preserving the peppers, Ben set out to make a sauce that had extra fresh flavor and the heat he so desired.

A friend allowed him to use his restaurant's kitchen, so Ben went to work making hot sauce. Over the next few years, he learned a lot about the specialty food business and enjoyed some amount of success selling his sauce at summer fairs and fall festivals. Realizing that it was time to spread his wings, he moved to Vermont in July 2008. He was drawn to the Green Mountain State, with its emphasis on locally made products that support the local economy, nurtured by a strong commitment to sustainable agriculture. Ben knew that he had found the perfect setting to start his new business.

Over the years, Ben has developed strong relationships with farmers throughout Vermont. Since 2009, he has been using 100 percent Vermont-grown chiles in all of his sauces. Benito's Hot Sauce now sources over 2,000 pounds of Vermont-grown chiles and other vegetables, as well as approximately 250 gallons of maple syrup, all of which are obtained from six local farms. People often tell him that his hot sauce tastes like fresh vegetables, which is music to his ears. He wants folks to recognize that flavor is just as important as heat level.

Ben is constantly testing and creating products in a commercial kitchen in Morrisville, Vermont, where he prepares, bottles, and warehouses his product. With constant experimentation, he has developed a few new hot sauces and two certified organic chile pepper–infused Vermont maple syrups to add to his line. His goal is to incorporate a range of heat levels, along with various flavor profiles. He has been committed to the non-GMO movement since 2013, when the company obtained Non-GMO Project Verification. The project's objective is to safeguard the non-GMO food supply, thereby providing consumers with an option.

All sauces are made with non-GMO and organic ingredients. He does not use filler ingredients, artificial flavors, preservatives, gums, or starches.

The busy entrepreneur still prepares, cooks, and bottles every batch of his pure vegetable hot sauce by hand. Ben readily acknowledges that his business is not about big name recognition, but rather about producing a fresh and unique product that is always made with organic and non-GMO ingredients. The company's products are sold year-round at Vermont's Burlington Farmers' Market, organic and natural food stores, specialty and gift shops, festivals, and a number of restaurants and eateries.

Roasted Brussels Sprouts with Infused Vermont Maple Syrup

Serves 4 as a side dish

The chipotle-infused maple syrup has a medium, smoky sweet heat. It is made with pure Vermont Grade A Dark Amber maple syrup harvested in Jeffersonville, Vermont. It is then combined with organic chipotle peppers that are grown at Foote Brook Farm in Johnson, Vermont.

1 pound Brussels sprouts, trimmed and halved lengthwise
1 tablespoon extra virgin olive oil, plus extra for baking sheet
Sea salt and freshly ground black pepper
2 tablespoons organic chipotle-infused Vermont maple syrup, such as the one from Benito's Hot Sauce

Preheat the oven to 400 degrees Fahrenheit. Lightly oil a quarter size rimmed baking sheet.

In a medium bowl, combine the Brussels sprouts, oil, salt, and pepper to taste. Place the Brussels sprouts on the prepared baking sheet in a single layer, cut side down. Season with salt and pepper to taste. Bake in the oven, shaking the pan every 5–7 minutes until crispy and golden brown, about 20 minutes,

Transfer the Brussels sprouts to a metal or porcelain bowl. Add the syrup and gently toss until well combined. Adjust seasonings with salt and pepper to taste. Serve at once.

Recipe from Benito's Hot Sauce

Sweet and Savory Kale Salad with Apple Cider Vinaigrette

Serves 4

The red color from the apple skins and cranberries create a beautiful contrast with the green kale and white feta cheese. The kale must be started 1 day before it is served.

Dressing

3 tablespoons extra virgin olive oil
3 tablespoons fresh lemon juice
1 tablespoon organic unfiltered apple cider vinegar, preferably Vermont Village
2 teaspoons Vermont honey
Salt

Salad

5–6 cups kale, stems removed, chopped into bite-size pieces
½ apple, such as Gala or Golden Delicious, unpeeled, cored, and diced
½ cup dried cranberries
½ cup crumbled feta cheese
1 ripe avocado, peeled, pitted, and cubed
2 tablespoons minced red onion
¼ cup toasted sliced almonds
Salt

To make the dressing: In a small bowl, whisk together the oil, lemon juice, vinegar, and honey until well combined. Adjust seasonings with salt to taste.

To make the salad: In a large bowl, combine the kale and the salad dressing. Using a pair of tongs or your hands, massage the kale for 3 minutes. Cover with plastic wrap and let chill in the refrigerator overnight.

To assemble: Just before serving, add the apple, dried cranberries, feta cheese, avocado, onion, and almonds, tossing until well combined. Season with salt to taste and serve.

Recipe from Village Cannery of Vermont

Someday Farm Kale and Feta Cheese Salad

Serves 2 as a main dish or 4 as a side dish

This super easy prep lets nutritious kale steal the show. It's delicious on its own or as a side—even for breakfast with a farm fresh fried egg or soft scramble.

3 tablespoons extra virgin olive oil
3 medium garlic cloves, peeled and finely chopped
1 quart coarsely chopped kale, stems removed (about 1 pound, 3 ounces before stemming and chopping)
1 cup grated carrots
½ cup sunflower seeds, lightly toasted
¾ cup crumbled feta cheese or farm cheese curds, plus extra for garnish
Sea salt and freshly ground black pepper

Heat the oil in a large skillet over medium heat. Add the garlic and cook until fragrant, about 1 minute. Add the kale in batches and stir until the greens are evenly coated with oil. Continue to sauté until bright green but not wilted, about 2 minutes. Stir in the grated carrots, sunflower seeds, and cheese, tossing until well combined. Adjust seasoning with salt and pepper to taste. Garnish with additional cheese if desired.

Recipe from Someday Farm

Executive Chef Rhys Lewis & Master Gardener Benjamin Pauly

Woodstock Inn & Resort

The Woodstock Inn & Resort Executive Chef Rhys Lewis and Master Gardener Benjamin Pauly work hand in hand to bring guests farm-fresh cuisine using regional recipes that showcase Vermont's bounty. In 2013, the Woodstock Inn & Resort created the 2½-acre Kelly Way Gardens as a means of supplying the resort's two restaurants with food produced on-site. Ben manages the kitchen garden, working with Chef Rhys and the resort's culinary team to produce a unique variety of vegetables and fruit that reflect the essence of Vermont and its seasons.

Chef Rhys has worked in restaurants for most of his life. He loves the challenge of bringing out the natural flavor of the foods that he is crafting. Each is a product of nature's canvas from which this skilled chef creates a culinary work of art. Chef Rhys considers the resort's AAA Four Diamond Award-winning Red Rooster Restaurant to be "a celebration of the ingredients found in the Northeast, with respect to the gardeners, farmers, fishermen, and foragers—all presented with country elegance." Cozy Richardson's Tavern is the resort's more casual dining option, offering cuisine that exemplifies the landscape of American food.

A mile down the road, at Kelly Way Gardens, Master Gardener Ben Pauly grows more than 200 varieties of vegetables, 50 types of herbs and edible flowers, 75 kinds of berries and fruit, a mushroom glen, and a collection of 200 types of cut flowers—all of which are grown exclusively for use at the Woodstock Inn & Resort. The small acreage specializes in unique and heirloom produce. Ben hand-cultivates using elements of permaculture and nutrient-dense farming to create certified organic produce. Crops are picked daily and delivered, often still warm from the sun, to Chef Rhys and his culinary team.

Every January Ben meets with Chef Rhys and his team to go through the upcoming season's production plan. Plants are discussed from A-Z, and a strategy is prepared for ordering seeds. The chefs are given a graph that designates when each produce item will be available throughout the growing season. This strategy gives Chef Rhys and his staff time to plan their menus in advance.

This farm-to-table approach has made the Woodstock Inn & Resort a favorite among locals and out-of-town visitors. Drawing from the best purveyors in New England and the freshest homegrown produce, Chef Rhys and Master Gardener Ben Pauly have created an epicurean's paradise with gourmet dishes that capture the very nature of Vermont. It is a certainty that with this dynamic duo at the helm, each year promises to be a new and exciting culinary odyssey.

Roasted Kelly Way Gardens Beet Salad with Herbed Chèvre, Arugula, and Pesto

Serves 4

"I really enjoy using the organic beets, skinny beans, and arugula that are hand grown in our Kelly Way Gardens by Benjamin Pauly, our Master Gardener. The incredible flavors of the vegetables are paired with Garden Herbed Vermont Goat Cheese, truly a delight" —*Executive Chef Rhys Lewis, Woodstock Inn & Resort*

Roasted Beets

5 medium red beets, scrubbed (about 1 pound, 3 ounces)
1½ tablespoons extra virgin olive oil
Kosher salt and freshly ground black pepper

Parsnip Curls

2 cups vegetable oil for frying
1 medium parsnip, trimmed and peeled

French Green Beans (haricot vert)

6 ounces French green beans (haricot vert), trimmed

Fresh Goat Cheese

1 4-ounce log fresh goat cheese, or chèvre
2 tablespoons heavy cream
1 teaspoon fresh coarsely chopped rosemary
1 teaspoon fresh coarsely chopped thyme
Kosher salt and freshly ground black pepper

Basil Pesto

½ cup packed basil leaves
2 medium garlic cloves, peeled
2 tablespoons extra virgin olive oil, or as needed
Kosher salt and freshly ground black pepper

Salad

2 tablespoons fresh lemon juice
1 tablespoon extra virgin olive oil
Kosher salt and freshly ground black pepper
½ pound arugula, stems removed, washed and dried

To make the roasted beets: Preheat the oven to 400 degrees Fahrenheit. Remove the beet greens, reserving them for another purpose. Transfer the beets to a large bowl and toss with the olive oil. Season with salt and pepper. Wrap the beets loosely in foil, then transfer to a baking sheet. Roast until fork tender, about 60 minutes, depending on the size of the beets. When the beets are cool enough to handle, wrap one beet at a time in paper towels and rub the skins away. Slice the beets into ¼-inch-thick slices and chill in the refrigerator.

BEETS
EARLY WONDER
TALL TOP

While the beets are cooling, make the parsnip curls: In a large skillet, heat the vegetable oil to 350 degrees Fahrenheit over medium-high heat. While the oil is heating, bring a medium saucepan of water to a boil. Using a peeler, peel the parsnips into fine curls. Add the curls to the boiling water and cook for 30 seconds. Using a slotted spoon, remove the parsnip curls and transfer to a paper towel-lined plate. Carefully blot dry the parsnip curls, making sure they are completely dry. Set aside. Working in batches, carefully add the parsnip curls to the hot oil and fry for about 1 minute. Using a slotted spoon, carefully remove the parsnip curls and drain on a paper towel-lined plate. Repeat with the remaining parsnip curls.

While the parsnips are draining, blanch the green beans. Using the same saucepan and water for the parsnips, bring the water back to a boil over medium-high heat. Add the beans and cook for 30 seconds. Drain well. Transfer the beans to a small bowl of ice water and chill in the refrigerator.

To make the goat cheese: In a small bowl, combine the cheese, cream, rosemary, and thyme until smooth. Season with salt and pepper to taste. Transfer to the refrigerator until ready to use.

To make the pesto: Process the basil and garlic in a food processor until well combined. While the processor is running, slowly add the oil in a steady stream until well blended, scraping down the sides as needed. Season with salt and pepper to taste.

To make the salad: In a small bowl, whisk together the lemon juice and oil. Season with salt and pepper to taste. Transfer the arugula and beans to a medium bowl and toss with the lemon juice mixture. Season with salt and pepper to taste.

To assemble: Using a spoon, portion the goat cheese into the center of 4 serving plates. Arrange the roasted beet slices on top of the goat cheese. Top the beets with salad. Garnish with parsnip curls and dot the pesto around the salad. Serve at once.

Recipe from Executive Chef Rhys Lewis of the Woodstock Inn & Resort
Photograph by Oliver Parini

Executive Chef Scot Emerson

Coleman Brook Tavern at Okemo Mountain Resort

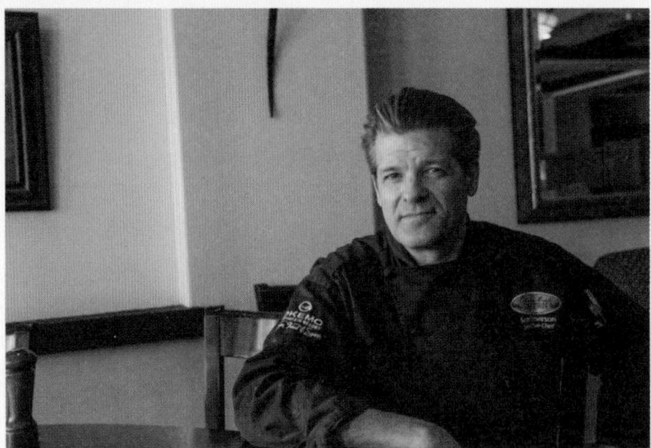

Visitors to Okemo Mountain Resort in Ludlow, Vermont, have an exciting variety of outdoor activities to choose from and a diverse collection of dining options as well. One such restaurant is the Coleman Brook Tavern, located in the Jackson Gore Hotel. Executive Chef Scot Emerson is in charge of all that is food at this upscale, comfortable eating establishment.

The talented chef is a graduate of the Culinary Institute of New York. His love for cooking started at a young age, working in the kitchen alongside his grandfather. A restaurant job at age 16 helped to seal the deal, paving the way to the executive chef position he holds today.

Everything at the tavern's restaurant is carefully sourced, with the majority coming from local farms and food producers. Chef Scot works with dozens of these hardworking folks, bringing a farm-to-table approach to the eatery and his culinary creations. Before agreeing to partner with a farm, the chef will visit to see firsthand the farmer's commitment to sustainability, land stewardship, and organic and non-GMO methods of food production. In turn, the farmer must stop by the restaurant to meet the team that will be using his products, viewing the heart of the kitchen's culinary practices, and getting a feel for what the restaurant's mission is all about: "providing guests with an exceptional meal and great service."

Since Chef Scot's arrival, Coleman Brook Tavern has become a member of the Vermont Fresh Network and the American Culinary Federation. The chef himself is a Vermont Fresh Network Gold Barn Honoree. To qualify, a nominee must source ingredients from fifteen or more Vermont Fresh Network farmers. Thirty-five percent of their restaurant's annual food expenditures need to be purchased from Vermont farmers and producers, or an annual monetary amount of $200,000 spent on Vermont-grown food products.

Celebrating Vermont's bounty, the tavern serves food that is sure to please every palate and lifestyle. It is Chef Scot's personal mission to help America change the way it looks at food and how it is produced, encouraging consumers to interact more with their local food community.

Photograph courtesy of Chef Scot Emerson

Coleman Brook Tavern Salad

Serves 4

The arrangement of the lettuce leaves to resemble flower petals makes this refreshing salad an elegant presentation. The honey wine vinegar is the perfect complement to the delicate buttery flavor of the hydroponic butter lettuce and the toasted nut sweetness of the Bayley Hazen Blue cheese. The tavern uses a local honey wine vinegar in the marinade that has bold peppery yet floral flavors produced by Artesano LLC, located in Grafton, Vermont.

Marinade

1 cup honey wine vinegar (mead vinegar), such as Artesano
2 tablespoons organic cane sugar
1¾ tablespoons kosher salt
1 pound (about 3½ cups) heirloom tomatoes, cored and cut into 1-inch chunks
1 pound cucumbers (about 3 cups), such as Holland Hothouse, peeled and cut into 1-inch chunks
½ pound (1 medium-large) red onion, peeled and thinly sliced

Salad

1 head lettuce, such as Vermont Hydroponic butter, divided 4 ways
2 ounces (about ¾ cup) crumbled blue cheese, such as Bayley Hazen, divided 4 ways
1 ounce (½ cup) carrot curls, divided 4 ways
½ teaspoon freshly ground black pepper, divided 4 ways
2 tablespoons extra virgin olive oil, such as Arbequina, divided 4 ways
Salt

In a medium bowl, whisk together the vinegar, sugar, and salt until well combined. Add the tomatoes, cucumbers, and onion, tossing until well combined. Cover with plastic wrap and let the vegetables marinate in the refrigerator for at least 1 hour.

To assemble: On 4 individual salad plates, arrange the lettuce leaves equally in a circle to resemble flower petals. Using a slotted spoon, pile 1½ cups of the vegetable mixture onto each plate in the center of the lettuce leaves. Sprinkle with ⅛ cup of cheese and a few grinds of pepper around each salad. Top each salad with ⅛ cup of carrot curls. Drizzle each salad with ½ tablespoon of olive oil. Adjust seasonings with salt and pepper to taste.

Recipe from Coleman Brook Tavern for Okemo Mountain Resort
Photograph courtesy of Wood's Market Garden

Kohlrabi Chips with Sherpa Pink Himalayan Salt

Peeling a kohlrabi bulb may present a challenge to the novice. Some folks like to use a vegetable peeler, but find trying to maneuver around the plant's knobby areas, where the leaves were once connected, can be quite a trying task. Others prefer using their favorite paring knife to do the job. See what works best for you. Begin by trimming off the stem end, then removing the skin and any inner areas that may be woody.

2½ pounds kohlrabi, peeled and halved
3 tablespoons extra virgin olive oil, or as needed
Sherpa Pink Himalayan salt fine grain, as needed

Preheat the oven to 375 degrees Fahrenheit. Lightly grease 2 baking sheets with cooking spray; set aside.

Using a mandoline or handheld slicer, slice the kohlrabi into 1⁄16- to ⅛-inch-thick rounds. Place the rounds in a large bowl and lightly drizzle with olive oil, tossing to coat well.

Working in batches, arrange the kohlrabi rounds in a single layer on the prepared baking sheets. Bake until golden brown and crispy, turning once, about 30 minutes. Transfer to a paper towel-lined plate. Sprinkle with salt to taste. Repeat with the remaining rounds.

Serve immediately with the Creamy Sriracha Dipping Sauce **(see recipe on page 127)** or your favorite dip of choice.

Recipe from Tracey Medeiros

Note: It is highly recommended to check the chips at 5-minute intervals, removing chips that cook faster than others.

Kohlrabi

While kohlrabi has a following in the United States, it's more popular in Germany, India, and Eastern Europe. The name comes from the German "kohl," meaning cabbage, and "rabi," meaning turnip, due to the fact that the plant's swollen stem looks like a turnip. However, this vegetable is neither and stands on its own merits with a hint of broccoli flavor. Kohlrabi, a member of the *Brassicaceae* family, is also known as German turnip, stem turnip, and cabbage turnip.

There are two main varieties of kohlrabi—white and purple—but the interiors of both are a creamy yellowish color. The kohlrabi family is made up of the white and purple Vienna, white and purple Danube, Grand Duke, and Gigante. The Gigante is the only variety that grows to a large size without becoming woody in texture. A good rule of thumb when purchasing kohlrabi is to remember that the bigger it is, the woodier the texture will be.

If you find bulbs with their leaves still attached, don't pass them by; the greens are edible, making them an excellent dietary choice. The greens are delicious sautéed, steamed, or eaten raw. Haakh kohlrabi does not have a swollen stem; it consists of only leaves and a thin stem.

When shopping for kohlrabi try to find medium bulbs with a sphere-like shape that feel heavy for their size. Avoid bulbs with cracks, cuts, soft spots, or brown areas. If the leaves are attached, check to see that they appear fresh and green and show no signs of wilting or mold. Younger kohlrabi is usually 2–3 inches in diameter. These plants tend to be more tender.

Kohlrabi is similar in texture to cabbage hearts or broccoli stems, but with a milder, sweeter flavor. When eaten raw, the vegetable has a bit of a kick. This versatile vegetable can be prepared in a variety of ways; try it steamed, boiled, pureed, or baked. Cut it into quarters then give a toss or two in olive oil, salt, and pepper and roast like potatoes. It's also a delicious addition to vegetable soup or perhaps potato or broccoli cream soups.

The growing season stretches from late spring through late fall. The bulbs will keep in your refrigerator's vegetable bin for several weeks, or freeze it for later use. Remove any attached leaves before storing.

Peeling a kohlrabi bulb may present a challenge for the novice. Using a vegetable peeler or paring knife, begin by trimming off the stem end, then removing the skin and any woody inner areas. Remember, to peel thoroughly - first, the hard outer skin, then the fibrous layer that lies beneath. A good rule to follow when peeling kohlrabi is to peel once, then peel again. The goal is to reach the fleshy part of the vegetable.

Kohlrabi is a great source of vitamin C and contains good amounts of many B complex vitamins such as niacin, B_6, thiamin, and pantothenic acid. There are also healthy levels of minerals such as copper, calcium, potassium, manganese, iron, and phosphorus. This knobby little vegetable has soared to the top of my list of healthy eating choices because it contains zero cholesterol, little fat, and few calories. Count me as the newest member of the Kohlrabi Fan Club!

Roasted Peppers with Salsa Taquera, Queso Fresco, and Charred Sweet Corn Crema

Serves 6

This recipe is warm and inviting with a very soft texture. The smoky and tangy flavors of the Salsa Taquera is the perfect complement to the roasted peppers, mild queso fresco, and sweet corn crema!

Peppers

6 large poblano or Carmen peppers
1 tablespoon extra virgin olive oil
8 ounces queso fresco, finely shredded

Salsa Taquera

Makes about 2 cups

1 pound tomatillos, papery husks removed, rinsed, and patted dry
1 medium tomato, diced (about 1 cup)
¼ cup diced onion
1 tablespoon minced garlic
1 teaspoon ancho chile powder
1 teaspoon fresh lemon juice
1 teaspoon fresh lime juice
1 teaspoon agave
¼ cup fresh chopped cilantro leaves
½ teaspoon salt

Charred Sweet Corn Crema

2 medium ears sweet corn, husks and silks removed, kernels cut from cobs, or about 1½ cups frozen corn
1 tablespoon extra virgin olive oil
½ cup crème fraiche
½ cup ripe mashed avocado (1 medium)
Zest and juice from 1 organic lime
1 teaspoon ground coriander
1 tablespoon chopped fresh cilantro leaves
½ teaspoon salt

Fresh minced cilantro leaves for garnish
Tortilla chips

Move your oven rack to the highest possible position in the oven. Preheat the oven broiler to high. Line a baking sheet with aluminum foil. Set aside.

Place the peppers in a medium bowl and rub with oil, then arrange in a single layer on the prepared baking sheet. Broil until the skins are charred and bubbly on all sides, turning occasionally with tongs, about 15 minutes. Transfer to a bowl, cover with plastic wrap, and let sit

at room temperature for 20 minutes. Carefully peel the skins off. Using a sharp knife, carefully cut a slit in the peppers lengthwise, being careful not to go all the way through, and keeping the stems intact, ribs and seeds completely removed. Set aside. **Note:** The roasted peppers are very fragile and should be handled very gently.

While the peppers are broiling, start the salsa taquera. Heat a skillet over medium-high heat. Add the tomatillos and char on all sides, turning frequently with tongs, about 12 minutes, depending on the size of the tomatillos. Transfer the tomatillos, tomatoes, onions, garlic, ancho chile powder, lemon and lime juices, agave, cilantro, and salt in a blender and pulse to a coarse puree. Adjust seasonings with salt to taste.

Reposition your rack in the center of the oven. Preheat the oven to 350 degrees Fahrenheit. Line a baking sheet with aluminum foil. Arrange the peppers in a single layer on the prepared baking sheet. Using a spoon, stuff each pepper using a scant ⅓ cup of cheese. Bake in the oven until the cheese is melted and the center is hot, about 10 minutes.

While the peppers are baking, make the charred sweet corn crema. Heat the oil in a medium cast-iron skillet over medium-high heat. Add the kernels and cook, shaking the skillet often, until light golden brown, about 8–10 minutes. Set aside and allow the corn to rest to room temperature. While the corn is cooling, in a medium bowl, stir together the crème fraiche, avocado, lime zest and juice, coriander, cilantro, and salt until well combined. Fold in the corn until well combined. Adjust seasonings with salt.

To assemble: While the corn is charring, heat the salsa taquera in a small saucepan over medium heat until heated through. Spoon some of the salsa taquera over the peppers. Top each pepper with a dollop of the crema and garnish with cilantro. Serve warm with tortilla chips on the side.

Recipe from El Cortijo Taqueria Y Cantina for The Farmhouse Group
Photograph by Oliver Parini

Roasting variation: Stem, seed, and rib the peppers before they are roasted, leaving a fragile sort of vessel that the cheese could carefully be stuffed into.

Heirloom Tomato and Mixed Green Salad

Serves 4 as a side

This salad is a great way to showcase ripe summer heirloom tomatoes and cucumbers! Serve this salad as a side dish alongside the Oven-Baked Burgers found on page 213.

Balsamic Vinaigrette

1 tablespoon organic balsamic vinegar
¼ cup organic extra virgin olive oil
2 tablespoons coarsely chopped fresh basil leaves
Salt and freshly ground black pepper to taste

Salad

1 cup baby arugula, tightly packed
2 cups assorted mixed greens, such as baby kale, tatsoi, mizunas, mustards, or Asian greens, tightly packed
1 heirloom cucumber, such as Bella, cut into cubes
½ pound assorted heirloom tomatoes, such beefsteak, Pruden's Purple, Cherokee Purple, Brandywine, or Valencia, cut into wedges
Salt and freshly ground black pepper

In a small bowl, whisk together the balsamic vinegar, oil, and basil. Season with salt and pepper to taste. In a large bowl, combine the arugula, mixed greens, cucumber, and half of the vinaigrette. Toss well and add more vinaigrette if desired. Top with tomatoes. Season with salt and pepper to taste.

Recipe from Naked Acre Farm

Roasted Gilfeather Turnips, Beets, and Farro Salad with Goat Cheese

Serves 6

"The Gilfeather turnip, one of many Vermont jewels, makes a perfect warm appetizer. In this recipe, paired with equally delicious roasted beets, it is enhanced with farro to create a delicious, healthy salad. A few shavings of a local goat milk tomme-style cheese from the Big Picture Farm will make it all come together." *—Executive Chef Frederic Kieffer, Artisan Restaurant Tavern & Garden at Four Columns Inn*

Farro
Makes 6 cups
2 cups of farro, preferably Anson Mills
2 quarts vegetable stock
¼ teaspoon salt

Roasted Gilfeather Turnips and Beets
6 medium golden beets, scrubbed
6 medium red beets, scrubbed
2 tablespoons extra virgin olive oil, plus extra for drizzling
6 medium Gilfeather turnips, ends trimmed, peeled and cut into ½-inch wedges
2 tablespoons local raw honey, plus extra for drizzling

Cider Reduction
Makes about 1 cup
½ cup organic unfiltered apple cider vinegar
2 cups fresh apple cider
3 ounces organic light brown sugar
3 cups packed organic arugula, washed
8-ounce hard aged raw goat tomme, such as Big Picture Farm's Sonnet, rind removed and shaved
Fleur de sel or Maldon sea salt flakes

Preheat the oven to 400 degrees Fahrenheit.

To make the farro: Place the farro in a medium bowl and pour enough hot water to cover it by 1 inch. Set aside for 20 minutes. Drain in a fine-mesh strainer. Transfer the farro to a 3½-quart saucepan. Add the vegetable stock and ¼ teaspoon salt. Bring to a simmer, cover, and cook until tender but still chewy, about 45 minutes.

While the farro is soaking, start making the roasted beets and turnips. Remove the beet greens, reserving them for another purpose. Transfer the beets to a large bowl and toss with 1 tablespoon olive oil. Season with salt and pepper. Wrap the beets loosely in foil, then transfer to a baking sheet. Roast until fork tender, about 65 minutes, depending on the size of the beets. When the beets are cool enough to handle, remove the skins with a paring knife. Cut into ¾-inch pieces.

Start the Gilfeather turnips during the last 30 minutes of the cooking time for the beets. Place the turnips, remaining 1 tablespoon olive oil, and honey in a large bowl. Season with salt and pepper to taste. Toss to combine, making sure to coat well. Spread the turnips on a lightly greased baking sheet. Roast, stirring occasionally, until turnips are fork tender, about 25 minutes.

While the beets and turnips are roasting, start the cider reduction. Combine the vinegar, cider, and brown sugar in a saucepan and bring to a boil over medium heat, whisking often. Reduce the heat to a simmer and cook, whisking often, until cider mixture reduces to a syrup, about 35 minutes. Keep at room temperature.

To assemble: Place 1 cup of farro in the center of each plate. Evenly arrange the beets and turnips over the farro. Drizzle with olive oil, honey, and 1 tablespoon of the cider reduction on top and around each plate. Sprinkle the beets and turnips with sea salt to taste. Scatter the arugula leaves and shaved goat cheese on top and around the dish. Serve at once.

Recipe from Artisan Restaurant Tavern & Garden at Four Columns Inn

Tip: Slice your reserved beet greens into thin ribbons and toss into pasta or soup dishes.

CHAPTER 5

ORGANIC AND GRASS-FED BEEF, PORK, LAMB, VENISON, AND GOAT MAIN DISHES

Vermont Beef Short Ribs Over Hakurei Turnip Puree Topped with Chimichurri Sauce

Serves 4–5

The hakurei or Tokyo turnip is a member of the *Brassica* family. These Japanese baby turnips are tender, sweet, and mild in flavor. There is no need to peel these humble white globes, simply trim the ends and wash the roots under cold water. This recipe is a three-day process; however, the actual hands-on cooking time is minimal.

Dry Cure

1 tablespoon kosher salt
2 teaspoons coarsely ground black pepper
1¼ teaspoons ground fennel seeds
2 teaspoons freshly chopped thyme

Short Ribs

¼ cup extra virgin olive oil
4 pounds bone-in beef short ribs, trimmed of excess fat
2 cups coarsely chopped mirepoix (equal parts onions, carrot, and celery)
½ cup tomato paste
1 cup dry red wine, such as merlot
1 quart low-sodium beef broth
1 teaspoon salt

Hakurei Turnip Puree

2 pounds (about 3 bunches) hakurei turnips or baby turnips, greens removed, trimmed, unpeeled, and cut into 1-inch pieces
1 pound Yukon Gold potatoes, peeled and cut into 1-inch pieces
1 quart vegetable stock
4 tablespoon butter, cut into chunks, at room temperature
½ teaspoon sherry vinegar
Salt and freshly ground black pepper

Chimichurri Sauce

Makes about 1 cup

The chimichurri sauce can be made ahead. Cover and store in the refrigerator for up to 1 week.

3 medium garlic cloves, peeled and trimmed
1 cup packed fresh flat-leaf parsley
1 cup packed fresh cilantro
1 tablespoon fresh lemon juice
1 tablespoon sherry vinegar
½ teaspoon red pepper flakes
½ teaspoon salt
½ cup vegetable oil
¼ cup extra virgin olive oil

In a small bowl, combine the salt, pepper, fennel seeds, and thyme for the dry cure. Place the ribs in a shallow baking dish. Rub the ribs all over with the cure. Cover the dish with plastic wrap and place in the refrigerator overnight.

Preheat the oven to 300 degrees Fahrenheit.

Heat the oil in a large Dutch oven over medium-high heat until hot but not smoking. Add the ribs, in batches, to the pot and sear on one side, about 4 minutes. Using tongs, turn the ribs and sear on the other side until well browned, about 4 minutes. Remove from the heat and set aside on a large plate. Repeat with the remaining ribs.

Add the onions, carrots, and celery to the pot and cook, stirring frequently, until the onions are soft and translucent, about 5 minutes. Stir in the tomato paste until well combined. Whisk in the wine, scraping up the bits from the bottom of the pan, until well combined. Stir in the broth and salt. Transfer the ribs, along with any juices that have accumulated, back into the pot. Cover and cook in the oven until the meat is fork tender, about 3 hours, depending on the thickness of the ribs.

Using a large slotted spoon, transfer the ribs to a large plate and loosely tent with foil. Strain the liquid through a fine-mesh strainer, pushing all the liquid through with the back of a ladle, discarding the solids. Transfer the liquid back to the pot along with the ribs. Cover and chill in the refrigerator overnight. The next day, use a spoon to carefully scrape away and discard the hardened layer of fat that has risen to the top of the sauce.

To make the hakurei turnip puree: Place the turnips and potatoes in a large saucepan and cover with the vegetable stock. Bring to a simmer over medium-high heat and cook until the turnips and potatoes are fork tender, about 20 minutes. Drain and reserve half of the cooking liquid. Transfer the vegetables, ⅓ cup of the reserved cooking liquid, butter, and vinegar to a medium bowl. Using an immersion blender or food processor, puree the vegetables, adding more liquid as needed, until smooth. Adjust seasonings with salt and pepper to taste. Cover with plastic wrap until ready to use.

While the hakurei turnips are simmering, reheat the ribs over medium-low heat on the stovetop until the meat is heated through, about 20 minutes.

While the ribs are reheating, make the chimichurri sauce.

To make the chimichurri sauce: Process the garlic in a food processor until finely minced. Add the parsley, cilantro, lemon juice, vinegar, pepper flakes, and salt. While the processor is running, slowly add the oils in a steady stream until well blended, scraping down the sides as needed. Adjust seasonings with salt to taste.

To assemble: Spoon some of the turnip puree in the center of individual plates. Top with ribs and chimichurri sauce. Drizzle the braising liquid over and around the ribs. Serve at once.

Recipe from Guild Tavern for The Farmhouse Group
Photograph by Oliver Parini

Meat variations: Butcher's cut steak like skirt, flat iron, or hanger can be used in place of the ribs.

Hakurei turnip substitutes: Mashed potatoes, egg noodles, or crusty bread can be substituted for the hakurei turnip puree.

KISMET
eat/drink

Kismet, LLC

PROFILE

Kismet is located in lovely Montpelier, Vermont. Owner and chef Crystal Maderia is passionate about eating fresh, whole foods. This desire is the foundation for all that is good at Kismet Kitchen, the restaurant that she opened in 2006. "I consider it my moral responsibility to care for the earth and my community and do so through my relationship with food—from the field to the table," she explains.

As a young person, Crystal traveled throughout the United States, Australia, and New Zealand, working and living on a variety of farms. This experience helped prepare her for her current roles as chef and owner of Kismet, and it enabled her to forge strong relationships with the owners of local organic farms. Crystal strongly believes that the future of food and farming in Vermont is based on educating and providing on-farm experiences for teens and young adults entering the workforce. She stresses, "Since so much of Vermont is farmland, it is important that the next generation of farmers are ethically and morally motivated to care for it with the promise of sustainability in mind." Currently, she is working with Vermont Farm to Plate, which strives to connect food system businesses and education.

The menu at Kismet features a wide assortment of organic offerings. To help accomplish this, Crystal uses locally sourced products as well as her own produce, which she grows on a plot of land that she rents. Visitors to Kismet may choose from creative dishes that in some cases are internationally inspired. One of the restaurant's signature dishes is Bread Pudding made with 24-hour bone broth from Greenfield Highland Beef, whole grain sourdough, Vermont cheeses, and onion jam (made with onions from Kismet's garden). The creative chef claims, "It's like a classic French onion soup, but way better!"

Kismet has a strong local following and a devoted clientele that identifies with Crystal's mission and benefits from her integrity. "Kismet means fate or good karma. Simply put, this is the heart of our philosophy and is the food that we use to nurture and inspire a whole community," explains the hardworking chef. With an innovative menu combined with warm, friendly surroundings and the freshest ingredients available, what's not to like about Kismet!

Photograph by Oliver Parini

Southern Fried Beef Heart with Roasted Cherry Tomatoes, Pickled Fiddleheads, and Toasted Chili Brown Butter

Serves 4

This recipe has a variety of textures and flavors. Frying the beef heart in safflower oil gives it a crispy texture on the outside and succulent quality on the inside. Roasting the cherry tomatoes adds a nice intensified tomato flavor to the dish. All of these ingredients, combined with the Vermont cheddar cheese gravy, make this a deliciously satisfying meal.

Much of the heart's weight will be in the trimming, so the pre-trim weight total should be approximately 3½ pounds, and the post-trim weight will be approximately 2 pounds. To save on time, ask your butcher to trim and remove the sinew, valves, and veins.

Pickled Fiddleheads

2 tablespoons organic cane sugar
1 tablespoon salt
½ tablespoon mustard seeds
½ tablespoon black peppercorns
½ cinnamon stick
1¼ cups organic unfiltered apple cider vinegar
1¼ cups white vinegar
1 pound fiddleheads, cleaned
2½ cups ice

Roasted Cherry Tomatoes

½ cup olive oil
4 tablespoons pure maple syrup
2 teaspoons salt
4 cups cherry tomatoes

Beef Heart

3½ pounds beef heart, trimmed, sinew, valves, and veins removed

Marinade

½ cup organic unfiltered apple cider vinegar
4 cups ice water
1 tablespoon salt
½ tablespoon cayenne pepper

Vermont Cheddar Cheese Gravy

½ tablespoon butter
1 tablespoon organic all-purpose flour or non-GMO cornstarch
2 cups heavy cream
½ teaspoon freshly ground pepper
½ teaspoon chopped fresh summer savory
¼ teaspoon chopped fresh rosemary
½ teaspoon granulated garlic
⅛ teaspoon ground cinnamon
½ teaspoon fresh lemon juice
½ cup shredded cheddar cheese, preferably Butterworks Farm
Kosher salt

Seasoned Flour

1½ cups all-purpose organic flour or non-GMO gluten-free flour
1½ cups organic masa harina
½ tablespoon aluminum-free baking powder
¼ teaspoon organic cane sugar
¾ tablespoon cayenne
¾ tablespoon garlic powder
½ tablespoon sea salt
2 large eggs, lightly beaten
1 cup hard cider or beer

Toasted Chili Brown Butter

¼ pound (1 stick) unsalted butter
½ fresh spicy red pepper, such as red jalapeños or red cayenne, seeded and finely diced
⅛ teaspoon salt
¼ cup white vinegar

Frying

2 cups organic safflower oil, or as needed
½ cup fresh curly parsley leaves

To make the pickled fiddleheads: Combine the sugar, salt, mustard seeds, peppercorns, cinnamon stick, and vinegars in a saucepan and bring to a boil over medium-high heat. Reduce the heat to a simmer and cook, stirring frequently, for 10 minutes. Place the prepared fiddleheads in a large, deep bowl or a nonreactive stockpot, pour the marinade over the vegetables, add the ice, and toss to coat. Let cool to room temperature, then cover with plastic wrap and refrigerate, turning occasionally, for at least 3 hours or overnight.

To make the roasted cherry tomatoes: Preheat the oven to 425 degrees Fahrenheit. In a small bowl, whisk together the olive oil, maple syrup, and salt. Lightly oil a baking sheet. Place the tomatoes on the baking sheet and drizzle with the oil mixture, tossing until well combined. Roast until the tomatoes start to burst and begin to caramelize, about 25 minutes.

To make the beef heart: Using a sharp knife, carefully cut the heart into 2- or 3-ounce pieces. Place each heart piece between sheets of parchment paper and, using the back of a heavy pan, pound to ¼-inch thickness. Place the heart pieces in a medium stockpot of ice water and allow to sit for 15 minutes. Drain and set aside.

To marinate the beef heart: In the same stockpot used for the beef heart, whisk together the vinegar, water, salt, and cayenne pepper. Place the heart in the marinade, cover, and set aside for 30 minutes. Remove and pat dry with paper towels.

To make the gravy: While the beef heart is marinating, melt the butter in a medium saucepan over medium-low heat. Whisk in the flour and cook until the mixture has thickened and the flour is a pale golden color. Slowly whisk in the heavy cream, stirring until well combined. Whisk in the pepper, savory, rosemary, garlic, cinnamon, and lemon juice and cook until heated through. Stir in the cheese until melted and smooth and continue to cook until heated through. Season with salt to taste. Reheat when ready to use.

To make the toasted chili brown butter: In a small saucepan, melt the butter over medium heat. Continue to cook, stirring occasionally, until the butter turns a toasty brown color, about

11 minutes. Add the chili pepper and salt. Remove from the heat and carefully strain the butter through a fine-mesh strainer or cheesecloth into a measuring cup to remove all the solids. Allow the butter to cool to room temperature. Carefully pour the butter into a bowl, leaving as much of the sediment in the measuring cup as possible. Stir in the vinegar. Place the butter in the refrigerator and allow to completely cool. Using a handheld immersion blender, blend the butter. Set aside.

To make the seasoned flour: In a large bowl, stir together all the dry ingredients, then divide the flour equally between two shallow bowls. Whisk together the eggs and hard cider into a third shallow bowl. Lightly dip each heart piece in the first bowl of flour, then in the egg mixture, and finally in the third bowl of flour. Set beef heart pieces on a wire cooling rack.

Heat the oil in a large cast-iron skillet over medium-high heat until shimmering, but not smoking. Add the beef heart pieces, in batches if necessary, into the hot oil and fry until golden brown on both sides, 2–3 minutes per side for medium-rare. Using tongs, carefully remove the beef heart pieces and drain on paper towels.

Using paper towels, carefully and completely blot dry the fiddleheads and parsley leaves. In the same skillet and oil used for the beef heart pieces, carefully add the fiddleheads and parsley into the hot oil and fry for 30 seconds to 1 minute over medium-high heat. Using a slotted spoon, carefully remove the fiddleheads and parsley and drain on paper towels.

To assemble: Place 2 or 3 pieces of the beef heart on each plate, arrange the fiddleheads and parsley around the heart pieces. Scatter the tomatoes on top and around the hearts. Top with gravy and drizzle with the chili brown butter. Season with freshly ground black pepper to taste. Serve.

Recipe from Kismet, LLC
Photograph by Oliver Parini

Notes:

- The pickled fiddleheads can be made up to a day ahead before you intend to serve; just cover and refrigerate. For safety standards, boil or steam the fiddleheads before pickling them. Cook for approximately 15 minutes when boiling, or 10–12 minutes if steaming.
- Pounding the beef heart pieces will help break apart the muscle fibers, tenderizing the pieces.
- If you can't find fresh summer savory, you can substitute a dash of thyme combined with sage or mint.
- You can substitute asparagus for the fiddleheads. Fiddleheads should never be eaten raw and must be cooked before pickling for safety. Asparagus can be eaten raw and does not need to be cooked before pickling.

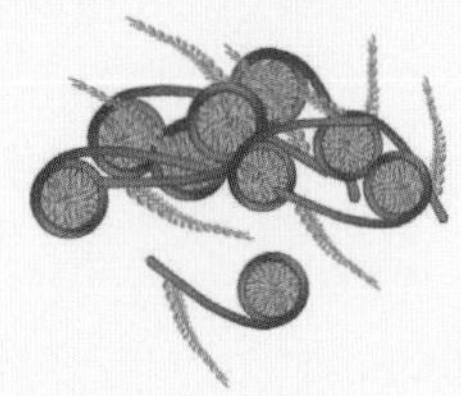

Ostrich Fern Fiddleheads: the Fabulous Fronds of Spring

Fiddlehead—the name in itself is intriguing. It is defined as the furled frond of a young fern, usually of the ostrich species, that is harvested for use as a vegetable. They're harvested in late April, May, and early June. The unusual name stems from the fact that the coiled frond has a similarity in shape to the curled scroll of a violin, hence the name fiddlehead. They are also known as "crosiers" or "croziers," after the crook-shaped staff of a bishop.

In North America, the Native Americans were the first to discover and eat these dainty delicacies. Fiddleheads have been part of the diet in Northern France since the beginning of the Middle Ages, and they're also popular in Asia. They may be found from Newfoundland to Alaska, from British Columbia south to Northern California, and in the Midwest and Southern Appalachians. The plant is abundant in the Upper Great Lakes and the Northeast, as well as southern Canada.

These ferns grow wild in wet areas, such as the banks of brooks, streams, rivers, and their floodplains. The most popular, the ostrich fern, likes partial shade and flourishes under an umbrella of tree boughs. Ask permission of the landowner before harvesting on someone else's property.

To identify the ostrich fern, look for a brown, papery, scale-like covering on the uncoiled fern. This covering is most easily removed when dry; shake gently and it will float away. Ostrich ferns are found in clusters; harvest when they're 2–6 inches tall and have a 1- to 2-inch portion of the stem attached to the tightly curled fiddlehead.

When harvesting pick only 3 tops per plant—each plant usually produces 7 tops. Pass on plants with only 1 or 2 tops. A plant will weaken, and eventually die if all of the fiddleheads on its crown are picked year after year.

In the early 1990s, the Centers for Disease Control discovered a food-borne illness that was determined to be caused by eating raw or undercooked fiddleheads. It has since been proven that proper handling and cooking reduces this risk. Fiddleheads should *never* be eaten raw. For safety standards, boil or steam them before using in most recipes.

After boiling or steaming, ostrich fern fiddleheads can be used in most recipes that call for green vegetables. Stir-fries, soups, and sautéing highlight their unique flavor. This vegetable is delicious when served with butter, lemon, or in egg dishes with hollandaise sauce. It goes well with cheeses, tomato sauce, and pasta dishes. For a tasty snack, marinate in vinegar and oil.

Nutritionally, fiddleheads have 34 calories per 100 grams and contain 72 percent of the daily requirement of vitamin A and 44 percent of vitamin C. Fiddleheads have no total fat or cholesterol and are low in sodium and rich in potassium. If you prefer to buy, rather than harvest your fiddleheads, they may be found at farmers' markets or grocery stores with a wild produce section. The flavor is best right after harvesting, although they will keep for around 10 days if wrapped tightly and refrigerated. Because fiddleheads are only available for a few weeks in the spring, they are rather expensive. If they are pickled or frozen, some grocery stores may carry them year-round. Ostrich fern fiddleheads: one more reason to look forward to spring!

Photograph by Tristan Von Duntz

Grilled Beef Tenderloin with Rutabaga Puree, Braised Cabbage, and Horseradish Cream

Serves 6

This recipe has a wide variation of textures and flavors from the sweet, acidic braised cabbage and slightly sweet and subtle earthiness of the rutabaga puree to the tender, savory beef tenderloin and the bright, peppery horseradish cream. The horseradish cream makes more than needed for this recipe. It also works well with chicken or fish. Store the tightly covered horseradish cream in the refrigerator for future use.

Dry-Age Beef Tenderloin

Start to dry-age the beef tenderloin four days before you intend to serve the meat.

1 (3- to 4-pound) beef tenderloin

Braised Cabbage

The braised cabbage can be made up to a day ahead before you intend to serve; just cover, refrigerate, and reheat.

1 cup pickle brine (from leftover store-bought or homemade pickle juice)
4 garlic cloves, peeled and minced
2 pounds cabbage (1 medium head), such as Savoy or Napa, shredded
½ teaspoon salt
1 teaspoon crushed black pepper

Rutabaga Puree

2½ pounds rutabaga, peeled and cut into 1-inch pieces
1 tablespoon heavy cream, preferably Butterworks Farm
4 tablespoons unsalted butter, cut into pieces, at room temperature
1 tablespoon Vermont hard cider
½ tablespoon salt
Freshly ground black pepper

Brown Butter

8 ounces unsalted butter

Horseradish Cream

2 cups sour cream
2 tablespoons freshly grated horseradish
½ tablespoon lemon juice
Salt and freshly ground black pepper
Chopped fresh thyme for garnish

To make the dry-age beef tenderloin: Rinse the beef tenderloin well under cold running water, then pat it dry with paper towels. Wrap the untrimmed beef tenderloin loosely in a layer of cheesecloth and place the beef on a wire rack over a rimmed baking sheet and transfer to the refrigerator for four days. To prevent the cheesecloth from sticking to the meat, after the first day, unwrap and rewrap with the same cheesecloth. On the fourth day, discard the cheesecloth and trim the beef tenderloin.

To make the braised cabbage: Place the pickle brine and garlic in a 14-inch cast-iron skillet and bring to a boil over medium heat. Add the cabbage, salt, and pepper and sauté, stirring occasionally, for 5 minutes. Reduce heat to medium-low, cover and cook, stirring occasionally, until the cabbage is tender, about 25 minutes. Season with salt and pepper to taste. Cover and set aside.

To make the rutabaga puree: Start the rutabaga puree 30 minutes before the beef tenderloin is ready. Place the rutabagas in a large saucepan with salted water. Bring to a boil over medium-high heat and cook until the rutabagas are fork tender, about 15 minutes. Drain and reserve ½ cup of the cooking liquid. Transfer the rutabagas, in batches if needed, to a food processor along with the heavy cream, butter, hard cider, and salt and pulse until smooth, adding reserved liquid as needed. Adjust seasonings with salt and pepper to taste. Transfer to a bowl and cover with foil until ready to serve.

To make the brown butter: While the gas grill is preheating, start the brown butter. In a small saucepan, melt the butter over medium heat. Stirring occasionally, cook until the butter turns a toasty brown color, about 14 minutes. Remove from the heat and allow to cool until just warm. Strain the butter through a fine-mesh strainer or cheesecloth to remove all the solids. Transfer to a small saucepan and keep warm until ready to use in the horseradish cream.

To make the horseradish cream: Whisk together the reserved brown butter, sour cream, horseradish, lemon juice, and salt and pepper to taste. Set aside until ready to serve.

To make the beef tenderloin: Preheat a gas grill over high heat and generously brush the cooking grate with oil. Tie the beef tenderloin with butcher's twine, securing the ends and center to form an even oblong shape. Season with salt and pepper. Grill until the internal temperature of the meat reaches 115 degrees Fahrenheit, about 7 minutes per side, depending on the size of the meat, or until desired doneness is reached. Let rest for 10 minutes, then slice into 1½-inch slices.

To assemble: Place a small mound of the cabbage in the center of the plate, spoon a small amount of the rutabaga puree next to the cabbage and top with two slices of the beef tenderloin. Top with a dollop of horseradish cream. Garnish with fresh thyme. Serve at once.

Recipe from Kismet, LLC
Photograph by Oliver Parini

Rutabagas

The rutabaga is a member of the cabbage family, and at first glance it resembles an odd-shaped turnip. It is a little larger at the base than its counterpart with a dark purple band at the crown, a lumpy irregular shape, and tan skin. The outer skin of a rutabaga is usually coated with wax to prevent moisture loss. It can be used in recipes as a tasty alternative to the turnip. Shoppers often confuse the two vegetables, although rutabagas are sweeter and do not taste as peppery as turnips. Their inside flesh has a yellow-orange color with a dense texture similar to that of the turnip. However, its flavor is more intense and has hints of the sweetness of cabbage. The rutabaga's leaves are entirely edible, with a mild flavor and soft texture much like turnip greens.

When selecting your rutabaga, make sure you choose one that is firm and smooth skinned, as well as solid to the touch. It should feel heavy for its size and have the root and stem ends intact. Avoid soft rutabagas or those with wrinkled skin or cracks. If you lean toward the theory that larger is better, the rutabaga you select may be tough and woody with less sweetness. Choose a medium-sized rutabaga whenever possible.

Since they have a lower water content than turnips, rutabagas will stay fresher longer. Place the unwashed vegetable in an airtight plastic bag and store in the coldest section of the refrigerator where it will keep for up to 3 weeks. If not refrigerated, it will last for about 1 week.

Rutabagas grow best in cool conditions and are considered a cool-season crop. Their flavor is intensified by a light frost. They are perfect for a fall crop in cooler regions and a winter crop in warmer zones.

Originally from Northern Europe, rutabagas were one of the few fresh foods available to the general population after World War I and World War II. A constant diet of rutabagas caused people to tire of eating the vegetable, and they soon became associated with poverty and starvation, gaining the unpopular title of "famine food." They are now primarily grown in the Northern United States, Europe, Great Britain, and Canada. It takes approximately 90 days for them to reach full size.

This versatile vegetable may be eaten raw or cooked. Since the outer skin is often waxed, use a paring knife to make the peeling process easier. Rutabagas can be baked, roasted, braised, steamed, stir-fried, microwaved, and boiled. When boiling, lift the lid of the pan to release the gases, which have an unpleasant odor. Releasing the gases will improve the taste of the rutabaga. There are a variety of ways to introduce this flavorful vegetable to your family or guests. Cook them with potatoes, either roasted or mashed, add them to stews and soups, or use as a delicious addition to salads. They also add a unique taste when grated into coleslaw or a carrot salad. Adding cinnamon, minced garlic, or lemon juice will enhance their flavor.

Rutabagas are high in antioxidants. The vegetable's most significant nutrient is vitamin C; one cup contains 53 percent of the recommended daily requirement. To make measuring easier, think of a cup of cubed vegetables as being equal to the size of your fist or a baseball. Rutabagas are low in sodium, saturated fat, and cholesterol and are an excellent source of dietary fiber, thiamin, vitamin B_6, calcium, magnesium, phosphorus, and potassium. One cup of cubed rutabagas is equal to 66 calories. All of these factors help to promote health throughout the body.

Health Hero Farm

PROFILE

Health Hero Farm's 180 rolling acres are located on West Shore Road in South Hero, Vermont. They stretch picturesquely along Lake Champlain with flat, open pastures that are ideal for grazing. Owners Hannah and Eric Noel, along with their new business partners, Joan Falcao and Robert Fireovid, run the certified organic farm. They grow a variety of vegetables, small fruits, herbs, and cut flowers on about ½ acre.

The farm is working on building its herd. There's currently about 60 head of cattle, which are pastured from May through December. The owners feel that their focus on healthy soil has resulted in wonderful grass-fed beef and delectable, nutritious organic vegetables. Their goal is to demonstrate how custom grazing and agronomics can build topsoil that will absorb storm water and prevent erosion.

Health Hero Farm offers traditional summer and year-round CSA shares through its community supported agricultural program. Some share options include eggs from pastured hens, 100 percent grass-fed beef, organic free-range whole chickens, artisanal bread, local honey, maple syrup, preserves, pasta, handcrafted salad dressings, granola, and Vermont cheese. Their unique multi-farm CSA offers goods from local vendors, as well as food from other Lake Champlain Island farms.

Believing that good health is a result of healthy soil, the business partners focus on the farm's soil. They know how important organic farming is and stress the dangers of chemicals. Being next to Lake Champlain has furthered their efforts, for they realize that one of the environmental benefits of healthy soil is better water holding capacity, which prevents water and nutrients from running off into the lake.

Eric and Hannah are consultants for other farmers and gardeners. They offer farm tours to show how their practices are building the soil and helping to clean up Lake Champlain. The owners of Health Hero Farm are positive role models for environmental stewardship. They farm to stay healthy so you can too!

Photograph by Oliver Parini

Grass-Fed Beef Shanks Osso Buco

Serves 4

This hearty, rustic dish is a perfect meal for fall or winter. The meat is fall-apart tender. Serve with a nice crusty bread.

Bouquet Garni
3 sprigs fresh sage
3 sprigs fresh Italian parsley
4 strips fresh lemon rind (preferably from an unwaxed lemon)
2 bay leaves

Beef Shanks
3 tablespoons extra virgin olive oil
2 teaspoons sea salt
1 teaspoon dried sage
1 teaspoon lemon pepper
4 cross-cut, bone-in beef shanks (about 3 pounds total)
½ cup all-purpose flour, for dredging
1 large Spanish onion, peeled and coarsely chopped
4 medium carrots, peeled and chopped
4 garlic cloves, peeled and minced
1 cup dry red wine
1 8-ounce jar high-quality organic tomato sauce
1 quart homemade or high-quality store-bought chicken stock, warmed, plus extra as needed
½ tablespoon fresh basil
½ tablespoon fresh oregano
1 teaspoon salt
1 teaspoon freshly ground black pepper

1 pound good-quality pasta, such as pappardelle

Gremolata
1½ tablespoons chopped fresh flat-leaf parsley
1 tablespoon finely grated lemon zest (preferably from an unwaxed lemon)
1 large garlic clove, peeled and minced

Crusty bread, for serving, optional

Preheat the oven to 300 degrees Fahrenheit.

To make the bouquet garni: Place the sage, parsley, lemon rind, and bay leaves in a piece of cheesecloth and tie into a bundle with kitchen twine. Set aside.

To make the beef shanks: Heat the oil in a Dutch oven over medium-high heat until hot, but not smoking. In a small bowl combine the salt, sage, and lemon pepper. Pat the shanks dry with paper towels and season with the salt mixture. Dredge the shanks in flour, shaking off any excess flour. Add the shanks, in batches if necessary, to the pot and brown them for 4–5 minutes on each side. Remove from the heat and set aside on a large plate, reserving the drippings in the pot.

Add the onions and carrots to the Dutch oven with the drippings, reduce the heat to medium and cook, stirring often, until the onions are soft and translucent, about 5 minutes. Add the garlic and cook until fragrant, about 1 minute. Stir in the wine, bring to a simmer, and cook until the wine is reduced by almost half, about 10 minutes. Stir in the tomato sauce, chicken stock, basil, oregano, salt, and pepper, and bring back to a simmer.

Transfer the beef shanks, along with any juices that have accumulated, back to the pot. Add the bouquet garni and additional stock as needed to cover three-quarters of the way up the beef shanks. Cover, then carefully transfer the pot to the oven and cook until the meat is fork tender, about 2 hours and 30 minutes, adding additional stock as needed. Once cooked, carefully remove the meat from the bones and coarsely chop. Discard the bones and fatty bits and return the meat back into the sauce. Remove the bouquet garni and discard. Season with salt and pepper to taste.

Bring a large pot of salted water to a boil, add the pasta, and cook until al dente. Drain and set aside.

To assemble: First, make the gremolata in a small bowl by combining the parsley, lemon zest, and garlic. Place some of the pasta in the center of individual bowls, then top with the onions, carrots, and meat. Spoon the sauce over the shanks. Garnish with gremolata. Serve at once.

Recipe from Health Hero Farm
Photograph by Oliver Parini

Bacon-Cheddar Venison Burgers with Oven-Baked Fingerling Fries and Garlic Aioli

Serves 4

Venison is a lean meat that contains high amounts of protein, iron, and B vitamins, making it a healthy alternative to beef. The tangy flavor of the extra-sharp Vermont cheddar cheese provides the perfect counterpoint to the "wild" venison flavor and garlicky aioli in these handsome burgers. The fingerling fries pair perfectly with the rich, smooth garlic aioli.

Venison Burgers

1 pound ground venison
1 egg, lightly beaten
Kosher salt and freshly ground black pepper
4 ounces extra-sharp Vermont cheddar cheese, thinly sliced

Garlic Aioli

2 tablespoons extra virgin olive oil
4 large garlic cloves, minced
1 cup high-quality mayonnaise
1 teaspoon fresh lemon juice
Kosher salt and freshly ground black pepper

Fingerling Fries

2 pounds fingerling potatoes cut into ½-by-½-by-3-inch-long rectangular sticks
Extra virgin olive oil, as needed
Kosher salt and freshly ground black pepper

Topping

4 slices applewood-smoked bacon
4 artisan rolls, sliced in half and toasted
2–3 large heirloom tomatoes, cut into ⅓-inch-thick slices
1 cup loosely packed greens, optional

To make the venison burgers: In a medium bowl, gently combine the venison, egg, salt, and pepper until just combined, being careful not overwork the meat. Using your hands, form the meat into four 1-inch-thick patties. Place the patties on a baking sheet lined with parchment paper, cover with plastic wrap, and partially freeze the meat for 1½ hours.

To make the garlic aioli: While the patties are freezing, start the garlic aioli. Heat the oil in a small sauté pan over medium-low heat. Add the garlic and cook, stirring frequently, until light golden brown, about 3 minutes. Transfer the garlic and any accumulated oil to a medium bowl. Stir in the mayonnaise, lemon juice, and season with salt and pepper to taste. Cover and refrigerate until ready to use.

To make the fingerling fries: Preheat the oven to 450 degrees Fahrenheit. Lightly oil a baking sheet and set aside. Place the cut potatoes in a medium bowl, drizzle oil over them, and toss until well combined. Season with salt and pepper and toss once more. Spread the potatoes out in a single layer on the prepared baking sheet. Bake, flipping every 4 minutes, until crispy on the outside and tender on the inside, about 20 minutes. Season with salt and pepper to taste.

While the fries are baking, cook the bacon. In a medium skillet, cook the bacon over medium-high heat, turning once, until crisp, about 7 minutes. Drain on paper towels, then carefully break each slice in half and set aside.

Heat a gas or electric grill to medium-high heat and generously brush the cooking grate with oil. Season the burgers with salt and pepper. Grill the burgers on one side for about 4 minutes. Using a large spatula, carefully flip the burgers, then top with the cheese. Cook until the desired doneness is reached, about 6 minutes for medium. Remove the burgers from the grill and let rest for 2 minutes.

To assemble: Spread the garlic aioli on the bottom of each roll. Place each burger on the bottom half of each roll and top with tomatoes, bacon, and greens, if desired. Top with the remaining half of each roll and serve with fries.

Recipe from Willow Brook Farm
Photograph by Oliver Parini

Note: Freezing the venison burgers before grilling will help keep them from falling apart on the grill.

Burelli Farm's Swiss Steak

Serves 6

Swiss steak is a classic dish where tough cuts of beef are braised in tomatoes until they are fork tender and falling apart. The "Swiss" in Swiss steak refers to the technique of tenderizing tough cuts of meat by pounding with a mallet or rolling with an electric tenderizer.

2 pounds boneless top round steak, preferably certified organic, pounded with a tenderizing hammer and cut into 1-inch pieces
Salt and freshly ground black pepper
⅓ cup all-purpose flour
½ tablespoon smoked sweet paprika
4 tablespoons certified organic leaf lard or vegetable oil, divided
1 large sweet onion, such as Vidalia or Walla Walla, chopped
3 medium carrots, peeled and cut diagonally into 1-inch pieces
3 medium celery stalks cut diagonally into 1-inch pieces
2 14-ounce cans diced tomatoes, undrained
1 tablespoon tomato paste
1 tablespoon Worcestershire sauce
2 tablespoons organic brown sugar
½ tablespoon fresh chopped thyme leaves
Fresh chopped parsley, for garnish

Pat the meat dry with paper towels and season liberally with salt and pepper. In a large, shallow bowl, combine the flour and paprika, stirring until well combined. Dredge the pieces of meat in the flour mixture, shaking off any excess flour.

In a large heavy pot or Dutch oven, heat 3 tablespoons of lard over medium-high heat until hot but not smoking. Working in batches, brown the meat on all sides, adding additional lard if needed, about 6 minutes. Using a slotted spoon, remove the meat from the pot and set aside on a large plate, reserving any meat drippings in the pot. Reduce the heat to medium. In the same pot with the meat drippings, add the remaining 1 tablespoon lard and onion and sauté until soft and translucent, about 5 minutes. Add the carrots and celery and sauté for another 3 minutes. Transfer the vegetables and meat along with any accumulated juices to a slow cooker. Stir in the tomatoes along with their juice, tomato paste, Worcestershire sauce, brown sugar, and thyme. Cover, and cook on low until the meat is fork tender and falling apart, about 8 hours. Adjust seasonings with salt and pepper to taste. Garnish with parsley and serve with mashed potatoes or egg noodles and crusty bread.

Recipe from Burelli Farm

Woodbelly Pizza

"Have Oven Will Travel" should be the slogan of Woodbelly Pizza. This Vermont-based business became a worker-owned cooperative in 2014, when a collaborative bought the business. Owners David and Celeste Huck and David Dickson are the current member-owners, along with two employees who are pursuing membership. The business was originally located on Provender farm in Cabot, Vermont, until spring 2017, but is now looking for a new place to call home. The owners serve in executive roles that involve responsibility for management and participation in the company's daily operations and event leadership. Because of the seasonal nature of the work, their long-range goal of making the business primarily owner-operated has been put on the back burner for now.

Both men have had previous experience working in the restaurant industry, and this expertise has helped them with the everyday activities of the catering company. Woodbelly provides both pizza and full catering services for rehearsal dinners, weddings, birthdays, graduations, festivals, farmers' markets, and a variety of other memorable occasions. Their specialty is wood-fired pizza, which is baked in one of the company's three mobile ovens. These ovens are mounted on trailers that travel throughout the state bringing nourishment and laughter wherever they go.

All vegetables are sourced from local organic farms, with cheese coming from area cheesemakers. Meats are selected from the best organic pastured beef, chicken, pork, and goose. The organic flour used for their dough is freshly milled in Vermont. Woodbelly's dough does not contain GMOs and is naturally leavened and hand-mixed for flavor and nutrition. The sourdough pizza uses time-honored techniques, enhanced by toppings ranging from classic to more diverse combinations.

The catering menu offers both casual and more upscale options, with appetizers, salads, side dishes, and desserts available upon request. There are also choices for folks who need gluten-free, celiac, or vegetarian options. Woodbelly's farm-grown salads and pizza toppings change with the seasons, making for an exciting variety of selections.

You can find Woodbelly at the Montpelier and Stowe farmers' markets—just look for their mobile pizza oven and trailer. Favorite pies include peach, apple, or pear and Bayley Hazen Blue cheese, sausage with sage parsley pesto, and lengua plus arugula. The names and toppings are intriguing, flavor-filled combinations that make folks want to return for yet another slice . . . or two!

Photograph courtesy of Woodbelly Pizza

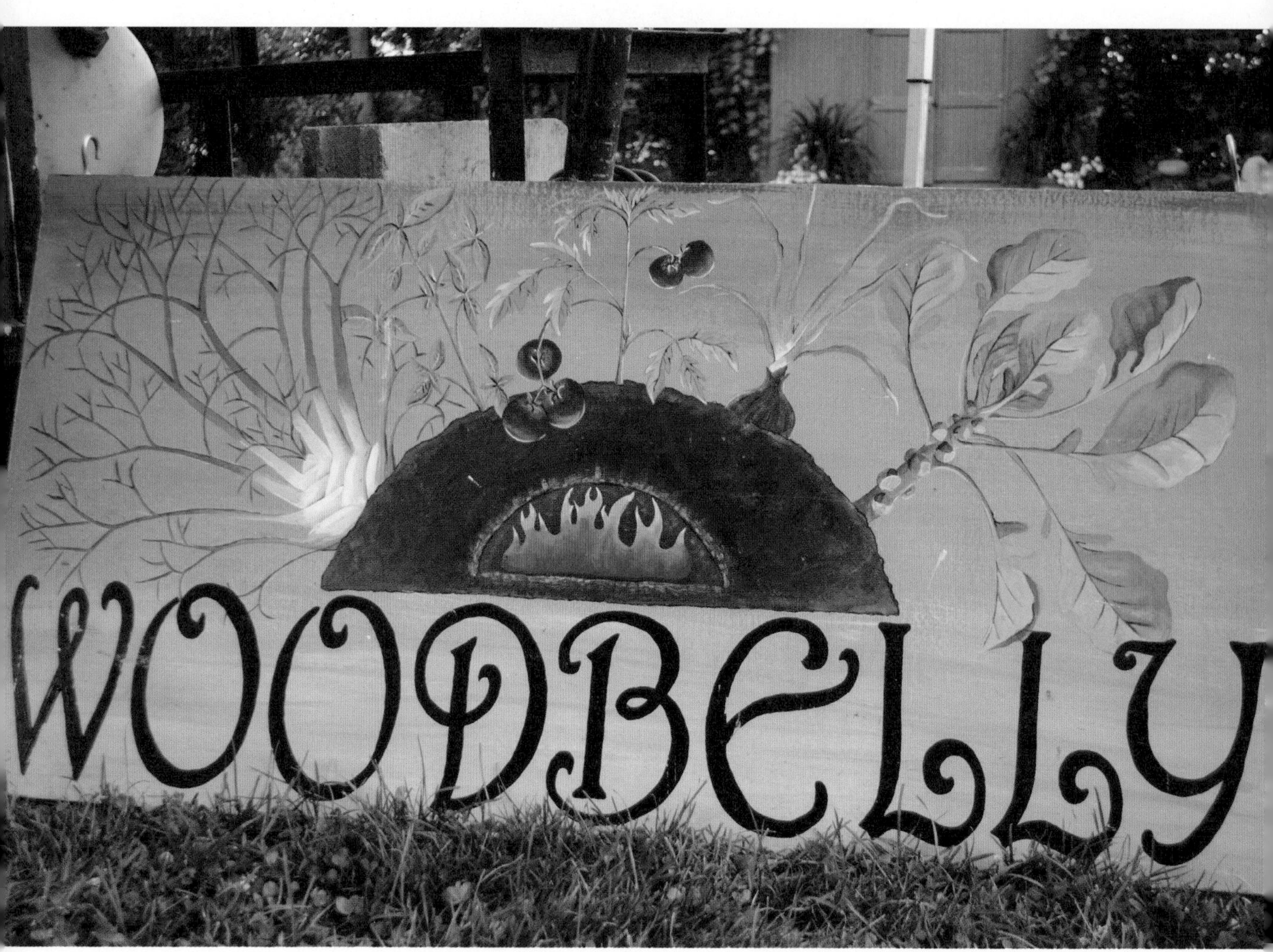
WOODBELLY

Honey-Glazed Pork Bellies

Serves 4

"Before bacon is cured and smoked, it's a slab of pork belly. When roasted, the meat bathes in its own fat and becomes meltingly tender. These pork bellies have a rich flavor and succulent texture. The ancho chile powder adds a fruity and smoky component reminiscent of raisins to the rub, while the honey adds a sweet flavor. Because the meat is so rich, it's best served with bright and acidic side dishes (think salad with vinaigrette or coleslaw) and goes really well with fruity sauces." —*Suzanne Podhaizer, Woodbelly Pizza*

Pork Bellies

2 pork bellies (1 pound each)

1 tablespoon extra virgin olive oil

Spice Mix

1 tablespoon salt

½ teaspoon ancho chile powder

¼ teaspoon ground coriander seeds

¼ teaspoon cinnamon

1¼ teaspoons freshly ground black pepper

1 large onion, peeled, sliced, and cut into thick half-moons

½ cup honey

1 tablespoon butter

To make the pork bellies: Pat each pork belly thoroughly dry with paper towels. Place the pork bellies, skin side up, on a cutting board and score the skin with a sharp knife in a crosshatch pattern, piercing about 1 inch deep through the tough skin.

In a small bowl, combine the salt, ancho chile powder, coriander, cinnamon, and pepper. Rub the pork bellies with the spice mix evenly over all sides.

Place half of the onions in a baking dish. Place the pork bellies, skin side down, on top of the onions and top with the remaining onions. Cover and refrigerate overnight.

Remove the pork bellies from the baking dish, reserving the onions. Place the pork bellies, skin side up, in a deep oven-safe frying pan and let the meat come to room temperature.

Preheat the oven to 450 degrees Fahrenheit.

Drizzle the pork bellies with olive oil and roast in the oven until the pork starts to bubble and turn a deep golden brown, about 30 minutes. Reduce the temperature to 325 degrees Fahrenheit and leave the oven door slightly ajar so the temperature will drop. Using a spatula, remove the pork bellies from the oven and drizzle with the honey evenly on all sides.

Return the pork bellies to the oven and cook, with the oven door closed, for 45 minutes. Remove from the oven and add the onions to the pan. Cook the pork bellies and onions for another 45 minutes, stirring the onions after 20 minutes. Continue to cook until the meat pulls apart easily, checking every 15 minutes until the desired doneness is achieved.

Transfer the pork bellies to a clean pan and allow to rest for 20 minutes. Wrap the pork bellies in plastic wrap, return to the pan, and weigh the pork down with another heavy pan for 10 minutes, reserving any accumulating juices.

Strain the cooking liquid through a fine-mesh strainer and into a fat separator or a clear liquid measuring cup, skimming any visible fat from the cooking liquid. Reserve the onions and set aside. Separate the fat from the cooking liquid, reserving the fat for another use, such as cornbread or flavoring a bean salad.

Transfer the onions, reserved accumulated juices, and 2 tablespoons water to a food processor and pulse, adding more liquid as needed, until smooth. Season with salt and pepper to taste. Transfer to a small saucepan and bring to a simmer over medium-high heat, whisking frequently, until the liquid is reduced by almost half, about 8 minutes. Add the butter and continue to whisk until melted. Season with salt and pepper to taste.

Slice the pork bellies, drizzle the sauce over the meat, and serve.

Recipe from Suzanne Podhaizer for Woodbelly Pizza
Photograph courtesy of Woodbelly Pizza

Shadow Creek Farm

PROFILE

Shadow Creek Farm is a small farm incubator operated by Eli Hersh. He started the business in 2015 on 1½ acres of land he leased from a much larger organic farm where he works as field manager. The University of Vermont Extension, Intervale Center, NOFA-VT, and Carrot Project have offered a variety of technical assistance during his start-up. With both mentoring and a start-up loan, Eli is on the way to establishing a successful farm business.

He has an extensive background in commercial produce, from organic production to retail sales to restaurant preparation. Eight seasons of experience growing organic vegetables for CSAs, farmers' markets, and wholesale production, as well as many years working in restaurants preparing meals, has helped to give him the basic skills needed to run a small farm operation. Eli knows that this background, and the knowledge gained farming at Shadow Creek, will eventually enable him to purchase a property of his own.

The busy farmer feels that growing vegetables is a natural fit for him. His love of the endless variety of colors, textures, shapes, and tastes have made what he grows a source of never-ending joy and wonder—not to mention the fringe benefits of sunshine and fresh air! Hot peppers, with their bright colors and bold flavor, are one of his favorite crops. He also sells cucumbers, beets, and other crops to local restaurants and wholesale accounts.

Organic farming is important to this new grower, who focuses his farming practices on soil health. Being on leased land does not allow him to make a long-term soil management plan, but during the time he has worked the land he is taking care of the soil in the best way possible. To Eli, the importance of organic practices seems like common sense; therefore, he feeds the soil with composted manure, builds soil structure with cover crops, and controls pests and diseases through crop rotation.

Eli feels that Vermont food processors are the foundation of his business and has established a great relationship with some amazing local kitchens. After spending years working in commercial kitchens and now transitioning into production farming, he appreciates the perspective gained from working on both sides of the supply chain. With hard work and dedication, Eli hopes that his future in farming will be as bright as the colorful vegetables that he grows!

Vermont Late Winter Cottage Pie

Serves 6–8

"This dish is a staple from my childhood, and a perfect comfort food for a cold winter night. I find it fun to cook because I can adapt the recipe to use almost any vegetable and ground meat that I have handy. And it never fails to make a hearty and delicious meal. My favorite additions are winter squash in the top layer and grated beets and radishes in with the meat." —*Eli Hersh, owner, Shadow Creek Farm*

Topping

1½ pounds Yukon Gold potatoes, preferably organic, peeled and cut into 1-inch pieces
1 purple top turnip, peeled and cut into 1-inch pieces, about ½ pound
2 medium parsnips, peeled and cut into 1-inch pieces
¼ cup organic cream, warmed
2 tablespoons salted butter, preferably organic
Salt and freshly ground black pepper to taste

Filling

2 tablespoons extra virgin olive oil
1 small sweet onion, peeled and diced
2 medium carrots, peeled and diced
1 cup thinly sliced shiitake mushrooms caps
½ pound grass-fed ground beef
½ pound pastured pork sausage, preferably hot Italian, casings removed
2 cups frozen peas
2 tablespoons butter
2 tablespoons all-purpose flour
2 medium garlic cloves, peeled and minced
1 tablespoon fresh chopped Italian parsley leaves, plus extra for garnish
½ teaspoon dry oregano
½ teaspoon dry basil
¾ cup low-sodium beef broth
2 tablespoons tomato paste
1½ tablespoons fresh lemon juice
Salt and freshly ground black pepper
1 cup shredded sharp cheddar cheese

Preheat the oven to 350 degrees Fahrenheit. Lightly grease a 9-by-13-inch baking dish.

To make the mashed potato topping: Combine the potatoes, turnip, parsnips and ½ teaspoon salt in a large pot of water and bring to a boil over medium-high heat. Reduce the heat to a simmer and cook until the vegetables are fork tender, about 20 minutes. Drain the vegetables in a colander and transfer to a large bowl. Add the cream and butter and mash with an old-fashioned masher or immersion blender until smooth. Adjust seasonings with salt and pepper to taste. Cover the bowl with plastic wrap and set aside.

While the potatoes are cooking, start the filling. Heat the oil in a large sauté pan over medium heat. Add the onions and carrots and cook, stirring occasionally, until the onions are soft and translucent, about 10 minutes. Add the mushrooms and cook, stirring occasionally, for 5 minutes. Add the beef and sausage, and cook, breaking up with a fork, until the meat begins to brown, about 7 minutes. Carefully pour off and discard some of the fat. Add the peas, stirring until well combined, and cook for 2 minutes. Add the butter and cook, stirring often, until melted. Add the flour, garlic, parsley, oregano, and basil and cook, stirring often, for 2 minutes. Stir in the broth, tomato paste, and lemon juice and cook until liquid slightly thickens, about 2 minutes. Adjust seasonings with salt and pepper to taste.

Pour filling evenly into the prepared baking dish. Drop spoonfuls of the mashed vegetables evenly over the filling, then smooth the top into an even layer with a rubber spatula. Place the baking dish on a baking sheet and bake, uncovered, until the potatoes are golden brown and the filling is heated through, about 30 minutes. Sprinkle the cheese over the top and bake for 10 more minutes. Let rest for 10 minutes. Garnish with parsley and serve.

Recipe from Shadow Creek Farm

PROFILE

Freighthouse Market & Café

As the owners of both Tamarlane Farm and the Freighthouse Market & Café in Lyndonville, Vermont, Eric and Cathy Paris have established a unique connection to the local farming community. Their story dates back to 1956, when Eric's parents bought Tamarlane Farm, a welcoming place to raise a family and call home. Now, finding themselves second-generation farm owners, Eric and Cathy have expanded their horizons with the founding of their quaint café and market in 2004. The market offers a wide variety of local and organic foods, including Tamarlane Farm's own certified organic, grass-fed beef and produce. Both businesses are located in a historic freight house, hence the name Freighthouse Market & Café. With an innovative farm-to-table approach, Tamarlane Farm supplies the restaurant and market with many of the organic food items. The owners describe the process as, "Food prepared by the same hands that grew it."

Their daughter, Bonnie, starts each day by helping out with the farm chores before beginning her second job as manager of the café. As the third generation of the family to be involved with the farming business, she carries on a tradition that started so many years ago. The Paris family believes that the secret of serving delicious food is very simple: source your ingredients with a care and appreciation for how and where they are grown. To accomplish this, they have established strong relationships with local farms, using their freshly picked offerings for both the café and market. Seeking seasonal, locally grown and produced products is always the order of the day.

The restaurant's menu consists of organic ingredients obtained from Tamarlane Farm and other area producers. The café's award-winning Tamarlane Burger is made from the farm's grass-fed beef and served on a handmade bun created with King Arthur organic flour. Accompanied by a side order of fresh organic vegetables, this dish is an all-time favorite. In the fall, customers often ask for the café's beet hash, which is made with the farm's own organic beets, the perfect partner when served with poached organic eggs. The café menu is extensive, showcasing a variety of selections made with organic meats, cheeses, and vegetables.

The Paris family has known some of their neighboring farmers for decades, witnessing how these hardworking folks join forces whenever possible to help each other out. As a farm family, they recognize the dedication that goes into growing and producing quality organic food. The Freighthouse Market & Café, with its "green commitment," is devoted to selling the best that Vermont has to offer. By being good stewards of the land, using sustainable and organic farming practices, and supporting their local food community, they hope to make the world a little better than they found it.

Organic Shepherd's Pie

Serves 8

"This recipe is one of those classic dishes that has many variations. Add seasonal vegetables, such as wild foraged leeks in the spring, which can be sautéed into the beef mixture, or freshly dug parsnips in addition to the carrots. Leftovers will keep for up to 1 week in the refrigerator, or tightly cover with foil and freeze for up to 2 months." *—Bonnie Paris, owner, Freighthouse Market & Café*

Topping

2 pounds Yukon Gold potatoes, preferably organic, peeled and cut into 1-inch pieces
¼–½ cup organic milk, warmed
4 tablespoons salted butter, preferably organic
⅛ teaspoon grated nutmeg, optional
Salt and freshly ground black pepper

Filling

2 tablespoons extra virgin olive oil
1 medium sweet onion, preferably organic, peeled and diced
2 medium carrots, preferably organic, peeled and diced
2 pounds organic ground lamb or beef, preferably grass-fed
1 tablespoon heavy cream, preferably organic
1 cup organic low-sodium beef or vegetable broth
1 cup green peas, preferably organic, frozen and thawed or fresh
1 cup sweet corn, preferably organic, frozen and thawed or fresh
2 tablespoons tomato paste
1 teaspoon granulated garlic
1 teaspoon onion powder
1 tablespoon minced fresh basil leaves or 1 teaspoon dried basil leaves
Salt and freshly ground black pepper
1 cup shredded cheddar cheese
Fresh chopped parsley for garnish

Preheat the oven to 350 degrees Fahrenheit. Lightly grease an 11-by-8-inch baking dish.

To make the mashed potato topping: Combine the potatoes and ½ teaspoon salt in a large pot of water and bring to a boil over high heat. Reduce the heat to a simmer and cook until the potatoes are fork tender, about 20 minutes. Drain the potatoes in a colander and transfer to a

large bowl. Add the milk, butter, and nutmeg. Mash with an old-fashioned masher or immersion blender until smooth. Season with salt and pepper to taste. Cover the bowl with plastic wrap and set aside.

While the potatoes are cooking, start the filling. Heat the oil in a large sauté pan over medium heat. Add the onion and cook, stirring occasionally, until the onion is soft and translucent, about 7 minutes. Add the carrots and cook, stirring occasionally, for 3 minutes. Add the lamb or beef and cream and cook, breaking up the meat with a fork, until the meat begins to brown, about 7 minutes. Carefully pour off and discard some of the fat.

Add the broth and bring to a boil over medium-high heat. Reduce the heat to medium-low and cook, stirring frequently, for 3–4 minutes. Add the peas, corn, tomato paste, granulated garlic, onion powder, and basil, stirring until well combined. Adjust seasonings with salt and pepper to taste.

Pour the filling evenly into the prepared baking dish. Drop spoonfuls of the potato topping evenly over the filling, then smooth the top into an even layer with a rubber spatula. Place the baking dish on a baking sheet and bake, uncovered, until the potatoes are golden brown and the filling is heated through, about 30 minutes. Sprinkle the cheese over the top and bake for 10 more minutes. Let rest for 10 minutes. Garnish with parsley and serve.

Recipe from Freighthouse Market & Café
Photograph by Oliver Parini

Tourterelle Restaurant & Inn

William Snell, owner of the Tourterelle Restaurant & Inn, knew early on that he was destined to be a chef. His love for fresh, distinctly different foods was inherited from his father, who was an avid fisherman and hunter. In 1990, Bill began his culinary training in the kitchen of The Frog and The Peach Restaurant in New Jersey before moving to New York City in 1994 to work at Robert DeNiro's Tribeca Grill. Driven by the desire to continue his education, he worked as both sous and head chef, followed by a short stint as a restaurant consultant.

After meeting, and marrying, his wife Christine in 1998, the twosome opened their first French bistro, Loulou, in Brooklyn, New York. This was soon followed by their second eatery, Cocotte's. Deciding to pursue a lifelong dream of owning a restaurant and inn, the restaurateurs purchased Roland's Place in New Haven, Vermont, in 2009. They changed the name to Tourterelle, the French word for turtle dove, a seemingly perfect choice, as turtle doves are monogamous and mate for life. The small gray bird pictured on the inn's welcoming sign is representative of the couple and the family values they hold most dear.

The quaint inn houses a country-chic French bistro. Visitors are treated to a breathtaking panorama of the Green and Adirondack Mountains, further enhanced by the nearby pond with its beautifully illuminated fountain. The surrounding grounds contain a variety of lovely gardens, adding to the inn's romantic appeal.

The inn's three elegant bedrooms all look out on the picture-perfect countryside. The bistro's French country cuisine is made with local Vermont products that are purchased from neighboring organic farms. As Bill explains, "We are always working together to stay ahead of the farm-to-table movement." The busy chef appreciates the fact that his providers are also his neighbors, minimizing the distance he has to travel to purchase products for his restaurant.

The restaurant offers four dining options: The Brick Room, The Stone Dining Room, The Front Porch, or The Deck. Visitors are treated to a variety of gourmet French cuisine, such as Tourterelle's signature dish, bouillabaisse, a seafood stew with red curry and saffron aioli that has been a menu favorite for 17 years. There are vegetarian selections as well, including tartiflette, a modern twist on a traditional casserole recipe that contains Vermont produce and French cheese from the Haute Savoie Mountains. Sunday brunch is a weekend favorite, providing an array of choices, including a toothsome assortment of sweet and savory crepes.

Christine is not only the restaurant's charming host, she also keeps the busy inn running smoothly while Chef Bill performs wonders in the kitchen. After all, there are weddings, birthdays, graduations, retirements, and all manner of happy occasions celebrated there. With its simple elegant ambience, awe-inspiring views, and outstanding seasonally driven menu, is it any wonder that folks come from near and far to visit this idyllic countryside gem?

Photograph courtesy of Tourterelle Restaurant & Inn

Braised Lamb Shoulder with Ramp Pesto and Toasted Quinoa Topped with a Poached Farm-Fresh Egg

Serves 6

"Springtime in Vermont means finally getting out of the house to enjoy the warmer weather. One of my favorite pastimes is to forage for leeks that grow like crazy on the mountainsides. Leeks grow in abundance during the few weeks that they are available. We get our supply of spring lambs from a number of farmers who are located within a mile of our restaurant." —*Chef William Snell, owner, Tourterelle Restaurant & Inn*

Braised Lamb

1 5-pound boned lamb shoulder rolled and tied*
2 tablespoons canola oil, or as needed
2 cups coarsely chopped celery
2 cups coarsely chopped carrots
2 leeks, washed, trimmed, and coarsely chopped
1 large onion, peeled and coarsely chopped, about 1½ cups
8 medium garlic cloves, peeled
5 fresh thyme sprigs
Salt and freshly ground black pepper
5 cups vegetables stock, or as needed

Ramp Pesto

Makes 1½ cups pesto

2 tablespoons toasted walnuts, coarsely chopped
3 medium garlic cloves, peeled
½ pound ramps or other wild onion, trimmed and coarsely chopped
¼ cup extra virgin olive oil
¼ cup canola oil
1 tablespoon sherry vinegar
Salt and freshly ground black pepper

Toasted Quinoa

1 cup quinoa, rinsed and drained
1½ cups vegetable stock
2 teaspoons unsalted butter
Salt and freshly ground black pepper

Poached Eggs

4–6 farm-fresh eggs

Chopped fresh parsley, for garnish, optional

Preheat the oven to 300 degrees Fahrenheit. Using paper towels, pat the lamb dry of any extra juices. Season the lamb with salt and pepper.

Heat the oil in a large Dutch oven or heavy-bottomed pot over medium heat. Add the lamb and sear on all sides, about 3 minutes per side.

Transfer the lamb to a plate and tent with foil. Reduce the heat to medium and add the celery, carrots, leeks, onion, garlic, and thyme to the pot and cook, stirring often, for 8 minutes.

Return the lamb to the pot with the vegetables. Add the stock and bring to a boil. Cover and braise in the oven until the meat is fork tender, about 4½ hours. Transfer the meat to a cutting board and allow to rest for 15 minutes. While the lamb is resting on the cutting board, strain the braising liquid through a fine-mesh strainer. Return the strained liquid to the same pot and bring to a simmer and cook until the sauce thickens and reduces. Season with salt and pepper to taste.

While the lamb is braising, make the ramp pesto. Process the walnuts and garlic in a food processor until minced. Add the ramps, oils, and vinegar and continue to process until the desired texture is achieved, scraping down the side of the bowl as needed. Adjust seasonings with salt and pepper. Spoon the pesto into a bowl, cover with plastic wrap, and set aside.

While the lamb is resting, start the quinoa. Cook the quinoa in a 10-inch skillet, shaking the skillet often to prevent the quinoa from sticking, over medium-high heat, until toasted, about 5 minutes. The quinoa will make a slight popping sound when almost done. Combine the toasted quinoa, vegetable stock, and butter in a small saucepan and bring to a boil over high heat. Cover, reduce the heat, and simmer until the quinoa is tender and the water is absorbed, about 15 minutes. Fluff with a fork. Season with salt and pepper to taste.

While the quinoa is cooking, start the poached eggs. Bring 3 inches of water to a simmer in a large saucepan over medium heat. Crack the eggs into individual small bowls or ramekins. Carefully slide the eggs into the water, making sure they do not touch. Turn off the heat, cover, and cook for 4 minutes. Using a slotted spoon, carefully remove the eggs from the saucepan.

To assemble: Place about ¾ cup of quinoa in the center of each plate. Slice the lamb across the grain and arrange on top. Drizzle with sauce to taste. Spoon ¼ cup of the pesto over the meat. Top with a poached egg. Garnish with parsley. Serve at once.

Recipe from Tourterelle Restaurant & Inn

Note: You can ask your butcher to remove the bone from the lamb.

PROFILE

3 Squares Café

Native Vermonter Matthew Birong, owner of 3 Squares Café, has always been fascinated with food. While in high school, he worked at the New England Culinary Institute's Essex campus washing dishes and working banquets. He loved the creative food environment and sense of camaraderie among the staff. In his mind a culinary career perfectly fit the plans for his future.

After attending New England Culinary Institute in Vermont, he left to gain experience in kitchens in places like New York City and Boston, all the while saving up money to start his own restaurant. Upon returning to Vermont in 2007, he opened 3 Squares Café. Located in the historic town of Vergennes, the casual café serves breakfast, lunch, and dinner seven days a week. Matthew takes great pride in the fact that virtually everything he creates is made from scratch.

His bond with the area's organic farmers is of the utmost importance to him. As he explains, "None of us got into our lines of work for the great pay and cushy hours." Because of their commitment to fresh, healthy food, the local farmers and Chef Matthew have a mutual respect for each other. Matthew knows he's fortunate to live in a place where the farmers and food producers have as much love for good food as he does.

For the owner of 3 Squares Café, organic and non-GMO products are a vital part of the way he views the future of agriculture, believing that the two support the vision for a sustainable future. He feels that accountability for our treatment of the environment will move our food systems away from the use of chemicals and other unsafe ways of growing crops, thereby encouraging responsible land stewardship, which will help to protect our farmlands for generations to come. In Matthew's opinion, the equation for a safer, healthier food system also includes the promotion of socially responsible labor practices.

After 10 years in the same spot, the café moved a short distance up the street to a location that can better accommodate its catering business. Matthew caters all types of occasions and will even rent out the café for a special event. Both the café and catering service offer gluten-free and vegan-friendly options.

Hungry patrons may choose from a wide variety of culinary selections, some with an international flavor. There are tasty soups, juicy burgers and sandwiches, and a variety of entrées and appetizers that will please even the most finicky eater. Steaming cups of locally roasted coffee and espresso warm folks while they wait for their meal. Matthew believes that food not only fuels our bodies, but it is also a tool to educate. It is his belief that if you want to learn about a region, country, or culture you should first start by exploring their food, with a visit to 3 Squares Café as the perfect place to start.

Goat Shank Tostada with Roasted Corn Salsa, Queso Fresco, and Stewed Black Beans

Makes 10 (4-inch) yellow dent corn tortillas

"Crispy, salty corn tortillas, earthy braised goat, and fresh corn salsa with lots of pop come together in a traditional Mexican approach to a tostada. This dish offers an introduction to the world's most common red meat; excellent on a hot summer day or a chilly winter night, the goat's versatility is very evident here." —*Chef Matthew Birong, owner, 3 Squares Café*

Goat Shanks

2 tablespoons extra virgin olive oil
Kosher salt and freshly ground black pepper
4 goat shanks (about 5 pounds total), preferably from VT Chevon
1 large onion, sliced
8 medium garlic cloves, peeled and coarsely chopped
4 dried guajillo chile peppers, seeded and thinly sliced
4 dried ancho chile peppers, seeded and thinly sliced
1½ tablespoons whole coriander seeds
1½ tablespoons whole cumin seeds
3 quarts low-sodium chicken stock, or just enough to cover the shanks
1¼ cups fresh lime juice

Corn Salsa

Makes about 7 cups

6 ears of corn, kernels cut from cobs
3 tablespoons extra virgin olive oil, divided
Salt and freshly ground black pepper
2 poblano peppers, seeded and diced
1 red onion, minced
½ bunch cilantro leaves, coarsely chopped
⅓ cup fresh lime juice

Stewed Black Beans

1 tablespoon extra virgin olive oil
1 large Spanish onion, diced
2½ tablespoons minced garlic
1–2 tablespoons ground cumin
1–2 tablespoons ground coriander
1–2 tablespoons smoked paprika
2 10-ounce cans organic black beans, undrained
Salt and freshly ground black pepper

Yellow Dent Corn Tortillas

10 4-inch yellow dent corn tortillas, preferably from the Vermont Tortilla Company
1½ cups oil, or as needed for frying
Salt

Crumbled Queso Fresco
¼ cup thinly sliced scallions, for garnish

Preheat the oven to 300 degrees Fahrenheit. Place a baking sheet in the oven and heat until it's very hot.

To make the goat shanks: Heat the oil in a 10-quart Dutch oven over medium-high heat until hot, but not smoking. Generously season the shanks with salt and pepper. Add the shanks to the pot and brown each side for 3–4 minutes. Transfer the shanks to a large plate, reserving the drippings in the Dutch oven.

Reduce the heat to medium. Add the onion and garlic to the same pot used for the shanks and cook, stirring frequently, until the onions are soft and translucent, about 5 minutes. Season with salt and pepper to taste. Add the peppers, coriander seeds, and cumin and cook, stirring frequently, until fragrant, about 2 minutes.

Add 1 quart of the stock and the lime juice, scraping up the bits from the bottom of the pot, and bring to a boil over medium-high heat. Transfer the shanks, along with any accumulated juices, back into the pot. Add enough stock to just cover the shanks. Cover, transfer to the oven, and cook until the meat is fork tender, about 3 hours.

Using tongs, remove the meat from the liquid and set aside for 30 minutes. Using your fingers or forks, pull the meat from the bones and shred, discarding the bones. Transfer the meat to a large bowl and add ¾ cup of the braising liquid, stirring until well combined.

Allow the remaining braising liquid to cool slightly, then puree with an emulsion blender. Strain the liquid through a fine-mesh strainer. Transfer the liquid back to the pot and season with salt and pepper to taste. Set aside until ready to use.

While the meat is braising, make the corn salsa. Place the corn kernels in a large bowl and toss with 2 tablespoons olive oil. Season with salt and pepper to taste. Place the corn kernels on the preheated baking sheet and cook, stirring occasionally, until light golden brown, about 8 minutes. Remove from the oven and set aside to cool. Transfer the corn kernels to a medium bowl. Add the peppers, onions, cilantro, and lime juice. Cover and let sit at room temperature for 3 hours. Add the remaining 1 tablespoon olive oil and toss until well combined. Adjust seasonings with cilantro, lime juice, and salt and pepper to taste.

To make the stewed black beans: Heat the oil in a large saucepan over medium heat. Add the onions and cook, stirring often, until soft and translucent, about 7 minutes. Add the garlic and cook, stirring often for 1 minute. Add the cumin, coriander, and paprika and cook, stirring often, until fragrant, about 1 minute. Add the beans and the liquid and simmer for 25 minutes. Adjust seasonings with salt and pepper to taste.

To make the yellow dent corn tortillas: In a large cast-iron skillet, heat 1 inch of oil to 325 degrees Fahrenheit, over medium-high heat. Using tongs, carefully add the tortillas, in batches if necessary, and cook until golden brown and crisp, about 2 minutes each side. Transfer to a paper towel-lined plate and season with salt to taste.

While the oil is heating for the tortillas, reheat the braising liquid.

To assemble: Place ½ cup black beans on a tortilla. Top with 1–2 tablespoons cheese, ½ cup meat, and ½ cup corn salsa. Drizzle with 2–3 tablespoons of braising liquid over the top. Season with salt to taste. Garnish with scallions and serve at once.

Recipe from 3 Squares Café
Photography by Oliver Parini

Notes:

- Save the extra braising liquid as a soup base for bean soup.
- Serve the extra salsa with your favorite corn chips.

Goat Meat

Although goat meat is a staple of many cultures, it has taken a long time for it to gain popularity in the United States. Today, goats provide the principle source of meat and part of the daily diet for three-quarters of the world's inhabitants. Known as chevon in Northern Europe, capretto in Australia and Southern Europe, and as cabrito in the Hispanic culture, the demand for goat meat in the States has been on the rise, as a variety of ethnic groups have migrated to our shores.

Health-conscious individuals find goat meat to be a welcome alternative to beef, chicken, or pork, because it is lower in calories, fat, and cholesterol. A 3-ounce portion of goat meat has approximately 122 calories and is much leaner than other meats. It has only 63.8 milligrams of cholesterol and contains higher amounts of iron, potassium, and thiamine with less sodium than other meats. The goat meat sold in stores is inspected by the United States Department of Agriculture. Because the USDA has not approved the use of growth hormones, goat meat is free of such additives.

Goat meat can be fried, stewed, baked, grilled, barbecued, minced, curried, smoked, or made into sausage. However, because goat has a low fat content, the meat may toughen at high temperatures unless additional moisture is added. Most goat meat aficionados agree that the best meat comes from 6- to 9-month-old goats, often called cabrito, which tastes very much like spring lamb. Depending upon the age of the goat, the meat may be similar in taste to veal or venison.

If you want to cook your goat meat quickly, use ribs, loins, and tenderloin; the other parts are better for braising.

When buying goat meat, look for a light pink or bright red color. The flesh should be firm and fine-grained with white fat that is evenly distributed. Some like the meat from older goats because it is juicy and has more flavor than kid; on the other hand, this meat is darker and less tender. The meat from the female goat is better for steaks and chops because it is more tender.

Goat meat should be used within three to five days when stored in the refrigerator. When frozen, use within 4 months.

Burlington, Vermont, is home to a cross-section of African, South Asian, and Central European cultures that are accustomed to eating goat meat as a regular part of their diet. Finding an accessible supply is a problem for these groups, so the United States must import goat meat from Australia and New Zealand.

Vermont Chevon, formed in 2011 by Shirley Richardson, is working to fill this void. Richardson and her partner, Jan Westervelt, strive to turn the abundance of Vermont dairy goats into a "value-added meat product." Their goal is to represent goat meat as a healthy option to beef, pork, and chicken and encourage local chefs and restaurants to add goat dishes to their menu. Vermont Chevon hopes that the increasing demand for goat meat in recent years might enable the state to become a significant supplier of the product.

This stance will benefit the dairy goat industry. Most importantly, when we enable farmers to become self-sustaining, consumers also benefit, which is a surefire recipe for success.

Goat Stew in Red Wine Sauce

Serves 6

This hearty, rustic, one-pot meal has a rich flavor and tender texture. You will not need to cook the stew as long if using cabrito meat. Serve this comforting dish with a nice crusty bread to help mop up the delicious red wine sauce on your plate. Feel free to substitute organic grass-fed beef stew meat for goat, if you prefer.

Ingredients

2 strips thick-cut bacon, coarsely chopped
2 pounds boneless goat meat, cut into 1-inch pieces
⅓ cup all-purpose flour
½ tablespoon smoked sweet paprika
½ tablespoon salt
½ tablespoon freshly ground black pepper
3 tablespoons olive oil, or as needed
1 medium sweet onion, such as Vidalia or Walla Walla, thinly sliced
3 medium garlic cloves, peeled and minced
2½ cups dry red wine
1 28-ounce can whole tomatoes in juice
¾ cup low-sodium beef stock, plus more if needed
1 tablespoon tomato paste
2 teaspoons pure maple syrup
⅛ teaspoon ground cinnamon
⅛ teaspoon dried red pepper flakes
1 teaspoon Worcestershire sauce
1 tablespoon chopped fresh thyme leaves
2 bay leaves
1 pound carrots, peeled and sliced diagonally into 1-inch pieces
1 pound new potatoes, scrubbed, unpeeled, and cut into ½-inch-wide wedges
1 tablespoon unsalted butter
1 tablespoon fresh chopped parsley, plus extra for garnish

Crusty bread

Preheat the oven to 300 degrees Fahrenheit.

Cook the bacon in a heavy-bottomed pot or Dutch oven over medium heat until crisp and browned, about 10 minutes.

Using a slotted spoon, remove the bacon and drain on paper towels. Reserve the bacon drippings in the pot.

Pat the goat meat dry with paper towels. In a medium bowl, combine the flour, paprika, salt, and pepper, then dredge the meat in the flour mixture.

In the same pot used to cook the bacon, heat the reserved bacon fat and 2 tablespoons olive oil over medium-high heat until hot but not smoking. Working in batches, brown the meat on all sides, adding additional oil if needed, about 6 minutes. Remove the meat from the pot and set aside. Add the remaining 1 tablespoon oil and onion and sauté, stirring often, until soft and translucent, about 5 minutes. Add the garlic and cook, stirring frequently, until fragrant, about 1 minute.

Stir in the wine, tomatoes and juice, beef stock, tomato paste, maple syrup, cinnamon, red pepper flakes, Worcestershire sauce, thyme, and bay leaves, scraping up any brown bits on the bottom of the pot. Break up the tomatoes with a fork.

Bring to a boil over medium-high heat. Return the meat to the pot along with any accumulated juices, cover, and transfer to the oven. Cook, stirring occasionally, until the meat is fork tender, about 3 hours for chevon meat. After 2 hours of cooking, add the carrots and potatoes.

Remove from the oven and whisk in the butter until melted. Discard the bay leaves and adjust seasonings with salt and pepper to taste. Garnish with parsley and reserved bacon. Serve with crusty bread.

Recipe from Tracey Medeiros
Photograph by Brent Harrewyn

Note: You can adjust the heat by using more or less smoked sweet paprika and dried red pepper flakes.

Haymaker's Roast Pork

Serves 4

Some folks used to call switchel Haymaker's Punch, as the beverage was widely consumed by farmers and family members while out haying the fields on long, hot summer days.

Marinade

½ cup Vermont Switchel
⅓ cup extra virgin olive oil
1 medium shallot, coarsely chopped
2 tablespoons chopped fresh sage leaves, plus extra for garnish
4 medium garlic cloves, peeled and minced
½ teaspoon sea salt
¼ teaspoon freshly ground black pepper

Pork Loin

1 2-pound boneless center cut pork loin, trimmed and tied
2 cups thinly sliced apples, such as Cortland, Jonagold, or Reinette, unpeeled
1 cup thinly sliced carrots
1 cup thinly sliced onions
½ cup thinly sliced celery
1½ tablespoons extra virgin olive oil
½ cup Vermont Switchel
1 tablespoon butter

Add the marinade ingredients to a blender and process until smooth. Transfer the pork to an extra-large zipper-lock plastic bag then add the marinade. Refrigerate for 24 hours, occasionally turning the bag.

Preheat the oven to 350 degrees Fahrenheit. Lightly grease a 13-by-9-by-2-inch baking dish. Set aside.

In a large bowl, combine the apples, carrots, onions, celery, and oil, tossing until well combined. Season with salt and pepper to taste. Place the vegetables in the prepared baking dish. Remove the pork from the marinade and place on top of the vegetables.

Place the marinade in a small saucepan and bring to a boil over medium-high heat.

Roast the pork, basting with the marinade every 15 minutes, until an instant-read thermometer registers 140–150 degrees Fahrenheit, about 45 minutes, depending on the desired doneness. Transfer the pork to a cutting board and allow it to rest for 15 minutes.

While the pork is resting, make the sauce: Add the switchel to the roasting pan and deglaze the pan, stirring frequently, scraping up any brown bits on the bottom of the pan, over medium-high heat until it is reduced by half, about 4 minutes. Whisk in the butter until well incorporated. Season with salt and pepper to taste.

Cut the pork into ½-inch-thick diagonal slices and arrange on a platter. Drizzle the sauce over the pork and garnish with sage then serve.

Recipe by KC Wright for The Vermont Switchel Company, LLC

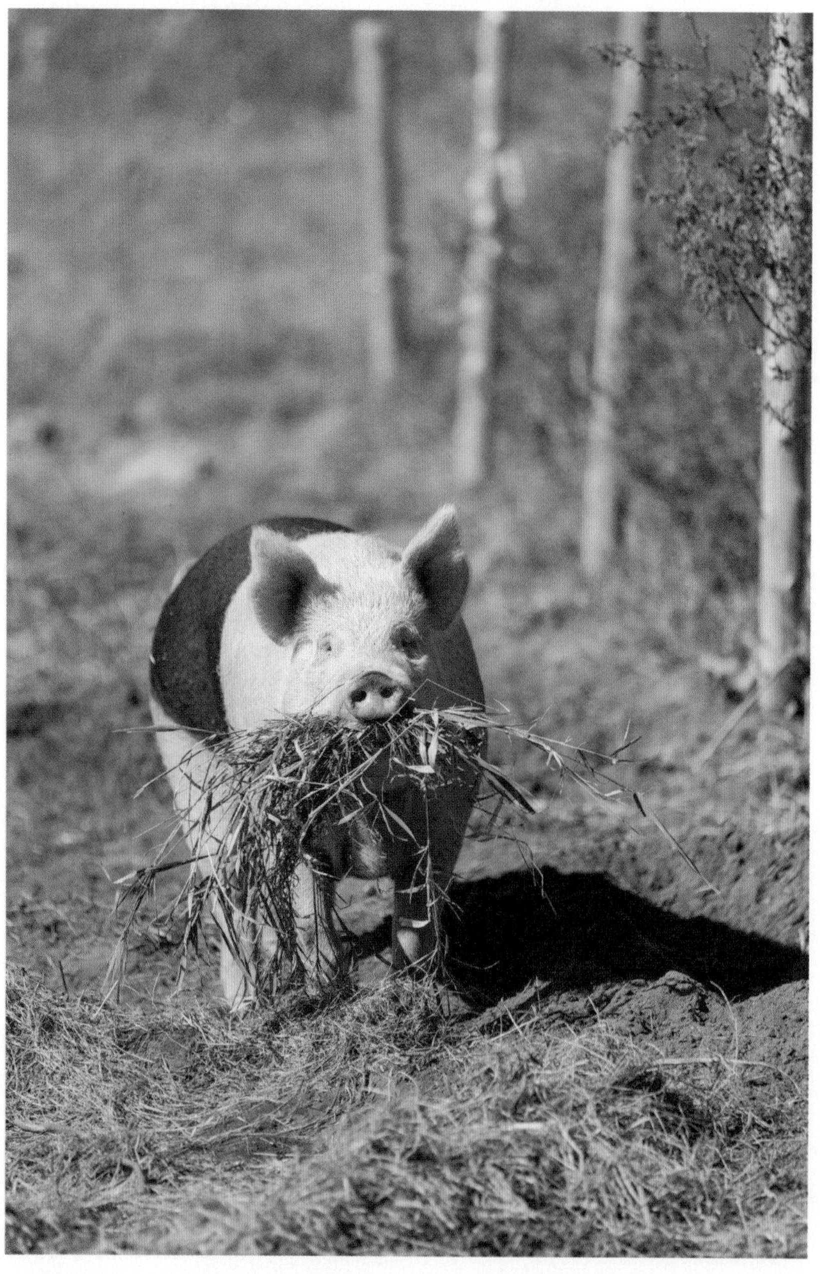

Spiced Vermont Lamb Burgers with Feta and Olive Relish and Herb Yogurt

Serves 5

These succulent and vibrantly flavored lamb burgers have a Greek twist reminiscent of a lamb gyro pita sandwich.

Herb Yogurt
1 cup whole milk yogurt
1 teaspoon minced garlic
1 teaspoon chopped fresh dill
1 teaspoon chopped fresh parsley
1 teaspoon fresh lemon juice

Feta and Olive Relish
½ cup feta cheese, crumbled or diced into ¼-inch cubes
½ cup Castelvetrano olives, pitted and diced into ¼-inch cubes
¼ cup fresh basil leaves, minced
2 tablespoons extra virgin olive oil
½ teaspoon sherry vinegar

Lamb Burger Rub
1 teaspoon salt
1 teaspoon ground coriander
1 teaspoon dried oregano
1 teaspoon ground cumin
1 teaspoon garlic powder
1 teaspoon onion powder
1 teaspoon coarsely ground black pepper

Lamb Burgers
2 pounds ground Vermont lamb
5 buns, such as challah or brioche
Unsalted butter, softened
Pickles

For the herbed yogurt: Line a fine-mesh strainer with two layers of cheesecloth. Ladle the yogurt into the prepared strainer and let drain at room temperature for 2 hours. Discard the whey and transfer the yogurt to a small bowl. Stir in the garlic, dill, parsley, and lemon juice until well combined.

While the yogurt is draining, make the feta and olive relish. In a medium bowl, combine the cheese, olives, basil, olive oil, and vinegar. Cover with plastic wrap and refrigerate for at least 1 hour before serving.

While the relish is in the refrigerator, make the lamb burger rub. In a small bowl, combine the salt, coriander, oregano, cumin, garlic powder, onion powder, and pepper. Set aside.

For the lamb burgers: Using your hands, form the meat into five 6-ounce balls and carefully knead each ball for about 1 minute. Form the balls into 1¼-inch-thick patties. Sprinkle the burgers lightly on both sides with some of the rub, then let them sit at room temperature for 20 minutes.

While the burgers are sitting at room temperature, heat a gas or electric grill to medium-high heat and generously brush the cooking grate with oil. Grill the burgers on one side until a nice crust forms, about 4 minutes. Using a large spatula, carefully flip the burgers and cook until a meat thermometer reads 125–130 degrees Fahrenheit for medium rare, about 5 minutes, or to your desired doneness. Remove the burgers from the grill and let rest for 2 minutes.

While the burgers are resting, grill the buns. Brush the inside of each bun with butter and grill for about 1 minute on each side. To assemble, spread each bottom bun with about 1 tablespoon yogurt, or to taste. Top each bun bottom with a burger. Spread each burger top with about 2 tablespoons relish. Cover the burgers with the bun tops and serve with pickles on the side.

Recipe from The Farmhouse Tap and Grill for The Farmhouse Group
Photograph by Oliver Parini

PROFILE

Naked Acre Farm

Naked Acre Farm derived its name from the field that Ryan Demarest leases for his farming operation. Completely bare, having not been used for planting in decades, it struck him that the word "naked," with its dual meaning, fit the bill. A bare field that would need few inputs to successfully grow organic vegetables, an empty canvas, so to speak. The 2-acre, small-scale organic farm is located in Waterbury Center, Vermont.

Ryan grows a wide variety of vegetables. He also runs a small CSA, and the members visit the farm each week to pick up their shares and chat for a while. The busy farmer enjoys this connection with his customers, which allows for some downtime to exchange news about family and farming.

With his belief that "health begins with the soil and is carried through a cycle to our plates," Ryan carefully treats his soil by mimicking natural systems of growth as much as possible. He says, "By growing organically, I am contributing to a regionally focused food economy and severing some dependence on an environmentally harmful industrial food system." He uses a tractor when needed, but does as much of the work as possible by hand.

The small boutique farm focuses on high quality and details, selling its organic vegetables to several local restaurants and markets in the area. Although the work is hard, Ryan loves farming. He adds, "Through the work of raising vegetables, I seek to feel a deep personal fulfillment, develop meaningful relationships, enhance the community, and contribute to a growing interest in food autonomy."

Oven-Baked Burgers served with Maple-Braised Greens and Heirloom Tomato and Mixed Green Salad

Serves 4

"After a long day in the field, I often want nothing more than fresh vegetables and a grass-fed burger. This recipe is fairly simple to cook and provides many of the staple flavors of a Vermont-style diet: beef, bacon, maple, butter, fresh heirloom tomatoes, and hardy greens. As the sun sets over the Green Mountains, I usually find a comfortable spot on the lawn to eat and reflect on the day. Having a strong Vermont-brewed IPA in hand will definitely complement this meal." *—Ryan Demarest, owner, Naked Acre Farm*

Grass-Fed Burgers

2 tablespoons olive oil, divided
¼ cup finely diced sweet onion, such as Vidalia or Walla Walla
2 medium garlic cloves, minced
1 pound ground beef, preferably organic grass-fed
Salt and freshly ground black pepper
2 ounces extra-sharp Vermont cheddar cheese, thinly sliced
4 artisan rolls, sliced in half and toasted

Maple-Braised Greens

4 ounces (about 4 slices) organic bacon, minced
Extra virgin olive oil
¾ pound assorted braising greens, such as kale, collards, Asian greens, mustard, mizuna, and arugula, tough stems removed and cut into 2-inch pieces
½ cup organic low-sodium chicken broth
¾ tablespoon Vermont maple syrup
Salt and freshly ground black pepper

Preheat the oven to 400 degrees Fahrenheit.

Heat 1 tablespoon of the oil in a medium skillet over medium heat. Add the onion and cook, stirring occasionally, until soft and translucent, about 5 minutes. Add the garlic and cook, stirring often, until fragrant, about 1 minute. Set aside.

Gently mix together the beef, onion, and garlic until just combined, being careful not to overwork the meat. Using your hands, form the meat into four 1-inch-thick patties. Heat the remaining tablespoon of oil in a cast-iron skillet over medium-high heat. Season the burgers with salt and pepper. Transfer the burgers to the skillet and cook for 2 minutes. Using a large spatula, carefully flip the burgers and cook for 2 more minutes. Transfer to the oven and bake until an

instant-read thermometer reaches 160 degrees Fahrenheit, about 15 minutes, turning once. Turn off the oven, top with cheese, and let rest in the oven until the cheese has melted, about 4 minutes.

While the burgers are baking in the oven, start the maple-braised greens. Sauté the bacon in a medium skillet over medium heat until crisp, about 12 minutes. Using a slotted spoon, transfer the bacon to a paper towel–lined plate. Reserve 2 tablespoons of the bacon drippings in the skillet. **Note:** If you do not have 2 tablespoons of bacon drippings, add enough olive oil to bring the drippings up to 2 tablespoons. Add the braising greens and toss to coat well. Add the broth, then cover and cook over medium heat until the broth is reduced and the greens are very tender, about 5 minutes. Add the maple syrup, salt, and pepper, and toss to coat well. Garnish with bacon.

To assemble the burgers: Place each burger on the bottom half of each roll and top with your favorite condiments. Top with the remaining half of each roll. Serve with braising greens and the Heirloom Tomato and Mixed Green Salad **(see page 153)** on the side.

Recipes from Naked Acre Farm
Photograph by Oliver Parini

PROFILE

Meeting Place Pastures

Meeting Place Pastures in Cornwall, Vermont, is a partnership owned by Cheryl and Marc Cesario. Although they're not native Vermonters, the couple met at a Northeast Organic Farming Conference in 2008, and a year later they decided to purchase the land in Cornwall and begin their agricultural venture. Searching for the perfect name for this new undertaking, they recalled that the pastures were their favorite meeting place when dating, which inspired the property's unique name.

A grass-fed, grass-finished beef operation, Meeting Place Pastures manages approximately 200 animals—their herd as well as other producers' cattle—which they graze on 500 acres. The grass-fed system they use replicates the grasslands that bison and other herds used for grazing years ago, in which herds moved frequently to avoid predators. Today, grass-fed production is assisted by the use of temporary fences, so cows can be moved multiple times a day. The fence that is being moved is lightweight "polywire" on reels that can be rolled out and strung on ⅝-inch round fiberglass posts. The wire can be rolled up, and the posts picked up, relatively quickly. They also use something called "tumblewheels" in which the wire is run through spoke-like contraptions that then roll as the line is pulled forward. This makes a new grazing strip and literally takes only minutes. The method is pretty typical of management-intensive grazing, which helps to avoid overgrazing damage and provides quality forage.

In the farm's early days, all products were sold directly to consumers, but this has become more difficult to do as the operation has grown in size. At this juncture, the decision has been made to focus on beef production, as there is now more available land on which to grow forage. The organic egg business has also been expanded to meet increasing demand. In addition to their very popular organic eggs, the free-roaming hens also provide the pastures with extra fertility.

Cheryl states, "Many people think of organic as what you can't do, but to us it's all about what we can do." At Meeting Place Pastures, the goal is to promote soil health by keeping the land in perennial grass production, which creates strong roots that hold the soil in place. To help this process, they rely on non-synthetic soil inputs, such as wood ash and chicken manure, to increase fertility. The frequent movement of cattle means manure is spread more uniformly over the pastures, eliminating the need for chemical fertilizers.

The cows are kept healthy by providing them with a diverse mix of grasses, clovers, and broad-leaved plants that supply the animals with sugar, protein, and minerals. They are also vaccinated to protect them from disease. The chickens help with fly control, which reduces the stress level of the cows and serves to prevent production loss. Marc and Cheryl have joined a regional beef co-op, a move that has worked out well and given them a much more consistent means of income. With happy animals, healthy soil, and good land stewardship, the Cesarios are doing their part to make a difference in our world for today and for all the tomorrows to come.

Grass-Fed Flat Iron Steak and Egg Salad with Sauerkraut and Apples

Serves 4

"As we always have a freezer full of beef, it is easy sometimes to end up with meat on a plate for dinner. We are always looking for ways to incorporate a diversity of 'green things' into our diet. This salad works well for us at the end of the day, as it is easy to put together from ingredients we always have on hand. We get the protein and omega-3s from our beef and eggs, while the salad ingredients provide additional vitamins, minerals, and probiotics for a complete and filling meal."
—*Cheryl Cessario, owner, Meeting Place Pastures*

Spice Mixture
1 teaspoon black peppercorns, coarsely ground
1 teaspoon juniper berries, coarsely ground
½ teaspoon kosher salt

Steak
1 tablespoon extra virgin olive oil
1 pound flat iron steak, 1-inch thick

Salad
½ pound packed mixed greens
1 medium carrot, trimmed and peeled
1 small red or golden beet, scrubbed, trimmed, and peeled
Creamy balsamic vinaigrette, store-bought or homemade
1 cup lacto-fermented sauerkraut, rinsed and drain
1 medium tart apple, such as Granny Smith, cored and thinly sliced
1 medium ripe avocado, cut in half lengthwise, pit removed, and cut into ¼-inch-thick slices
3 hard-boiled eggs, peeled and quartered
Salt and freshly ground black pepper

To make the spice mixture: In a small bowl, combine the peppercorns, juniper berries, and salt for the spice mixture. Set aside.

Heat the oil in a heavy skillet over medium-high heat until hot but not smoking. Season the steak on both sides with the spice mixture to taste. Place the steak in the skillet and cook for 4 minutes. Turn once and cook for another 4 minutes. Remove the skillet from the heat, cover, and let the steak sit in the skillet for 4 minutes. Transfer the steak to a cutting board and let rest for 10 minutes. Thinly slice the steak across the grain.

While the steak is cooking, grate the carrot and beet in a food processor fitted with the shredding blade. Set aside.

To assemble the salad: Place the greens, shredded carrots, and beets in a large bowl. Toss with the vinaigrette to taste. Scatter the meat along with any accumulated juices, sauerkraut, apple slices, avocado slices, and egg slices on top of the lettuce. Drizzle with additional vinaigrette if desired. Season with salt and pepper to taste. Serve at once.

Recipe from Meeting Place Pastures
Photograph by Oliver Parini

CHAPTER 6

ORGANIC AND PASTURE-RAISED POULTRY, TURKEY, AND PHEASANT MAIN DISHES

Full Moon Farm, Inc.

PROFILE

Husband and wife David Zuckerman and Rachel Nevitt are co-owners of Full Moon Farm, a 155-acre certified organic farm located on the southern edge of Hinesburg, Vermont. David started Full Moon Farm in Burlington's Intervale Center in 1999. Rachel, also an organic farmer, joined forces with him in 2001. In 2008, the couple graduated from the Intervale Center's Farm Program, one of the oldest incubator farm programs in the United States, and purchased a new farm, thanks to financial help from several conservation organizations.

Full Moon Farm is a Vermont Organic Farmers (VOF) certified organic farm that grows a variety of organic vegetables on 25 acres and raises certified organic pigs and chickens on the property's stunningly beautiful acreage. Three-quarters of their products are sold directly to consumers through the farm's 250-member CSA program and the Burlington Farmers' Market. The rest is sold wholesale to local stores or food shelves through their "Buy Food Not Crap" program. Both David and Rachel caution the reliance on the word "local" when determining which products to buy. They urge folks, when dining out, to ask which items on the menu are local and certified organic. Both of them stress that it is important to remember that local merely means where food is produced, not how. They clarify that only "certified organic" means no conventional chemical sprays or non-GMO seeds are used, and there is an inspection process in place to verify these claims.

David and Rachel are passionate about conservation, land stewardship, and politics, and they are active members of their community. David, who has worked on farms for most of his adult life, served as a Burlington representative and then as a Chittenden County senator before being elected lieutenant governor of Vermont in 2016. Rachel is a firm believer that less is more. She is adept at many folk arts and loves to share her knowledge of them in environmental and cultural education classes taught on the farm. Both are working hard to rebuild an agricultural economy that benefits the state's farm community, all its consumers, and, most importantly, Vermont's soil and water.

Photography by Oliver Parini

YOUR-OWN
NIC

Rustic Chicken Pot Pie

Serves 6–8

"If you have someone that you want to make fall in love with you or, perhaps, feel indebted to you for life, this recipe will work magic. It is made from scratch, the hard way, right down to the rendering of the lard, which is made almost entirely with ingredients from our farm. The vegetables are not the usual chicken pot pie suspects, but root veggies that offer a deep, rustic, slightly sweet comfort food—perfect for a cold fall or winter day. Full disclosure, the aforementioned magical power can only work if the cook uses certified organic ingredients from Full Moon Farm. The recipe will still be good if you use substitutions, but the magic will be lost." *—Rachel Nevitt, co-owner, Full Moon Farm*

Chicken

2 whole (4 split) organic chicken breasts, bone-in, skin-on (about 4 pounds), preferably Full Moon Farm
3 tablespoons organic butter, melted
Salt and freshly ground black pepper

Dough

2 cups organic all-purpose flour
1 teaspoon salt
⅔ cup organic pork leaf lard, chilled, preferably Full Moon Farm, divided
2 tablespoons organic butter, chilled, preferably Organic Valley
¼ cup cold water

Filling

1¼ cups parsnips, peeled, ends removed, and diced into ½-inch pieces
1¼ cups sweet potatoes, peeled and diced into ½-inch pieces
½ cup plus 2 tablespoons organic butter, divided, preferably Organic Valley
1 medium yellow onion, peeled and diced into ½-inch pieces
1 cup celeriac root, peeled and diced into ½-inch pieces
¾ teaspoon dried thyme
3 cups low-sodium chicken broth, warmed and divided
½ cup organic all-purpose flour
1½ teaspoons salt
Freshly ground black pepper

Egg Wash

1 egg, lightly beaten
2 tablespoons water

Preheat the oven to 350 degrees Fahrenheit. Line a baking sheet with foil. Place the chicken on the prepared baking sheet and drizzle evenly with the melted butter. Season with salt and pepper. Bake until a meat thermometer reads 160 degrees, about 50 minutes. Transfer to a cutting board and let the chicken rest for 20 minutes, then cut into 1-inch cubes. Set aside.

To make the dough: Place the flour and salt in a large bowl. Cut in half of the lard with a pastry blender or two knives until it has the consistency of cornmeal. Cut in the remaining lard and butter until the mixture begins to form pea-sized pieces. While mixing the dough with your fingers, add the water in a slow and steady stream until the dough holds together, adding additional water if necessary. Turn the dough out onto a clean, lightly floured work surface and form into two disks. Wrap in plastic wrap and refrigerate for at least 1 hour. When ready to use, let the dough sit at room temperature for 20 minutes before rolling the disks out.

While the dough is chilling in the refrigerator, start the filling. Place the parsnips and sweet potatoes in a medium pot of salted water and bring to a boil over medium-high heat and cook until just fork tender, about 5 minutes. Drain and set aside.

Meanwhile, melt 2 tablespoons of the butter in a Dutch oven over medium heat. Add the onions and celeriac root and sauté until soft and translucent, about 10 minutes. Add the parsnips and sweet potatoes and cook for 2 minutes. Add the thyme and 1 cup of chicken broth and bring to a simmer over medium-high heat for 10 minutes. Fold in the chicken until well combined. Adjust seasoning with thyme, salt, and pepper to taste. Set aside.

In a medium saucepan, melt the remaining ½ cup butter over medium heat. Whisk in the flour and cook, whisking often, until light golden brown, about 4 minutes. Whisking continuously, slowly add the remaining 2 cups chicken broth, ½ teaspoon salt, and pepper, to taste, until the sauce is thick and bubbling, about 3 minutes.

Preheat the oven to 350 degrees Fahrenheit. On a lightly floured surface, roll one disk of dough out into a 12-inch round. Transfer to a 9-inch deep-dish pie pan, trim the excess dough, leaving ½ inch past the edge of the pan. Combine the vegetables with the sauce until well combined. Adjust seasonings with salt and pepper to taste. Carefully spoon the vegetable mixture into the pie crust, making sure not to overflow the crust. Roll the second disk of dough out into a 12-inch round, then place it over the vegetable filling. Trim the excess dough along the edge, so there's ½ inch of dough past the edge of the pan. Fold the edges of the dough under, then crimp to seal. Whisk the egg and 2 tablespoons water in a small bowl. Brush the egg wash over the surface of the crust, then cut small slits into the top crust.

Place the pie pan on a baking sheet and bake until the crust is golden brown and the filling is bubbling, about 40 minutes. Transfer to a cooling rack and let rest for 15 minutes before serving.

Recipe from Full Moon Farm, Inc.
Photograph by Oliver Parini

Cedar Circle Farm & Education Center

Back in 1990, when the Vermont Land Trust bought the development rights to Cedar Circle Farm, it assumed responsibility for the preservation of this pristine piece of property. The terms of the sale ensure that the land can only be used for farming or forestry enterprises in perpetuity. This agreement protects the farm from being divided into house lots or sold for other commercial purposes. Today, the acreage encompasses a good-sized area of cropland, greenhouses, a farm stand, coffee shop, licensed commercial kitchen, and the Education Center. Cedar Circle Farm's mission is to increase public awareness of organic agriculture and its health benefits, while spreading the word that eating organic is the best way to ensure that the food you choose is free of genetically modified ingredients.

The farm is situated along Connecticut River in East Thetford, Vermont. Its commercial kitchen was built in 2011, offering customers access to the fresh vegetables and berries grown at Cedar Circle Farm throughout the year. A variety of classes are offered, including how to make jarred preserves, pickles, and pesto—all made with high-quality organic ingredients grown on the farm. There are lessons in the art of canning using the day's freshly picked crop, which will perhaps be served during the long, cold winter—a tasty reminder of summer's bounty.

School programs for grades 1–12 offer engaging lessons on organic agriculture, climate change, soil science, and nature in agriculture. There is something for all age groups, from the Little Farmers' Toddler Program investigating bugs, plants, and chickens, to home school programs that use the farm as an outdoor classroom. Cedar Circle also matches classrooms with farmers based on interests and grade level. During the quiet winter months, the farmer and children in the classroom become pen pals, writing to each other about life and work on the farm. The Education Center hosts classes for adults and children, and offers farm tours, seasonal workshops, summer camp, and harvest festivals.

Cedar Circle's rustic farm stand sells fresh organic vegetables, berries, and flowers. They even do beautiful flower arrangements for weddings, and it's no surprise that their cut flowers are also organic. Customers may join the popular CSA program or gather certified organic berries, pumpkins, or flowers from the pick-your-own fields.

The folks at Cedar Circle Farm & Education Center firmly believe that healthy soil is the product of regenerative organic practices, which, in turn, are the key to growing good food. They strongly support the movement to halt GMOs, toxic pesticides, and factory animal production. For many years, farmer activists from Cedar Circle Farm have been involved in the movement against GMOs in agricultural crops, fighting for the labeling of food products that contain GMOs. Their message is loud and clear: "Eating organic is the simplest way to ensure that what you eat is free of genetically modified ingredients." The people at Cedar Circle Farm want their customers to know that the healthy food choices they make can ultimately have a positive effect on the well-being of our planet.

Spinach and Smoked Chicken Gratin

Serves 6

"This is an excellent recipe to make in the late winter using a hardy storage potato, like a russet, along with spinach from farm greenhouses. Good cheese and cream and smoked chicken round out the mix in this dish for those last chilly evenings. Gratin recipes can get pretty involved; we came up with an easy and delicious one that can be mixed in a single dish and baked up hot to serve alongside tangy winter greens for an easy supper." *—Alison Baker, former kitchen manager and chef, Cedar Circle Farm & Education Center*

1 tablespoon olive oil
1 yellow onion, peeled and chopped
2 garlic cloves, peeled and thinly sliced
5 cups loosely packed baby spinach
1 cup sliced smoked chicken
1 cup sour cream or crème fraiche
1 teaspoon fine sea salt
½ teaspoon freshly ground black pepper
3 large russet potatoes, peeled and sliced into ⅛-inch-thick circles
⅔ cup half-and-half
½ cup shredded cheddar cheese

Preheat the oven to 375 degrees Fahrenheit. Lightly grease an 8-by-11-inch baking dish with nonstick cooking spray. Set aside.

Heat the oil in a large skillet over medium heat. Add the onion and cook, stirring occasionally, until soft and translucent, about 10 minutes. Add the garlic and cook, stirring frequently, for 1 minute. Transfer to a large bowl and mix in the spinach and smoked chicken until well combined. Stir in the sour cream, salt, and pepper, mixing until well combined.

Arrange a layer of the potatoes evenly on the bottom of the prepared dish, overlapping the slices. Spread some of the spinach mixture over the top. Continue layering the potatoes and spinach mixture, ending with the spinach mixture. Carefully pour the half-and-half over the spinach mixture; it should just rise up the sides but not cover the potatoes. Sprinkle the cheese over the top. Bake, uncovered, until golden brown and bubbly, about 35 minutes. Remove from the oven and allow to rest for 10 minutes before serving.

Recipe from Cedar Circle Farm & Education Center
Photograph by Oliver Parini

PROFILE

Burelli Farm

After spending many years working in New York and New Jersey, Peter Burmeister and his wife, Katherine Fanelli, decided that it was time to change their lifestyle. Many years prior to this decision, Peter's very first job had been on a farm making hay and cutting corn by hand. He always loved the agricultural way of life, which made moving to Vermont in 2003 seem like a dream come true.

Peter and Katherine began their present organic farming career in 2007 with a small herd of cattle. Their first farm was in Marshfield. They purchased Burelli Farm in Berlin, Vermont, in 2010. The couple raise Normande beef, whose heritage can be traced back to the fifth century, when the Vikings brought them to France. These animals, which are very popular in Europe, have now gained recognition in the United States because they produce superior beef on a diet that consists entirely of grasses. They are the perfect fit for Burelli Farm's 85 acres located not too far from downtown Montpelier. Pigs and chickens are also part of this NOFA-certified farm's animal and bird community.

In 2014, a certified organic Vermont state–inspected chicken processing facility was built on the property. It is the only facility of its kind in Central Vermont. The farm's organic meat birds are processed there with the service offered to other area farms as well. All of the farm's chickens are raised on feed that is organically grown on the farm or from other nearby local sources.

Peter and Katherine practice organic and regenerative agriculture, raising hay and grain for their animals and birds, who then give back to the land through their waste products. Peter points out, "We believe in building our soil, rather than depleting it. It is our intention to leave the land in a much better condition than when we first settled on it. In my opinion, organic agriculture will be the salvation of our planet."

Burelli Farm and its high-quality meats are well known in the surrounding culinary community. Peter proudly declares, "What better compliment then to have local chefs buy your meats and praise the quality of the farm's meat products? And, of course, it's great when they generously share their recipes with me!" As those in the food community have discovered, when you have excellent ingredients, it is almost impossible not to create the perfect dish.

Burelli Farm's Pan-Seared Oven-Roasted Whole Chicken

Serves 4

"We love roast chicken at Burelli Farm dinners. It's one of our very favorite meals. The problem with most roast chicken is that it is either too dry, or the skin never really gets brown and crisp. Over time, we've experimented with multiple variations on this delicious dish, and we believe we've come up with the very best way to solve the dryness/crispness dilemma. We are delighted to share this recipe with our family, our friends, our neighbors, and our customers." *—Peter Burmeister, owner, Burelli Farm*

Ingredients

1 whole chicken (about 3½-pounds), giblets and neck discarded

2 tablespoons certified organic rendered lard or ⅛ cup vegetable oil

1 teaspoon poultry seasoning, homemade or store-bought

Coarsely ground salt and freshly ground black pepper

Place the oven rack in the lower-middle of the oven. Preheat the oven to 375 degrees Fahrenheit. Rinse the chicken inside and out. Pat the chicken dry with paper towels and set aside.

Heat the lard in a 12-inch cast-iron skillet over medium-high heat until hot but not smoking. Season the chicken with poultry seasoning, salt, and pepper, to taste. Reduce the heat to medium. Place the chicken, breast side down, in the skillet and cook until the skin is a deep golden brown, about 5 minutes. Using a large metal spatula, carefully flip the chicken breast side up, tucking the wingtips behind the back, and cook, pressing gently on the breastbone to slightly flatten, until the skin is well browned, about 5 minutes.

Roast the chicken in the oven until the juices run clear and the internal temperature of the thickest part of the thigh reaches 165 degrees Fahrenheit, about 75 minutes. Transfer to a cutting board and let rest for 20 minutes. Carve the chicken into breast, thighs, and drumsticks. Serve with organic brown rice and a fresh salad, if desired.

Recipe from Burelli Farm
Photograph by Oliver Parini

Someday Farm

It's been said that it takes a village to raise a child. Surprisingly, this philosophy also holds true when it comes managing a successful farming operation like Someday Farm in East Dorset, Vermont, a prime example of commitment and cooperation. The farm has been in owner Scout Proft's family since the 1930s. It is where she raised and home-schooled her five children.

Scout, a graduate of the University of Vermont, is the primary caretaker of the farm. She also serves as a consultant and farm-to-community mentor for the Northeast Organic Farming Association of Vermont (NOFA-VT), which diligently promotes a Vermont food system that works both economically and ecologically for present and future generations. With this goal in mind, Scout has initiated a highly successful farm-to-school correspondence program that links local students to the area's farming community.

Eben Proft, her second eldest son, owns Woodbury Game Birds and works in cooperation with Someday Farm. He has traveled the world to learn from the best game bird producers and uses this knowledge to nurture and raise the pheasants in his care. The farm has its own state-inspected processing facility that handles 3,000 pheasants, 1,500 roasting chickens, and 500 turkeys each year.

Maria Buteux Reade is a working partner at Someday Farm, helping with field work, poultry processing, and compost operations while balancing a freelance writing career. Mara Hearst focuses on the management of the farm's poultry processing system and assists with the game bird operation. Mara also serves as farm advisor to the Rutland Area Farm and Food Link. The farm stand and CSA program are supervised by Angela Saccamango. She also helps run the greenhouses, preserves food, and cooks for the whole farm family, all while caring for her two young sons. There are a number of other hardworking folks who contribute to the success of the farm's daily operations. Yes, indeed, it does takes a village!

At Someday Farm, they grow more than 100 varieties of organic vegetables and fruits on 6 acres, and raise thousands of poultry and game birds in two locations. At the Home Farm in East Dorset, they raise poultry and grow produce in six greenhouses, while Three Farms is used for growing hardy crops and raising pheasants and turkeys. The farm also has Certified Tree Status and sustainably logs about 120 acres of land.

The farm is a closed-loop system, building soil fertility through the use of cover crops and compost, which incorporates all the poultry processing residuals and other animal manures. The farm's 700 free-range hens provide nitrogen-rich manure, which aids in compost. Some compost is delivered to area gardeners and businesses, with the rest reserved for the farm's use.

The CSA program, established in 1984, is free choice and allows shareholders to visit the farm stand or self-serve store to choose from produce, poultry, eggs, fruits, honey, and bread.

Someday Farm strives to share the profession of farming with students of all ages through mentoring and the farm-to-school correspondence project, along with several agricultural programs. Hoping that the young people of today will be inspired by their example, the Profts are carrying on a family farming tradition that has spanned more than 80 years, employing sound farming techniques and environmental stewardship to produce fresh, healthy, organic food. Coaxing the best from the land, they treat the soil as nature intended it to be: fertile, productive, and chemical-free.

How to Roast a Turkey

Preheat the oven to 375 degrees Fahrenheit. Prepare the bird by removing the giblets in the neck cavity and the neck from the main cavity. Using cold water, rinse the cavities, then pat the turkey dry with paper towels. Generously season the turkey cavities with salt and pepper, then stuff your bird. Place the bird in a roasting pan, breast side up.

Cook the bird for 12½ to 15 minutes per pound. A bird that is 15 pounds and larger will cook closer to the 12½ minute per pound time frame. **Note:** This time frame is for a stuffed turkey. Calculate your cooking time on the minimum minutes per pound and check the bird 1 hour before the calculated finish time.

Basting the bird during cooking will add color to the skin.

To test if the bird is done, stick a paring knife into the thickest part of the thigh at an upward angle so you can view the juices as they exit the incision. The juices will run almost clear when the bird is done. We like to see little droplets of pink in the juice, not too much, just enough to indicate that the bird is not overdone.

When it's done cooking, remove the bird from the oven. Loosely cover it with foil, then place two clean tea towels over the foil to keep the bird warm while it rests. Resting will allow the bird to reabsorb juices that are between the skin and meat, as well as finish cooking with the heat that is already in the bird, which gets rid of that little bit of pink juice detected in the thigh. While the bird rests, use this time to heat your side dishes in the oven. Once the bird has rested for 30 minutes, uncover it and transfer it to a cutting board, then recover loosely with foil and clean tea towels, and allow the bird to rest for an additional 30–60 minutes. Carve and serve.

From Someday Farm
Photograph by Oliver Parini

Woodbury Gamebirds Roast Pheasant

Serves 2–3

"Remember that farm-raised or wild pheasant, with its higher fat content, should be treated more as a red meat rather than a white meat in the kitchen. The breast meat will become very dry if cooked too long. The pheasant will cook a bit more once it's pulled out of the oven, so don't worry if the thigh meat is pink. The juices from the breast should run nearly clear. As long as the internal temperature is at least 154 degrees Fahrenheit and the meat is not translucent, the thighs will be perfectly safe to eat and much tastier than if overcooked." —*Maria Buteux Reade, working partner, Someday Farm*

1 whole pheasant (about 3 pounds), rinsed inside and out, patted dry
1 cup pitted and diced plums (about 2)
½ medium apple, cored and diced
½ cup brandy
7 juniper berries, ground
Salt
Freshly ground black pepper
6 small potatoes, such as multicolored fingerlings
½ tablespoon extra virgin olive oil
1 teaspoon fresh chopped rosemary

Up to 24 hours before roasting, place the pheasant on a cooling rack in the refrigerator, uncovered, to allow the pheasant to air-dry.

Preheat the oven to 375 degrees Fahrenheit. Lightly oil an 8-by-11-inch baking dish. Set aside.

In a small saucepan, cook down the plums, apple, and brandy on medium heat until the apples have become a sauce and the plums are softened, about 10 minutes. Add the juniper berries, ½ teaspoon salt, and pepper to taste. There should be a small amount of fruit juices on the bottom of the saucepan. Let cool. Strain the fruit through a fine-mesh strainer, pushing all the liquid through with the back of a ladle, reserving the solids.

Meanwhile, place the potatoes in a medium pot of water and bring to a boil over high heat. Reduce the heat to a simmer and cook until the potatoes are barely fork tender, about 10 minutes. Drain the potatoes in a colander and transfer to a medium bowl and toss with olive oil, salt, and rosemary, until well combined. Set aside while you prepare the pheasant.

Stuff the pheasant cavity with the strained cooked fruit. Generously brush the strained fruit juices evenly over the skin of the bird. Season the skin with salt and pepper. Place the pheasant, breast side down, on a rack in the prepared baking dish. Tuck the wings back behind the shoulders to keep them close to the main part of the body. Using kitchen twine, tie the legs together. Arrange the potatoes around the pheasant.

Roast, uncovered, for 20 minutes. Turn the pheasant breast side up, then generously baste with the reserved fruit juices and continue to roast, basting occasionally, until the juices run clear and the internal breast temperature reaches 154–58 degrees Fahrenheit, about 35 minutes, or until desired doneness is achieved.

Let rest for 15–20 minutes. Remove and discard the kitchen twine. Carve the meat into 8 serving pieces and place on a decorative platter. Spoon some of the fruit stuffing on top and place the potatoes around the meat. Serve.

Recipe from Woodbury Gamebirds

Notes:

- Ask the butcher to de-tendon the legs for you; it makes such a difference in the quality of the meat.
- The "fruit stuffing" is more of a relish. Serve remaining stuffing on the side, if desired.

CHAPTER 7

PASTA MAIN DISHES

PROFILE

Green Rabbit, LLC

Suzanne Slomin, owner of Green Rabbit, got her start baking bread when she took an intensive weeklong course in the art of bread making. This experience ignited her passion for the science of making bread. While farming in Central New York, she converted a small root cellar into a rudimentary bakery to begin learning the art of making sourdough. During winters (farming downtime), she reached out to other bakers around the country in an effort to perfect her craft.

Green Rabbit Bread is a small-batch, solar-powered bakery located in Waitsfield, the Mad River Valley area of Vermont. Suzanne specializes in the making of long fermented breads that are composed from organic grains, seeds, fruits, and sea salt.

To produce her naturally leavened bread, this skillful baker lets her dough ferment slowly in cool temperatures. What distinguishes Suzanne's bread from other naturally leavened loaves is the time-intensive process that is used. Most bakeries allow their dough to rise for approximately 6 hours in 70–100-degree-Fahrenheit heat; she gives her loaves 24 hours to ferment in a chilly 45-degree Fahrenheit room. The difference is noticeable.

Suzanne's bread making philosophy is slow cool through the fermentation of grains, generous hydration of all grains and seeds, pureness and simplicity of ingredients, and a great deal of patience. The end result is bread with a fluffy interior complemented by a thin and chewy crust; many artisan bakeries create crusts that are thick and crackly. Customers have discovered that a loaf of Green Rabbit's bread remains fresh for up to 1 week, compared to some crustier breads that are often unusable after 2–3 days.

The bakery offers a delicious variety of breads: Pan de Mais, Sunflower Flax, Olive Rosemary, Cinnamon Raisin, and their classic signature Levain (a mild sourdough). The Levain dough is the base for many creative combinations, such as a seasonal bâtard garnished with wilted ramp greens and Reggianito. Loaves may contain whatever is found in Suzanne's garden at the time she's preparing to bake, such as garlic scapes, potatoes, and shallots, as well as a host of other locally produced and foraged delicacies. Sweeter breads are moistened by chunks of chocolate or speckled with cinnamon and raisins. During the holidays, Green Rabbit offers breads that are reminiscent of the occasion, with cranberries a popular option. All of the bakery's breads are genuine artisanal quality, which allows the true bread flavor to shine through.

Suzanne has no plans to go gluten-free. She doesn't discount celiac disease, but feels that some folks who believe that they need gluten-free are just eating the wrong bread. It is not the gluten per say that causes discomfort, it is the speedy process by which conventional wheat products are made. In fact, some of her customers who are on gluten-free diets acknowledge that they are able to eat Green Rabbit's bread without experiencing any digestive issues.

The busy baker admits that she is still amazed every morning when the bread comes out of the oven, "It's magic to me—flour, salt, and water!" It must also seem like magic to those who purchase her loaves, because Green Rabbit Bread has become a little Vermont bakery with a big following. The bread is sold at local farm stands and stores, co-ops, small grocers, and through area CSA programs.

Smokey Lamb Bolognese

Serves 6

"Every year, we preserve our own tomatoes by roasting them over a wood fire and packing them into mason jars with garlic and herb sprigs. On a cold winter's night, we open a jarful of summer's harvest to conjure up this heartwarming sauce." —*Suzanne Slomin, owner, Green Rabbit*

1 28-ounce can high-quality whole, peeled tomatoes in juice, preferably San Marzano
¼ pound bacon, diced
3 tablespoons extra virgin olive oil, divided
1 small yellow onion, diced into small pieces
1 large carrot, peeled and diced into small pieces
1 small fennel bulb, fronds removed and reserved, bulb quartered and diced into ¼-inch pieces
1 dried chipotle pepper
½ cup fresh chopped parsley stems
4 fresh thyme sprigs
2 medium garlic cloves, peeled and finely chopped
1 pound ground pastured lamb
¾ cup fresh rough chopped flat leaf parsley leaves
Salt and freshly ground black pepper
⅓ cup freshly grated Parmigiano-Reggiano cheese
1 pound fresh pasta, such as broad egg noodles, pappardelle, or fettuccine

Coarsely chop the tomatoes and place them in a bowl with any accumulated juice. Set aside.

Sauté the bacon in a large pot or Dutch oven over medium heat until the fat begins to render. Add 2 tablespoons of the oil to the pot. Add the onion, carrot, fennel, chipotle pepper, parsley stems, and thyme sprigs. Season with salt and cook, stirring occasionally, until the onions are soft and translucent, about 10 minutes. Add the garlic and cook until fragrant, about 2 minutes.

Add the lamb and season with salt and pepper. Increase the heat to medium-high and cook, breaking up the meat with a fork, until it begins to brown, about 10 minutes. Add the tomatoes, along with any accumulated juice, and parsley leaves. Lower the heat and simmer, uncovered, stirring occasionally, until the sauce is thick, about 35 minutes. Season with salt and pepper to taste. Remove and discard the chipotle pepper and thyme sprigs.

When the Bolognese is almost done, bring a large pot of salted water to a boil. Add the pasta and cook until al dente. Drain, reserving ¼ cup of the pasta water. Return the pasta to the pot and toss with the remaining 1 tablespoon oil. Add half of the sauce and toss to coat well, adding more sauce as desired. If the sauce seems too dry, stir in the pasta water as needed. Garnish with some

of the reserved fennel fronds and sprinkles of Parmigiano-Reggiano cheese. Serve with Olive Oil and Sea Salt Crostini **(see page 242)**.

Recipe from Green Rabbit, LLC
Photograph by Oliver Parini

Olive Oil and Sea Salt Crostini

Makes 8 slices

"I highly recommend using day-old bread; there is no point in wasting fresh bread for crostini, as the slight loss of moisture helps the caramelization. There are so many wonderful ways to make use of older bread." —*Suzanne Slomin, owner, Green Rabbit*

2 tablespoons extra virgin olive oil, divided, plus more for drizzling
Sea salt
8 slices organic naturally leavened bread, about ¾ inches thick

Preheat the oven to 425 degrees Fahrenheit.

Brush each slice of bread with oil on both sides. Sprinkle each side with sea salt to taste. Place the bread slices directly on the oven rack and bake until caramelized on the outside and soft in the middle, about 5 minutes per side. Adjust seasoning with salt and a drizzle of oil, if desired.

Serve with Smokey Lamb Bolognese **(see page 239)**.

Recipe from Green Rabbit, LLC

J J Hapgood General Store and Eatery

Peru, Vermont, a small rural community with a population of 420, boasts a post office and one church within its tiny village. Conveniently located in the center of town is a quaint country store called J J Hapgood General Store and Eatery, a meeting place for residents and tourists alike. According to town records, the store opened in 1827 and is known to be the longest continuously running general store in Vermont. It was shuttered for five years before the present owners, Juliette and Tim Britton, revived the establishment in 2013.

The general store provides basic provisions, dry goods, Vermont produce, meat and dairy, local cheese, charcuterie, authentic wood-fired pizza, prepared meals, penny candy, and fine wine and beer. Juliette grew up in Peru and returned to the tiny hamlet with her husband after many years of owning a private chef service in the Boston area. Her decades of experience working in the food industry has helped tremendously in the culinary operations of the business.

The building was completely rebuilt, but they retained the look and feel of the old store by using artifacts from the original building. The Eatery's wood-fired oven was hand-built, its tables and chairs constructed from local sugar maple accented by custom cabinets that were designed by local artists. The comfortable atmosphere, with a gallery space and patio for outdoor dining, invites visitors to pause for a while, relax, and enjoy each other's company.

J J Hapgood General Store and Eatery has a solid relationship with local organic farmers, some of whom are family, others old friends, and a number who are new acquaintances. These food producers know they can call Juliette with details of freshly harvested crops, which she will readily incorporate into her menu. The busy chef relies on these healthy, fresh ingredients to bring out the best in the dishes she designs. Having studied fine art, she wants her food presentation to be colorful, beautiful, and delicious.

Breakfast, lunch, and dinner are served every day in an environment that encourages customers to learn more about the food they are eating. By doing this, the business honors and fosters relationships with farmers and food producers, helping to build a bridge between these hardworking folks and the community they serve. Patrons love the fact that their pizza dough, bread, and baked goods are made with local organic flour, and the coffee they drink is Fair Trade organic.

The Brittons have created a common space and everyday destination for eating, celebrating, and coming together with family and friends. Every town should be lucky enough to have a J J Hapgood General Store and Eatery in their own backyard!

Pappardelle with Pork Sugo, Roasted Shishito Peppers, and Garlic Bread Crumbs

Serves 8

Fresh Japanese shishito peppers are very sweet and mild and can be found at some farmers' markets and at Japanese markets. If you can't find Japanese shishito peppers, opt for some Spanish padron peppers, which have a similar flavor. Red or green bell peppers are also suitable substitutes.

Garlic Bread Crumbs
1 tablespoon extra virgin olive oil
1 cup panko bread crumbs
2 medium garlic cloves, peeled and finely grated
Salt and freshly ground black pepper

Roasted Shishito Peppers
10 Japanese shishito or Spanish padron peppers
1 tablespoon extra virgin olive oil
Salt

Pork Sugo
3 tablespoons extra virgin olive oil
2 pounds boneless pork shoulder or butt, trimmed and cut into 2-inch cubes
3 medium shallots, peeled and minced
6 medium garlic cloves, smashed and peeled
3 cups dry red wine
4 cups of canned whole peeled tomatoes, drained and crushed
3 cups milk
1 cup low-sodium chicken stock
8 sprigs of thyme, tied with kitchen twine
1 tablespoon fresh minced oregano
¼ teaspoon chile flakes
6 tablespoons unsalted butter, cut into chunks
1 cup freshly grated Grana Padano cheese, plus extra for serving
Salt and freshly ground black pepper
2 pounds pappardelle
Fresh minced parsley leaves for garnish
Finely grated lemon zest (preferably from an unwaxed lemon), optional

To make the garlic bread crumbs: Heat the oil in a medium skillet over medium-high heat. In a small bowl, combine the bread crumbs and garlic, tossing until well combined. When the oil is hot but not smoking, add the bread crumbs, stirring often, until golden brown, about 4 minutes. Season with salt and pepper to taste. Transfer to a bowl and set aside.

To make the roasted shishito peppers: Preheat the oven to 500 degrees Fahrenheit. Place the peppers and olive oil in a large bowl and season with salt to taste, tossing until evenly coated. Place the peppers in a single layer on a lightly greased baking sheet and roast, turning occasionally, until blisters form, about 7 minutes. When cool enough to handle, mince the peppers. Transfer to a bowl and set aside.

To make the pork sugo: Reduce the oven temperature to 350 degrees Fahrenheit. In a large Dutch oven or heavy-bottomed pot, heat the oil over medium-high heat until hot but not smoking. Working in batches, brown the pork cubes on all sides. Using a slotted spoon, transfer the meat to a large plate. Reduce the heat to medium. Add the shallots and garlic and cook, stirring often, until soft and translucent, about 3 minutes. Deglaze the pot with the wine. Return the pork and any accumulated juices back to the pot. Add the tomatoes along with any accumulated juices, milk, stock, thyme, oregano, and chile flakes and bring to a simmer. Cover and bake in the oven until the meat is fork tender, about 2½ hours.

When the pork sugo is almost done, bring a large pot of salted water to a boil. Add the pasta and cook until al dente. Drain the pasta and transfer to a large decorative serving bowl.

Using a slotted spoon, transfer the meat to a cutting board and shred it with a fork. Discard the thyme. Return the shredded meat back to pot. Add the peppers and stir in the butter and cheese. Adjust seasonings with salt and pepper to taste. Toss half of the pork sugo with the pasta, adding additional sauce as desired. Garnish with parsley, lemon zest, if using, and bread crumbs. Serve at once with additional cheese, if desired.

Recipe from JJ Hapgood General Store and Eatery
Photograph by Brie Passano

Notes:

- Parmesan or Asiago cheese can be substituted for the Grana Padano.
- This recipe makes more pork sugo than needed; freeze any leftovers in freezer bags.

Capellini Pasta with Garlic and Baby Spinach

Serves 4

This quick and easy pasta dish is perfect for those nights when you don't have a lot of time to cook. Serve with crusty bread.

¼ cup extra virgin olive oil, plus extra for drizzling
8 large garlic cloves, peeled and minced
10 ounces loosely packed baby spinach
¼ teaspoon red pepper flakes, optional
Salt and freshly ground black pepper
1 pound capellini pasta
½ cup freshly grated Parmigiano-Reggiano cheese, plus extra for serving
2 teaspoons finely grated lemon zest (preferably from an unwaxed lemon), plus extra for garnish

Bring a large pot of salted water to a boil over medium-high heat.

While waiting for the water to boil, heat the oil in a large skillet over medium-low heat. Add the garlic and cook, stirring occasionally, until it just begins to turn golden brown, about 5 minutes. Add the spinach and red pepper flakes (if using) and cook until the spinach begins to wilt, about 3 minutes. Season with salt and pepper to taste.

While the spinach is cooking, cook the pasta until al dente. Drain the pasta, reserving ½ cup of the pasta water. Combine the pasta and spinach mixture in a large serving bowl. Add the cheese, lemon zest, and ¼ cup of the reserved pasta water, adding more water until the desired consistency is reached. Toss until well combined. Adjust the seasonings with red pepper flakes, salt, and pepper.

Garnish with additional cheese and lemon zest, if desired. Drizzle with oil and serve at once.

Recipe from Pangea Farm, LLC

Juniper Bar & Restaurant, Hotel Vermont

Bleu Northeast Seafood

Hotel Vermont is located in the bustling city of Burlington, Vermont. Tucked away within its welcoming interior is the popular Juniper Bar & Restaurant, a go-to spot for both tourists and Vermonters. The restaurant, which opened in 2013, serves breakfast, lunch, and dinner, with a farm-to-table brunch offered on weekends. Next door to Hotel Vermont is Bleu Northeast Seafood, located inside the Burlington Harbor Courtyard Marriott. Bleu, Juniper's sister restaurant, focuses on sustainably sourced regional seafood.

Executive Chef Doug Paine oversees the workings at both restaurants and the bar, as well as all catering operations. The busy chef is always on the lookout for new local producers and providers who can supply the restaurant with the organic produce, cheeses, meats, and non-GMO eggs that the kitchen uses each day. With organic agriculture of the utmost importance to him, this dedicated chef thoroughly enjoys visiting local farmers, bakers, cheesemakers, and other area food producers to get to know them better and see firsthand how they operate.

Juniper and Bleu are run very much like independent restaurants, with Chef Paine having the freedom to experiment and create savory, seasonally driven recipes that showcase the community and its food producers. Earning the Snail of Approval Award from Slow Food Vermont is a feather in Paine's culinary cap. This much-sought-after recognition is given to a select number of eating establishments, only being awarded to the "best of the best." These outstanding recipients have all shown an unwavering commitment to fair and sustainable practices.

Located near beautiful Lake Champlain, Juniper has both indoor and outdoor seating, where diners can relax and soak in the beauty of this vibrant city. The eating area and bar blend together seamlessly, offering guests a combination of chic, modern, and rustic Vermont decor. By featuring Vermont-made spirits, the bar also does its part to support locally produced products. Bleu has wonderful seasonal views of the lake in a refined setting.

Chef Paine's philosophy on food is quite simple: "Find the best ingredients possible and make them into something fresh and delicious." With more than 40 farms sharing their produce and products with the award-winning restaurant, this ideology seems to be working quite well. Gathering inspiration from the juniper berry with its strong, unique flavor that has been used in making food and drink for centuries, this innovative eating establishment offers cuisine that appeals to all lifestyle choices, including vegan and vegetarian.

Photograph by Oliver Parini

Chèvre Gnocchi with a Mushroom, Sunchoke, and Garlic Cream Sauce

Makes about 2 quarts of gnocchi; serves 4–6

"Gnocchi is one of my favorite comfort foods. This version is a fall staple at Juniper. We get freshly picked wild mushrooms from local wild crafters and crisp new crop sunchokes from Half Pint Farm in Burlington's Intervale [Center]. It is nutty and slightly sweet with a ton of umami from the roasted mushrooms. The tartness of the goat cheese from Vermont Creamery balances it all out." —*Executive Chef Doug Paine, Juniper Restaurant and Bleu Northeast Seafood*

Gnocchi
Makes about 112 Gnocchi

1¼ pounds russet potatoes, peeled, cut into 1-inch pieces, and boiled until fork tender
3½ ounces chèvre, crumbled, plus more for garnish, such as Vermont Creamery
2 egg yolks
1¾ teaspoons melted butter
⅛ teaspoon freshly grated nutmeg
1½ teaspoons salt
¼ teaspoon freshly ground black pepper
3 cups organic all-purpose flour, such as King Arthur
⅛ cup extra virgin olive oil

Creamy Mushroom, Sunchoke, and Garlic Sauce
Makes 1 quart

½ pound sunchokes (Jerusalem artichokes), scrubbed, unpeeled, cut into ¼-inch-thick slices
2 tablespoons extra virgin olive oil, divided
1 pound mushrooms, such as oyster, maitake, or shiitake, trimmed and cut into ¼-inch-thick slices
1 medium garlic clove, peeled and chopped
½ cup dry white wine
1 cup heavy cream
2 tablespoons chopped mixed herbs, such as parsley, rosemary, sage, or thyme
Salt and freshly ground black pepper

4 tablespoons butter, divided, for browning 4 batches of gnocchi
Fresh parsley leaves, finely chopped
Edible flowers, optional

Preheat the oven to 375 degrees Fahrenheit. Lightly oil four baking sheets and set aside.

When cool enough to handle, place the potatoes into a ricer and rice them into a medium bowl. Set aside.

In a standing mixer, combine the potatoes, chèvre, egg yolks, melted butter, nutmeg, salt, and pepper until well combined. Add the flour and continue to mix until a stiff dough forms.

Bring 4 quarts of water and 1 tablespoon of salt to a simmer in a large stockpot.

Place the dough on a clean, lightly floured work surface. Using lightly floured hands, knead the dough until it's slightly elastic. The dough will be sticky.

Using a lightly floured knife or dough scraper, cut the dough into egg-size pieces. Roll each piece of dough into a ¼-inch-thick rope. Using a sharp, lightly floured knife, cut each rope into ½-by-¼-inch pieces. Transfer the gnocchi to one of the prepared baking sheets and repeat the process with the remaining dough.

Place a large bowl of ice water near your cooking area. Add the gnocchi in four batches to the simmering water and cook, stirring gently, until they float to the surface, about 4 minutes. Remove the gnocchi from the pot with a slotted spoon and transfer to the bowl of ice water, replenishing the ice in the bowl of water as necessary. Drain the cold gnocchi in a colander, transfer to a prepared baking sheet, and drizzle with the olive oil. Repeat with the remaining gnocchi.

To make the sauce: Place the sunchokes in a bowl. Add ½ tablespoon of the oil and season with salt and pepper to taste, tossing until well combined. Arrange the sunchokes in a single layer on the remaining prepared baking sheet and bake for 5 minutes. In the same bowl used for the sunchokes, add the mushrooms and toss with 1 tablespoon olive oil. Add the mushrooms to the baking sheet with the sunchokes. Bake until the sunchokes are fork tender and the moisture from the mushrooms has evaporated, about 25 minutes.

While the sunchokes and mushrooms are baking, heat the remaining ½ tablespoon of oil in a 2-quart saucepan over medium heat. Add the garlic and cook, stirring often until fragrant and light golden brown, about 1 minute. Increase the heat to medium-high, add the wine, and bring to a boil, stirring frequently, until reduced to ⅓ cup, about 4 minutes. Slowly whisk in the cream. Add the mushrooms, sunchokes, and herbs, lower the heat to a simmer, and cook until the mushrooms and sunchokes are heated through and the sauce thickens and reduces, about 15 minutes. Season with salt and pepper to taste.

While the sauce is thickening, brown the gnocchi. Heat 1 tablespoon of the butter in a large nonstick skillet over medium-high heat until hot but not smoking. Working in four batches, add the gnocchi and sauté until golden brown, about 5 minutes for each batch. Transfer the gnocchi to a large bowl. Repeat with the remaining gnocchi, adding an additional 1 tablespoon of butter per batch. Pour the sauce over the gnocchi. Season with salt and pepper to taste, tossing until well combined. Garnish with cherve, parsley, and edible flowers, if desired. Serve at once.

Recipe from Chef Doug Paine of Juniper Bar & Restaurant, Hotel Vermont
Photograph by Oliver Parini

The Farmhouse Group

The Farmhouse Group is a shining example of what can happen when restaurant owners, chefs, and farmers work as a team. The four restaurants owned by this group each have their own distinctive theme with a common thread that draws them together as one: a focus on locally produced food. The Farmhouse Tap and Grill is an award-winning gastro pub that serves up craft burgers and beers, while El Cortijo Taqueria, a farm-to-taco tequila bar, serves Mexican entrées in a retro 1950s diner. Folks who are in the mood for a steakhouse atmosphere will find that the Guild Tavern more than fills the bill with its craft cocktails and tavern fare. Handmade pastas, wood-fired Neapolitan pizzas, and an award-winning wine list make dining at Pascolo Ristorante *bellisimo*. All four distinctive dining establishments are located in the lively city of Burlington, Vermont.

Executive Chef Phillip Clayton has assisted with the openings of the group's four restaurants and now oversees each of them while also managing the kitchens at Guild Tavern and Pascolo. The busy chef is one of the four owners of the Farmhouse Group. Each member shares a profound commitment to the area's food community by supporting the use of locally produced farm products in each of the eating establishments. For these dedicated businessmen, buying local has proven to be the best way to guarantee the highest caliber of quality ingredients. They trust that their patrons will appreciate the outstanding food each of their restaurants has to offer and realize that the "buy local" movement is the driving force behind the delicious cuisine they're enjoying.

Along with its four diverse restaurants, the Farmhouse Group also operates a catering and events company. Always focused on buying local first, the group partners with many non-GMO and certificated organic farms and producers in the area. Sourcing locally is the core of the business, as the group firmly believes that by doing so they are helping to strengthen the health of the area's agriculture, environment, and community. This devotion to members of the neighboring food community has proven to be mutually beneficial. The Farmhouse Group supports organizations such as NOFA and the Intervale Center, investing in their farming operations with agricultural enhancements like the addition of greenhouses that help to extend the growing season.

Chef Phillip believes, "Great food is made in the field and enhanced in the kitchen." To achieve this goal, the restaurant owners have partnered with well over twenty area farms and expect that the number will increase as time goes on. The rewards of these agricultural relationships are twofold: great farm-fresh ingredients that are used in the creation of healthy, delicious recipes, and a means of showcasing the hardworking folks of Vermont's agricultural and culinary communities. With four popular restaurants, a catering and events management division, and innovative beverage program, the Farmhouse Group is moving full steam ahead. The journey for this culinary juggernaut is far from over.

Photograph by Oliver Parini

Fresh Pappardelle with Fennel Cream, Italian Sausage, and Sheep's Milk Tomme

Serves 4

The fried sage leaves make a nice visual contrast to the pale and rich looking pasta dish. "While working the dough, mist it liberally with a spray bottle filled with room temperature water to help moisten and bring the dough together." —*Executive Chef Phillip Clayton, The Farmhouse Group*

Pappardelle Pasta Dough

1½ cups all-purpose flour, plus extra for dusting
2 extra large eggs
6 egg yolks
Water as needed for spritzing the dough
1½ tablespoons extra virgin olive oil

Fennel Cream

2 tablespoons unsalted butter
1 medium onion, peeled and diced
Fennel fronds from 1 medium fennel bulb, reserving bulb for pasta sauce, coarsely chopped
2 ounces Pernod absinthe
1 quart heavy cream
½ tablespoon salt
1 bay leaf

Pasta Sauce

2 tablespoons extra virgin olive oil
8 ounces hot or sweet Italian sausage, casings removed
¼ cup packed whole fresh sage leaves, about 50 medium sized sage leaves
2 medium garlic cloves, peeled and smashed
1 medium fennel bulb, halved, cored and diced into ¼-inch pieces, reserving fronds for fennel cream
2 ounces brandy
¼ cup finely grated firm sheep's milk cheese, such as Vermont Shepherd's Verano or Invierno, plus extra for garnish

To make the pasta dough: On a large wooden cutting board or clean work surface, sift the flour. Make a well in the center of the flour. Break the eggs into the well and add the egg yolks. Using a fork, mix the eggs into the flour until thick. Kneading with your hands, continue mixing until a firm dough forms, spritzing the dough with water as needed. Lightly drizzle with olive oil. Wrap the dough in plastic wrap and chill in the refrigerator for 1 hour.

To make the fennel cream: Melt the butter in a medium saucepan over medium heat. Add the onion and cook, stirring often, until soft and translucent, about 5 minutes. Add the fronds and cook for 2 minutes. Add the Pernod and bring to a simmer over medium-high heat, scraping up the brown bits from the bottom of the pan with a wooden spoon, about 3 minutes. Add the cream in a slow and steady stream. Add the salt and bay leaf and simmer until the cream mixture is reduced to ⅔ cup, about 45 minutes. Strain through a fine-mesh strainer and set aside.

While the cream sauce is reducing, make the pappardelle pasta. On a lightly floured surface, knead the dough with your hands until smooth and elastic to the touch. Divide the dough into 6 pieces and dust with flour. Feed the first piece of dough through a pasta machine, starting on the first thickness setting (usually marked 1). Fold the dough into thirds and roll through this setting four more times, dusting with flour as needed. Continue feeding the pasta sheet through, adjusting to the next setting, one pass at a time, until the dough is between ⅛ and 1/16 inch thick. Using a lightly floured pasta cutter or knife, cut the dough into ⅝-inch-wide noodles. Drape the pasta in a single layer over a pasta rack, coat hangers, or the back of a chair. Repeat with the remaining dough pieces and let the pasta air dry until almost brittle, about 20 minutes.

While the fennel cream is reducing, make the pasta sauce. Heat the oil in a large skillet over medium-high heat. Add the sausage and cook, breaking it up with a fork, until browned, about 10 minutes. Season with salt and pepper to taste. Using a slotted spoon, transfer the sausage to a plate, reserving the sausage drippings in the skillet.

While the sausage is browning, bring 5 quarts of water and ½ tablespoon of salt to a boil in a large stockpot over medium-high heat.

Using paper towels, carefully and completely blot dry the sage leaves. Heat the reserved sausage drippings in skillet, adding additional olive oil, if needed, to bring the drippings up to 4 tablespoons, over medium-high heat. When the oil begins to shimmer, working in 6 batches, carefully add the sage leaves and garlic and fry for 10–12 seconds. Using a slotted spoon, carefully remove the sage leaves and drain on paper towels. Leaves will continue to crisp while cooling. Discard the garlic. Repeat with the remaining sage leaves, adding additional oil as needed. Reserve 1 tablespoon of the oil in the skillet, for the fennel. Add the fennel and cook, stirring often, until lightly browned and tender, about 4 minutes. Return the sausage back to the pan. Slowly and carefully add the brandy and simmer, scraping up the bits from the bottom of the pan with a wooden spoon, for 3 minutes. Add the fennel cream in a slow and steady stream and simmer, stirring occasionally, until the sauce is reduced to a third of its original volume, about 15 minutes.

While the sauce is reducing, cook the pasta until al dente, about 4 minutes. Drain the pasta in a colander, drizzle with olive oil, and transfer the pasta to the sauce. Add the cheese and gently toss until well combined. Adjust seasonings with salt and pepper to taste. Garnish with fried sage leaves and additional cheese, if desired.

Recipe from Pascolo Ristorante for The Farmhouse Group
Photograph by Oliver Parini

Cheesy Veggie Pasta Bake

Serves 6–8

"My five-year-old son calls this dish 'Popa.' My focus in cooking for the past few years has been all about finding palatable ways to get him to eat vegetables. Serve this dish with a nice crusty baguette on the side." —*Cindy Growney, owner, Pedalbarrow Farm*

Pasta

1 pound organic mini shell pasta
Salt
Olive oil

Cheese Sauce

2 tablespoons butter
2 tablespoons all-purpose flour
2¼ cups milk, warmed
1 head broccoli, florets cut into bite-sized pieces, stems peeled and sliced
3 large kale leaves, stems removed, and leaves sliced into 1-inch strips
12 ounces sharp cheddar cheese, finely shredded
1½ teaspoons prepared mustard
¼ teaspoon salt
Coarsely ground black pepper
¼ cup finely grated Parmigiano-Reggiano cheese, plus extra for serving
Fresh chopped parsley leaves, for garnish

Preheat the oven to 350 degrees Fahrenheit. Grease a 9-by-13-inch baking dish with butter. Set aside.

To make the pasta: Bring a large pot of salted water to a boil over medium-high heat. Add the pasta and cook until al dente, about 10 minutes. Drain in a colander and toss with olive oil. Return the pasta to the pot and set aside.

While the pasta is cooking, make the cheese sauce. Melt the butter in a 2-quart saucepan over medium-low heat. Whisk in the flour and cook, whisking often, until light golden brown, about 3 minutes. Whisking continuously, slowly add the milk until the sauce is thick and bubbling. Add the broccoli and kale and continue to cook, stirring often, for 5 minutes. Using an immersion blender, puree the vegetables until very smooth. Add 2½ cups of the cheddar cheese, mustard, and salt and continue to whisk until the cheese has completely melted, about 5 minutes. Adjust seasonings with salt and pepper to taste.

Pour the cheese sauce over the pasta and stir until well combined. Pour into the prepared baking dish, sprinkle with the remaining cheddar cheese and Parmigiano-Reggiano cheese over the top, and bake, uncovered, until hot and bubbly, about 25 minutes. Let rest for 10 minutes, sprinkle with parsley, and serve.

Recipe from Pedalbarrow Farm

CHAPTER 8

ORGANIC AND HEIRLOOM GRAINS AND BEANS

Black Bean and Sweet Corn Salad

Makes 2 quarts

This salad is delicious served chilled or at room temperature. "Our kitchen seems to be the happiest when making recipes with a Tex-Mex flair. This recipe is great for summer dinner parties and gatherings. It makes a nice big family-size bowl." —*Courtney Satz, owner, Wood's Market Garden*

Dressing

Makes about ¾ cup

½ cup extra virgin olive oil
5 tablespoons fresh lime juice
1 teaspoon finely grated lime zest
Salt and freshly ground black pepper

Salad

3 cups cooked black beans, drained, or 2 15-ounce cans, drained
2 cups sweet corn kernels, from about 4 ears of corn, parboiled, or frozen and thawed
1 pint multicolored cherry tomatoes, halved
½ cup red onion, thinly sliced
½ jalapeño pepper, seeded and diced
1 teaspoon salt
2 ripe Hass avocados, cut in half lengthwise, pit removed, peeled, and cut into 1-inch chunks
⅓ cup crumbled whole-milk cow feta cheese, preferably Maplebrook Farm
2 tablespoons fresh chopped cilantro leaves, plus extra for garnish
Freshly ground black pepper

To make the dressing: In a medium bowl, whisk together the oil, lime juice, and zest. Season with salt and pepper to taste. Set aside.

In a large bowl, combine the beans, corn, tomatoes, onions, jalapeño pepper, and salt until well combined. Add the dressing, tossing until well combined. Cover and chill in the refrigerator for at least 1 hour. Right before serving, gently fold in the avocados, cheese, and cilantro. Adjust seasonings with salt and pepper to taste. Garnish with additional cilantro and drizzles of lime juice, if desired.

Recipe from Wood's Market Garden
Photography by Oliver Parini

PROFILE

Stowe Street Café

The Stowe Street Café, nestled in scenic Waterbury, Vermont, welcomes folks to drop by for a warming cup of locally roasted coffee, barista-made espresso, or a selection of specialty teas. For those who are otherwise inclined, there is a tantalizing assortment of delicious freshly pressed juice drinks and silky smoothies. The full menu changes regularly, drawing customers back time after time to try a variety of made-from-scratch baked goods, handcrafted salads, soups, sandwiches, quiches, frittatas, empanadas, house-made sausage, and much more. A full menu is served all day or until, as some diners sadly learn, the kitchen runs out of one of the most popular selections.

Owner Nicole Grenier and Chef Stephanie Biczko are committed to building a sense of community by creating healthy food from locally sourced ingredients that draws people together. The two women supported neighboring farms and farmers long before the café opened its doors in 2015. They not only have a desire to source the freshest locally grown ingredients possible for the café's customers, but they have also tried their hand at growing their own food, experiencing both ends of the farm-to-table process.

The café has built strong relationships with a number of area farmers who supply them with everything from produce to maple syrup, tofu to peanut butter, and yogurt to honey. While many of these products are organic, all are grown using good land stewardship and responsible farming practices. Farmer friends may walk through the café's door to deliver freshly harvested produce and leave with a supply of Stowe Street Café's own creation, quality compost. The sense of reciprocity that flows between the café and its local providers fuels the feeling of loyalty and commitment to each other and the community they love. Working together has helped to strengthen community ties and benefited the local economy as well.

The beautiful artwork that is displayed throughout the restaurant showcases area artists and crafters. Paintings, prints, photography, jewelry, and other original works of art are offered for sale. These pieces, which beautify the café and make for interesting topics of conversation, sometimes leave with a new owner. The folks at Stowe Street Café are dedicated to "fostering community and celebrating local art in all forms." Stop by, enjoy a quiet bite to eat, and drink in the unique artwork and friendly, relaxing atmosphere of this cozy eatery.

Coconut Dhal

Makes 4 quarts; serves 6– 8

This bright and hearty freezer-friendly dish is very popular at the Stowe Street Café. It is both vegan and gluten-free! Before cooking the lentils, it is highly recommended to examine them for small debris and rocks.

Lentils
7 cups water
½ teaspoon kosher salt
3 cups red lentils, picked over and rinsed
¾ teaspoon cayenne pepper
¾ teaspoon ground turmeric

2 tablespoons virgin coconut oil
1 large onion, diced
3½ medium garlic cloves, minced
1 28-ounce can plus half a 14½-ounce can diced tomatoes, drained
¾ tablespoon cumin
¾ tablespoon garam masala

32 ounces organic unsweetened coconut milk
¼ cup minced cilantro, plus extra for garnish
Fresh lime juice
Salt
1 large lime, cut in 8 wedges
Naan bread, warmed

To make the lentils: Bring the 7 cups of water and salt to a boil in a large saucepan over medium-high heat. Add the lentils and stir occasionally, until the water returns to a boil. Boil the lentils for 20 minutes. Remove from the heat and allow to cool to room temperature. Once cooled, add the cayenne pepper and turmeric.

In a separate large saucepan, heat the coconut oil over medium heat. Add the onions and sauté until soft and translucent, about 10 minutes. Add the garlic and sauté until fragrant, about 1 minute. Stir in the tomatoes, cumin, and garam masala and simmer until thickened, caramelized, and the tomatoes have turned a dark red, about 25 minutes.

Using an immersion blender, puree the tomato mixture. Add the tomato puree to the lentils and cook, stirring occasionally, over medium-high heat until heated through, about 3 minutes. Whisk in the coconut milk, cilantro, and lime juice to taste and simmer until heated through, about 8 minutes. Season with salt to taste. Garnish with fresh cilantro. Serve on its own or over rice, if desired, with lime wedges and naan bread on the side.

Recipe from Stowe Street Café

Warm Lentil Salad with Roasted Butternut Squash, Sage, and Feta Cheese

Serves 6–8

"We use a high-quality local organic cow's milk feta in this popular fall salad, sage leaves from the garden, and organic French lentils. The sweetness of the squash is perfectly offset by the salty feta and the earthiness of sage." *—Alison Baker, former kitchen manager and chef, Cedar Circle Farm & Education Center*

Butternut Squash

1 butternut squash (about 2 pounds), halved lengthwise, seeded, peeled, and cut crosswise into ¼-inch-wide half-moon slices
2 tablespoons extra virgin olive oil
Kosher salt

Green Lentils

2 tablespoons extra virgin olive oil
2 cups dried green lentils, picked over
½ cup peeled and finely chopped carrot
½ cup finely chopped celery
3 cups water

Dressing

Makes 1¼ cups

1 garlic clove, peeled and minced
¾ teaspoon salt
½ cup lemon juice
½ cup olive oil

Fried Sage

2 tablespoons, tightly packed, whole fresh sage leaves, about 25 medium sage leaves
3 tablespoons extra virgin olive oil

½ cup thinly sliced red onion, cut into ½-inch pieces
6 ounces feta cheese, crumbled

Preheat the oven to 350 degrees Fahrenheit. Lightly oil a baking sheet and set aside.

Toss the squash with the oil in a medium bowl and season with salt to taste. Spread the squash on the prepared baking sheet. Roast, stirring every 15 minutes, until the squash is fork tender and golden brown, about 30 minutes. Set aside to cool.

Rinse the lentils under cold running water. Drain and set aside.

Heat the oil in a 2½-quart heavy-bottomed saucepan over medium heat. Add the lentils, carrot, and celery and sauté, stirring often, for 5 minutes. Cover the lentils with 3 cups of water and bring to a boil over medium-high heat. Reduce the heat to a simmer, cover, and cook, stirring occasionally, until the lentils are just tender and still hold their shape, 12–15 minutes. Turn off the heat, and leave the pot covered, allowing the lentils to absorb the extra cooking water.

While the lentils are cooking, make the dressing. Place the garlic in a small bowl and sprinkle with ½ teaspoon of salt and set aside for 5 minutes. In a medium bowl, add the garlic and lemon juice. Whisking vigorously, add the olive oil in a slow, steady stream. Season with the remaining ¼ teaspoon salt.

Drain any excess water from the lentils, then put them in a large bowl. Toss the lentils with ½ cup of the dressing. Season with salt and pepper to taste. Set aside.

To make the fried sage: Pat the sage leaves thoroughly dry with paper towels. Set aside. Heat the oil in a small frying pan over medium-high heat until hot but not smoking. When the oil begins to shimmer, working in batches, add the sage leaves and fry, watching carefully to avoid scorching, until the leaves turn crisp, about 10–12 seconds. Using a slotted spoon, carefully remove the leaves and drain on paper towels. Leaves will continue to crisp while cooling. Repeat with the remaining sage leaves, adding additional oil as needed.

Carefully crumble the sage into the lentils, stirring until well combined. Fold in the squash, cheese, and red onion, until well combined. Adjust seasonings with salt and pepper to taste. Serve with crusty bread.

Recipe from Cedar Circle Farm & Education Center
Photograph by Oliver Parini

Note: This dressing recipe makes more than you will need. Add the extra dressing to green beans or as the perfect complement to a garden salad.

PROFILE

Nitty Gritty Grain Company of Vermont

Tom Kenyon is a cofounder and owner of the Nitty Gritty Grain Company of Vermont. He has been using organic farming practices for more than 25 years on Aurora Farm in Charlotte, Vermont. The concept for Nitty Gritty Grain took hold when the owner of Red Hen Bakery approached Tom and several other farmers with the idea of having them plant a hard red winter wheat that would enable the bakery to produce an all-Vermont bread. The first two growing seasons the wheat did not meet organic standards due to uncooperative weather conditions. Without the right combination of precipitation, a wheat crop may fall short of perfect. In 2009, they successfully created the flour that is now used for Red Hen's Cyrus Pringle bread.

The company's production facility is located on Aurora Farm, in a refurbished milk house. Business is growing slowly, and there's no desire to become corporate. During the past decade, wheat growing has experienced a rebirth, and because of this a small group of farmers now independently grows limited quantities of high-quality wheat. Nitty Gritty minimally processes locally grown grains in small batches to preserve its flavor. The workforce is mostly comprised of family members, including Tom's sister, Catherine Kenyon, who is in charge of production. The goal of this small, family-run business is to produce the best product possible, with the hope that in doing so they are also helping to preserve their land for generations to come.

It has taken eight years for the company to reach its present level of success. Tom and his family have strong relationships with many chefs and restaurant owners who are also committed to the local food movement. Some of these businesses have been using Nitty Gritty's grains from early on, while others have become supporters. Local health food markets and co-ops are also taking notice, singing the praises of buying local and organic. Black River Produce does an outstanding job distributing and marketing the farm's grains, which are sold at local stores and on the Nitty Gritty Grain Company's website.

Tom Kenyon has been a member of the Vermont Fresh Network for many years, and because of this organization's help, the state's food industry has become aware of the company's unique Vermont-grown grains. These grains are all milled in small quantities to guarantee the product's freshness and excellent flavor. The Nitty Gritty Grain Company stresses the importance of knowing where your food comes from, hoping that you will taste the difference that care and hard work can create.

Ann's Super Moist 100% Whole Grain Corn Bread

Serves 10

Nitty Gritty's certified organic whole grain wheat flour is an unbleached, all-purpose flour milled from hard red winter wheat grown in Vermont. Hard red winter wheat has a slightly higher amount of protein than hard white wheat. Nitty Gritty's Organic Whole Wheat flour has a protein content of about 11.9%.

1 cup Nitty Gritty's Organic High Meadow Yellow cornmeal
½ cup Nitty Gritty's Organic Whole Grain Wheat flour
2 teaspoons aluminum-free baking powder
½ teaspoon salt
1 cup whole milk
2 large eggs, lightly beaten
⅓ cup canola oil
1 cup cream-style corn
3 teaspoons pure Vermont maple syrup

Preheat the oven to 350 degrees Fahrenheit. Spray an 8-inch square baking pan with nonstick cooking spray and set aside.

In a large bowl, whisk together the cornmeal, flour, baking powder, and salt.

In a medium bowl, whisk together the milk, eggs, oil, cream-style corn, and maple syrup. Stir the wet ingredients into the cornmeal mixture and mix until just combined. Pour the batter into the prepared pan and smooth with a spatula.

Bake until the top is lightly golden brown and a toothpick inserted into the center comes out clean, about 30 minutes. Serve hot or warm.

Recipe from Nitty Gritty Grain Company of Vermont

Note: If you enjoy a sweeter corn bread, feel free to add more maple syrup to taste.

Variation: Feel free to use 3 teaspoons of honey instead of pure maple syrup.

Avocado, Jalapeño, and Cheddar Cheese Corn Bread

Serves about 15

High Meadow Yellow cornmeal is produced from certified organic dent hybrid corn. The medium grind produces a pleasant chewiness with a mellow, corny flavor—a good general-purpose cornmeal.

- 1 cup Nitty Gritty's Organic High Meadow Yellow cornmeal
- ½ cup Nitty Gritty's Organic Whole Grain Wheat flour
- ½ cup Nitty Gritty's Pastry Flour
- ¼ cup organic cane sugar
- 1 teaspoon aluminum-free baking powder
- 1 teaspoon baking soda
- 1 teaspoon salt
- 3 large eggs, lightly beaten
- 1 cup low-fat buttermilk
- 4 tablespoons unsalted butter, melted, cooled to room temperature
- 1 ripe avocado, cut in half lengthwise, pit removed, peeled and mashed
- ¾ cup shredded mild or sharp Vermont cheddar cheese
- 2 jalapeño peppers, halved, stemmed, seeded, and minced

Preheat the oven to 350 degrees Fahrenheit. Spray an 8-by-11-inch baking pan with nonstick cooking spray and set aside.

In a large bowl, whisk together the cornmeal, flours, sugar, baking powder, baking soda, and salt.

In a medium bowl, stir together the eggs, buttermilk, butter, and avocado. Stir the wet ingredients into the cornmeal mixture until just combined. Fold in the cheese and peppers until just combined. Pour the batter into the prepared pan and smooth with a spatula.

Bake until the top is lightly golden brown and a toothpick inserted into the center comes out clean, about 25 minutes. Let cool in the pan on a wire rack for 10 minutes before cutting; serve warm.

Recipe from Nitty Gritty Grain Company of Vermont

PROFILE

Mint Restaurant and Tea Lounge

Iliyan Deskov and Savitri Bhagavati are the proud owners of the cheery Mint Restaurant and Tea Lounge found in Waitsfield, Vermont's picturesque Mad River Valley. The couple, who have always enjoyed being close to nature, decided to move from Los Angeles to Vermont in search of a more sustainable lifestyle. It seemed the perfect choice, as their own philosophy of life was in harmony with Vermont's ideology.

Savitri's cooking is pure, clean, and simple, yet rich in flavor. The restaurant serves vegetarian, vegan, gluten-free dishes made with produce from local farms that practice organic farming. Only the freshest ingredients are used in the creation of each dish. Vegetables are often prepared in layers to introduce a complexity of flavors. The inspired chef finds Italian, Indian, Middle Eastern, and East African cooking—with their bold, intriguing use of spices that are pure and not overpowering—exciting. The couple also offers a unique assortment of teas that pair well with the restaurants daily offerings.

Seasonal ingredients determine each day's menu, making every visit a culinary adventure. At the charming Mint Restaurant, they strive to support the sustainability of local farms, using the bounty from their fields as an inspiration for meals that make guests eager to return. As one satisfied diner exclaimed, "My only complaint is that I live so far away and can't come back more often."

Mexican Polenta

Serves 8

This dish is both pretty and festive! The recipe uses certified organic whole grain Wapsie Valley cornmeal from the Nitty Gritty Grain Company of Vermont. Wapsie Valley is an heirloom, open-pollinated variety of corn that's grown in Vermont. The corn grinds into a rich orange meal and has an earthy, robust flavor and super crunchy texture.

Polenta

12 cups vegetable stock
1 tablespoon salt
3 cups organic whole grain Wapsie Valley cornmeal, preferably Nitty Gritty Grain Company of Vermont
Salt and freshly ground black pepper

Filling

8 veggie sausage links, such as Field Roast's apple sage sausage, sliced ¼ inch thick on a bias
5 tablespoons extra virgin olive oil, divided
1 large onion, peeled and diced (about 1½ cups)
1 medium red or yellow bell pepper, seeded and diced
½ teaspoon whole cumin seeds
½ teaspoon dried Mexican oregano
3 cups fresh corn kernels (about four ears, depending on the size)
1 15-ounce can black beans, drained and rinsed
2 medium–large tomatoes, chopped
½ tablespoon regular paprika powder or smoked paprika powder
1 cup fresh cilantro leaves, coarsely chopped
3 tablespoons fresh lime juice
Salt and freshly ground black pepper
Oil for frying polenta circles
2 cups shredded cheddar cheese, preferably Grafton Village Cheese Company
8 lime wedges

To make the polenta: Bring the 12 cups of stock and salt to a boil in a large stockpot over medium-high heat. Whisking constantly, add the cornmeal in a slow, steady stream to prevent a lumpy mixture that is hard to fix. Continue stirring until the water returns to a boil. Reduce the heat to low and simmer, stirring occasionally with a wooden spoon, until thickened, about 45

minutes. The polenta should pull away from the sides of the pan. Season with salt and pepper to taste.

Liberally butter a rimmed baking sheet. Spoon the polenta into the prepared baking sheet. Set aside at room temperature for about 1 hour and 20 minutes. Then, cover with plastic wrap and allow to chill in the refrigerator for 1 hour.

Once the polenta has set, make the filling. Heat 1 tablespoon of the oil in a Dutch oven over medium heat. Working in four batches, add the sausage and 1 tablespoon of oil for each batch and cook, flipping once, until the sausage is browned, about 6 minutes. Using a slotted spoon, transfer the sausage to a large plate lined with paper towels. Repeat with the remaining sausage slices and 3 tablespoons oil. Heat the remaining 1 tablespoon of oil in the same Dutch oven over medium heat. Add the onions and peppers and cook, stirring occasionally, for 5 minutes. Add the cumin and oregano, stirring until well combined, and cook for 1 minute. Stir in the corn, beans, tomatoes, and paprika and cook until heated through, about 5 minutes. Remove from the heat and stir in the cilantro and lime juice. Adjust seasonings with additional lime juice, if desired, and salt and pepper to taste.

While the sausage slices are cooking, cut the polenta. Using a 2½-inch biscuit cutter, cut the polenta into circle shapes. Heat about 2 tablespoons of oil in a large skillet over medium heat. Working in batches, add the polenta circles and cook until slightly golden brown on one side, about 3 minutes, then carefully flip and cook for about 3 more minutes. Repeat with the remaining polenta circles, adding more oil as needed.

To assemble: Spoon 1 cup of the warm vegetable mixture in the center of each plate. Scatter 10–15 sausage slices on top. Sprinkle with cheese to taste. Place 3 polenta cakes evenly around the top. Serve with high-quality salsa and lime wedges on the side.

Recipe from Mint Restaurant and Tea Lounge
Photograph by Oliver Parini

Note: Using a smoked paprika will impart a rich, deep woodsy flavor to the veggie filling.

Polenta Cooking Tip: At the end of cooking, take a spoonful of the polenta and set it in the refrigerator for 2 minutes—if it solidifies the polenta is done. If the polenta's texture is somewhat soft and flowing, continue to cook for approximately another 15 minutes.

PROFILE

Pedalbarrow Farm

Cindy Growney believes that we all have an obligation to take care of our planet Earth, with organic farming being an important part of this responsibility. She feels that it is everyone's duty to know how our food is raised or grown and where it comes from. For this farmer, organic methods are a natural fit. Even as a child she had an interest in gardening, which turned into a life's passion when she got a job on a vegetable farm after high school.

She is the owner of Pedalbarrow Farm's 8½ acres in Bridport, Vermont, a rural farming community in the Champlain Valley. The farm's two greenhouses are used for growing greens in the winter and starter plants for the spring. Cindy is a certified organic farmer who primarily grows vegetables, sunflowers, and herbs on 1 acre of her property. She also raises chickens for eggs.

Farming is done without the use of a tractor; in fact, Cindy doesn't even own one. A one-woman operation, she walks behind a tiller, which helps her prep the beds for planting. She practices seven-year rotation to keep diseases under control, mulching with hay and straw as often as possible, and utilizing compost to build soil. Cindy's produce is available at the local natural food co-op and at her farm stand.

Brown Rice Bowls with Black Beans and Veggies

Serves 4

This dish offers warm and hearty comfort food with veggies peeking out invitingly from the rice and beans.

2 cups water
⅛ teaspoon kosher salt
1 cup long-grain brown rice, rinsed
2½ tablespoons extra virgin olive oil, divided
1 medium onion, diced into small pieces
2 carrots, trimmed, peeled and diced into small pieces
1 medium zucchini, trimmed and diced into small pieces
1 head broccoli or cauliflower, florets cut into bite-size pieces, stems peeled and sliced
¼ teaspoon salt
¼ cup frozen or fresh peas
¼ cup frozen or fresh corn
1 can black beans, drained and rinsed
2 tablespoons organic tamari soy sauce
4 ounces shredded cheddar cheese
Freshly ground black pepper
Salsa, homemade or store-bought
Sour cream
Chopped cilantro
Juice from 1 lime

In a 2-quart saucepan, bring 2 cups of water and ⅛ teaspoon of salt to a boil over medium-high heat. Add the rice, cover, and reduce the heat to a low simmer. Cook the rice until just tender, about 40 minutes. Fluff with a fork. Keep covered until ready to use.

While the rice is cooking, start the vegetables. Heat 2 tablespoons of oil in a large skillet over medium heat. Add the onions and cook, stirring occasionally, until soft and translucent, about 5 minutes. Add the carrots, zucchini, and broccoli and cook, stirring often, for 5 minutes. Season with ¼ teaspoon salt, gently stirring until well combined. Reduce the heat to medium-low and cook until the broccoli is crisp yet tender, about 12 minutes. Add the peas and corn, cover, and cook until tender, about 5 minutes.

Heat the remaining ½ tablespoon oil in a small saucepan over medium-low heat. Add the beans and cook, stirring occasionally, until heated through, about 5 minutes. Set aside.

Add the beans, vegetables, and tamari to the pot with the rice, stirring until well combined. Remove from the heat, sprinkle with cheese, cover, and let sit for 5 minutes. Adjust seasonings with additional soy sauce and salt and pepper to taste.

To assemble: Place the rice mixture into four serving bowls and top with salsa, a dollop of sour cream, and sprinkles of cilantro. Drizzle with lime juice.

Recipe from Pedalbarrow Farm
Photograph courtesy of Wood's Market Garden

Brotbakery

Heike Meyer grew up in Germany. Her love of baking was nurtured by her father, who spent every weekend in the kitchen baking. At a very young age, Heike developed a love of bread. When she was in kindergarten, she was already requesting crusty Vollkornbrot, a whole grain bread. During high school, she would bicycle across town to her favorite bakery to get a certain kind of bread, not minding that it was an hour-long ride.

In 2000, she moved to New York City and worked in the media business for several years. Finding the lifestyle very fast paced, she and her husband decided to buy some land in Vermont so they could enjoy nature and live a more sustained life by growing their own food. She missed the delicious sourdough and sprouted breads from her childhood in Germany, so she decided to build a bread oven and get back to baking. At first she and her husband just baked for themselves, but more and more people wanted to buy her bread. Eventually, they began selling the bread at a small farmers' market nearby.

The baking is done out of the couple's homestead in Fairfax, Vermont. They call the secluded 15 acres paradise, with its beautiful sunsets, chickens, honeybees, and family dogs. There's a large garden of herbs and vegetables, as well as a small grain field. Heike's baking philosophy is 100 percent organic, only naturally leavened breads using the best ingredients—no compromises! Brotbakery bread is delivered twice a week to the local food co-op and farm store.

At the Brot Bakehouse School and Kitchen, artisan baking and culinary classes are offered on weekends. The Brotbakery education project was launched in 2015 with anthropologist and food educator Anna Mays. Both women strongly believe in promoting the craft of artisanal baking, history and culture of regional specialties, and the centuries old techniques of culinary artisans from around the world, all of which they feel are at risk of dying out due to commercialization, industrialization, and standardization. Classes include narratives about the region of production, terroir, heritage of ingredients, and the history and culture that surround each bread, pastry, or dish.

Heike sources from local farms where the land, animals, and workers are treated with respect and integrity. She feels fortunate to live in a place where collaboration with like-minded people is a natural thing. Using non-GMO food is a no-brainer for her, and she can happily reassure her customers that when they eat her products nothing is genetically modified.

Every year, Heike travels to Europe and around the United States discovering traditions, researching new recipes, and learning new baking techniques. Of course, she is still baking flavorful crusty breads, such as sprouted and classic stone ground sourdough breads, Bierbot, Khorasan wheat bread, and buckwheat bread, along with pretzels, croissants, and some unusual pastries.

Heike supports farmers and mills that share her same philosophy when it comes to food, plants, and soil. When working as a member of a local food CSA, Heike saw firsthand that the work was long and exhausting, and she realized that with Vermont's climate the returns not to be taken for granted. As she wisely observes, "You gain a lot of respect for your food when you work on a farm!"

Photograph by Evi Abeler

Buckwheat Crackers with Black Walnuts

Makes approximately two 9-by-11-inch free-form crackers

"Buckwheat is often just used as a cover crop, but its taste in baked goods is marvelous! Groats can be toasted and used as whole grains or ground into fresh flour. Buckwheat provides a complete protein, which includes all the essential amino acids, and pairs nicely with nuts. Our neighbor here in Vermont grows black walnuts and kindly provides us with buckets full every year. They are a pain to crack, but incredibly delicious! We love them in this recipe, but also use whatever nuts may be found locally, such as hazelnuts, almonds, or regular walnuts." —*Heike Meyer, owner, Brotbakery*

1 cup whole kamut or rice flour
½ cup buckwheat flour
¾ cup black walnuts
½ cup minus 1 tablespoon ground flax meal
1 tablespoon organic cane sugar
1 teaspoon sourdough culture, such as King Arthur Flour's classic fresh or gluten-free sourdough starter
2 teaspoons aluminum-free baking powder
1½ teaspoons salt
¾ cup water
1 tablespoon distilled white vinegar
¼ cup olive oil
Sea salt
Fresh goat cheese, optional

Preheat the oven to 425 degrees Fahrenheit.

Process the flours, nuts, flax meal, sugar, sourdough culture, baking powder, and salt in a food processor until combined. Add the water and vinegar and blend on low speed until combined, about 30 seconds. While the machine is running, gradually add the oil, scraping down the sides of the bowl as needed, until the dough is fully combined, about 1–2 minutes. Divide the dough in half.

Place two 18-by-13-inch pieces of parchment paper on a clean work surface. Turn the first piece of dough out onto one piece of the parchment paper. Top with the second sheet of parchment paper and flatten with your hands, then roll the dough out in a free-form manner to ¼ inch thick. Carefully place the dough, along with the parchment paper, on a baking sheet, then carefully remove the top piece of parchment paper, leaving the bottom piece under the dough. Repeat with the second piece of dough. Bake until the crackers are golden brown, about 8 minutes.

When you remove a baking sheet from the oven, carefully place another baking sheet on top of it, sandwiching the cracker between the two sheets. Holding the sheets together with both hands at the edges, carefully flip them over so the cracker will gently land upside down on the surface of the second sheet. Carefully remove the top baking sheet and parchment paper, leaving the cracker on the new baking sheet. Sprinkle with sea salt to taste. Repeat this process with the second baking sheet. Return the baking sheets with the crackers on them to the oven and bake until the crackers are fully dry and golden brown around the edges, about 3–4 minutes.

Let cool completely, then break crackers into the desired size. The crackers may be stored in an airtight container for up to 1 week. When ready to serve, warm them in the oven at for 3–4 minutes at 400 degrees Fahrenheit.

Recipe from Brotbakery
Photograph courtesy of Evi Abeler

Note: The dough is very sticky and pieces will stick to the parchment paper. Using a small metal spatula, scrape the remaining bits of dough off the parchment paper, then carefully press the recovered bits of dough into the holes of the flattened dough.

CHAPTER 9

DRINKS

Salted Caramel Dark Sipping Chocolate

Makes 2 servings

"The fun thing about making the salted caramel sauce used in this dark sipping chocolate is that it has so many other applications! Use it as a topping for your favorite ice cream, stir it into your coffee, drizzle it over yogurt with bananas, or eat it with a spoon." —*Eliza La Rocca, co-owner, Farmhouse Chocolates + Ice Cream*

1⅔ cups whole organic cow's milk, or soy or nut milk
9 tablespoons high-quality cocoa powder
6 tablespoons organic cane sugar
⅛ teaspoon kosher or coarse sea salt
1 ounce organic Fair Trade chocolate, coarsely chopped
⅛ teaspoon pure vanilla extract
2 tablespoons salted caramel sauce **(see page 351)**, optional

In a 2-quart heavy-bottomed saucepan, bring the milk to a simmer, stirring occasionally, over medium-low heat. Using a wooden spoon or whisk, add the cocoa powder, sugar, and salt, stirring until well combined. Continue stirring until the sugar has dissolved, about 1 minute. Increase the heat to medium-high, scraping the bottom of the saucepan every couple of minutes to avoid scorching the milk. Remove from the heat. Add the chocolate and vanilla extract and stir until the chocolate has melted. Pour into 2 mugs and top with salted caramel sauce, if desired.

Recipe from Farmhouse Chocolates + Ice Cream
Photograph by Oliver Parini

Note: To make this recipe vegan, simply substitute water for the whole milk and leave out the caramel sauce.

Variations: Add freshly ground cardamom, nutmeg, cinnamon, or orange or lemon zest, to taste.

Butternut Mountain Farm

You might say that maple runs through the Marvin family's veins. Grandfather James Wallace Marvin, a research professor, dedicated his life to understanding the workings of sap flow in sugar maple trees. In 1953, he bought 600 acres of woodland in Johnson, Vermont. After graduating from college, his son, David, followed in his footsteps, purchasing land adjacent to his father's property in 1972. The next year he started tapping trees. Through the years, David and his wife, Lucy, have continued to acquire additional holdings, which today number somewhere in the neighborhood of 1,200 acres.

Local farmers have been selling their syrup to the Marvin family of Butternut Mountain Farm for 40 years. There have been many changes since David purchased his first 400 acres. Today, the 75,000-square-foot processing plant the family owns in Morrisville, Vermont, is one of the largest maple processors and distributors in the United States. Their facility and farm are certified organic, non-GMO, and kosher.

Forty years ago, the making of maple syrup was considered a hobby, most certainly not a way to make a living. Today, it is a shining star in Vermont's agricultural economy. David Marvin and his family, with their passion for maple, have worked hard and stayed committed in order to make their business endure and be successful. They now have a team of more than 90 employees who work with approximately 350 sugar makers and thousands of customers. The family has proven that you can indeed make a living from maple! Case in point, in 2016, Butternut Mountain Farm produced the most syrup ever, both in total number of gallons and pounds per tap.

Butternut Mountain Farm now handles more than 50 percent of Vermont's maple crop, although the farm itself produces less than 1 percent of the syrup that they process. David has a close relationship with the folks that he works with and stresses, "I've always thought it was better to collaborate and cooperate than to compete." The business has built its reputation on quality, service, and fair pricing. Because of this philosophy, they are helping to sustain local working forests and farmers.

The section of woods that David and his father cared for as seedlings 50 years ago was recently brought into production, which truly reflects the Marvin's stewardship of the land. The dedicated owner and his family feel an unbreakable connection to the land and its trees; making the farm productive is important, but the ultimate goal is sustainability.

Today, people are searching for natural, sustainably produced foods. Maple sweeteners fit this niche perfectly. The maple business is not just about syrup and candy anymore, now there's granulated maple sugar; syrup infused with cinnamon, vanilla, ginger, or chai; maple butter, mustard, barbecue sauce, pepper, and popcorn, showcasing maple at its best.

David and Lucy's children, Emma and Ira, are third-generation owners of Butternut Mountain Farm. Emma oversees the company's sales and PR department, as well as the retail store. Ira is responsible for the production side of things. David has pulled back a bit from the business end, but is still involved with all things maple while continuing to dedicate his days to preserving Vermont's forested landscape. The Marvin family firmly believes, "If we don't take care of the woodlands that supply us, we are not going to have a future," which is what the folks at Butternut Mountain Farm do each and every day.

Maple Grapefruit Margarita

Serves 4

This simple recipe is sweet, tart, and refreshing. Ice is welcome here to reduce the strength.

1 cup freshly squeezed pink grapefruit juice
½ cup freshly squeezed lime juice
1 cup orange liqueur, such as Cointreau
1 cup high-quality tequila
½ cup Grade A Dark Amber maple syrup
Granulated maple sugar or rock salt to rim glasses
Ice, optional
1 lime, cut into wedges

Chill 4 rocks glasses in the refrigerator.

Combine the grapefruit juice, lime juice, orange liqueur, tequila, and maple syrup in a pitcher and stir well.

Fill a saucer with about ¼ inch of maple sugar. Moisten the rims of each glass with a lime wedge. Press the rim of each glass into the sugar to rim the edges.

Fill the glasses with ice, if desired, and pour margarita into the prepared glasses; garnish with lime wedges and serve at once.

Recipe from Butternut Mountain Farm

Maple Milkshake

Serves 2

Pure Vermont maple syrup gives this recipe a decadently delicious twist on the classic vanilla milkshake.

1 pint high-quality vanilla ice cream
¼ cup organic whole milk
½ cup pure Vermont maple syrup
⅛ teaspoon salt
Whipped cream, optional

Blend together the ice cream, milk, maple syrup, and salt in a blender until smooth.

Pour into chilled glasses and top with a dollop of whipped cream, if desired. Serve immediately.

Recipe from Butternut Mountain Farm
Photograph by Oliver Parini

Strawberry-Basil Shrub

Makes about 4 cups

The word "shrub" comes from the Arabic *sharbah*, meaning "a drink." It is a fruit syrup preserved with vinegar and mixed with still or sparkling water or used as a cocktail mixer to create a tart yet refreshing drink. This recipe is the perfect way to use bruised, crushed, or overripe fruit. Store leftover shrub syrup in the refrigerator for up to 2 months.

1 pound fresh, very ripe strawberries or frozen, chopped
1 tablespoon chopped fresh basil, thyme, or mint
2 cups organic cane sugar
2 cups red wine vinegar or organic unfiltered apple cider vinegar
Club soda

Gently mash the strawberries and basil in a large bowl. Add the sugar and toss until well combined. Cover, and let sit at room temperature for 3 days, stirring once a day.

Using a fine-mesh strainer, strain the liquid syrup into a measuring cup, pressing the solids with the back of a ladle or spoon, discarding any solids.

Stir in the vinegar. Adjust taste with additional vinegar, if desired. Cover and refrigerate for 24 hours.

To serve: Mix 2 tablespoons of shrub syrup into an 8-ounce glass of club soda or water. Stir until well combined. Add ice, if desired. The shrub syrup may also be added as a cocktail mixer.

Recipe from Moonlight Farm
Photograph courtesy of Wood's Market Garden

Tonewood Twister

Serves 2

"As delicious as it is stylish, our pure maple sugar cube is the preferred option for adding a touch of sweetness to your favorite snack. A perfect cube that can be used to sprinkle some shavings over the top of oatmeal, fruit, or ice cream for a sweet delicate twist." —*Dori Ross, founder, Tonewood Maple*

3 ounces bourbon
1 ounce fresh lime juice
1 ounce pure maple syrup
Ice
1–2 ounces ginger beer
2 lime wheels
Grated maple sugar cube

Combine the bourbon, lime juice, and maple syrup in a cocktail shaker filled with ice. Shake several times. Strain into two glasses filled with ice. Top with ginger beer, to taste. Garnish with a lime wheel and grated maple sugar.

Recipe from Tonewood Maple
Photograph by Brent Harrewyn

Mad River Distillers

Mad River Distillers is the brainchild of a group of friends whose dream was to create an apple brandy that was native to their area of Vermont. John Egan, founder of the company and a lover of Calvados, the French apple brandy, volunteered to research apple brandy production. When Brett Little, who also shared John's passion for Calvados, came on board, the idea for creating a distillery at Cold Spring Farm was born. Brett is one of the company's founding members, as well as its chief distiller.

Cold Spring Farm, located in the heart of the picturesque Green Mountains in Warren, Vermont, dates back to the 1800s and was converted to a horse farm in the 1900s. Alex Hilton, who grew up in Warren, a stone's throw from Cold Spring Farm, was very familiar with the scenic location. Finding the scope of the project intriguing, Alex, a carpenter by trade, agreed to renovate the dilapidated old horse barn. The barn was transformed into a state-of-the-art distillery with the original horse stall doors, wall planking, beams, and hardware used whenever possible. Because of this attention to detail, the renovation took almost a year to complete, but the end result was well worth the effort. Alex continues to be part of the venture, and now serves as the company's general manager.

With Maura Connolly as co-founder and national sales director, the distillers began making Calvados-style apple brandy in 2011. Their flagship apple brandy, Malvados, is made with heirloom Vermont cider apples. In 2013, the business released its Mad River Rum and Corn Whiskey, soon followed by a Maple Rum. Bourbon was brought to the market in 2014 using locally sourced non-GMO corn. All spirits are distilled by hand from scratch in small batches, with a pure mountain spring on the property supplying the water for the fermentation process. As not all grains can be found in Vermont, some may be sourced regionally—non-GMO sources and Vermont ingredients are used whenever available. The sugar that is used in the rum is Fair Trade certified and sustainably harvested.

Mad River Distillery has a devoted team, which includes Mimi Buttenheim, who joined the staff in 2015 to serve as president. The company is hoping to expand its footprint with strong support from distillery assistants, Bennett Dee and Zack Fuller; Burlington retail store manager, Neil Goldberg; and Burlington marketing and events coordinator, Tristan Baribeau. All are committed to making high-quality, GMO-free spirits that highlight local producers and support sustainable agriculture.

The company's spirits are available at most Vermont liquor stores, as well as in Massachusetts, Connecticut, and Rhode Island. For those who would like to try a sampling before making a selection there are two tasting rooms, one in Burlington and one in Waitsfield, Vermont. During their visit, patrons can learn about distilling, shop for cocktail accessories, and taste samples of Mad River's spirits, which include Rye and Corn Whiskey, Bourbon, First Run Rum, Maple and Vanilla Rum, as well as the flagship brandy, Malvados. To view the whole process from start to finish, tours of the distillery are available by appointment. With a love of the science and art of distilling, the folks at Mad River Distillery are focused on producing high-quality spirits with character.

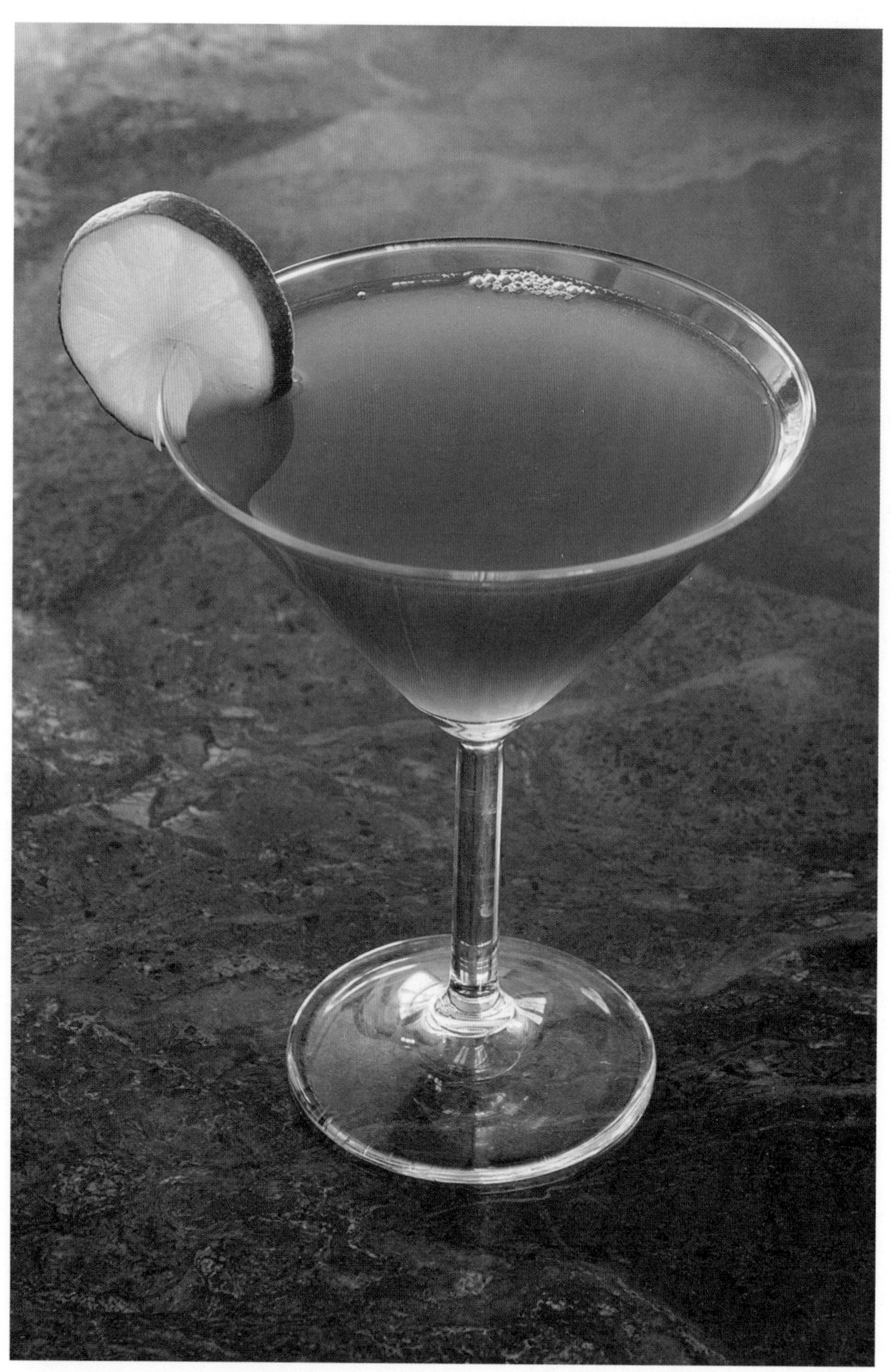

Jack Rose Cocktail

Serves 2

"Apple brandy is the original New England spirit. Upon arriving in North America, the traditional sources of starch and sugar for fermentation were hard to come by, and the apple proved hardy enough to thrive despite New England winters. Hard cider was consumed as a daily beverage from early colonial times. Seeking a more powerful product, New Englanders 'jacked' their cider by allowing the fermented juice to freeze, removing the ice to leave a more concentrated and alcoholic beverage behind. When stills were brought over by other immigrants, the cider was simply distilled into apple brandy. Because of the relative abundance of apples—and before the triangle trade brought in sugar products—apple brandy, or 'jack,' was the main source of distilled spirits in the colonies.

"Since Vermont is endowed with apple orchards and they represent part of our Green Mountain heritage, Mad River Distillers sources apples and cider locally, focusing on heirloom varieties to create the essence of Vermont, a salute to our state. We also use the apples from our farm—there are dozens of apple trees dotting the fields surrounding the distillery—a remnant of the Cold Spring Farm history.

"Our apple brandy is very 'fruit forward,' exactly how we had hoped when we sourced the still in Germany. We released our first limited batch of Malvados in October of 2014." *—Mimi Buttenheim, president, Mad River Distillers*

4 ounces Mad River Distillers Malvados Apple Brandy
2 ounces Small Batch Grenadine from Jack Rudy Cocktail Co.
1 ounce fresh lime juice
Ice
2 lime wedges, optional

Combine the apple brandy, grenadine, and lime juice in a cocktail shaker filled with ice. Shake several times. Strain into two coupe glasses. Garnish with lime wedges, if desired.

Recipe from Mad River Distillery
Photograph courtesy of Mad River Distillers

PROFILE

Vermont Switchel Company, LLC

Susan Alexander studied Forestry and Agriculture at Cornell University, so she believes that the job offer she received from the USDA Forest Service after graduation would be a good fit. As a child, she spent many family vacations in the Green Mountain State and was overjoyed at the prospect of returning. After marrying a sixth-generation Vermonter whose descendants had been dairy farmers, she realized that Vermont was to be her "forever" home.

For decades, the Alexander family and other dairy farmers kept themselves hydrated and energized during the summer's hot haying season by drinking quantities of a drink called switchel. In those days, every farmhouse had their own version of the drink, which was commonly called Farmers' Gatorade. Susan was first introduced to switchel at an Alexander family celebration many years ago. As she gleefully states, "For me, it was love at first sip!" The experience made her decide that she would one day bottle the refreshing, invigorating nectar so others could enjoy it. To realize this dream, she spent years researching, recipe testing, and sampling before she was satisfied with the taste, nutritional content, and ability to compete in the beverage market.

Susan was confident that her recipe could serve as a natural energy drink, sports drink, and a healthy alternative to soda. After all, she was using a recipe that had been in her husband's family for years, but with a modern twist. The original switchel recipe contained maple syrup, apple cider vinegar, ginger, and organic black strap molasses; Susan's inspired addition to the century-old recipe was organic lemon juice. She registered the product in 2008, and then began the organizational part of the project: hiring a graphic designer, and researching ingredients, bottles, caps, and boxes.

After much research, the busy entrepreneur felt there was a definite need for her product, largely due to our country's love affair with sugary drinks, which was contributing to an alarming increase in obesity and diabetes. Vermont Switchel is lower in sugar than most other sport and energy drinks, with the added benefit of anti-inflammatory properties, essential minerals, electrolytes, and antioxidants making it a healthy alternative. The maple syrup in the product adds a refreshing crisp, clean taste and is also non-GMO.

The Vermont Switchel Company is based out of Susan's home in Cabot, Vermont, with the real work being done at the Vermont Food Venture Center in Hardwick, where it is produced and warehoused. The product was first introduced at local farmers' markets, primarily because these locations appeal to the large number of tourists who travel from all over the country to try Vermont foods and products. The drink is now sold at markets, stores, and co-ops throughout New England and New York, as well as online.

Switchel is very versatile. Drink it cold when the weather's hot, and when temperatures drop, heat it up and add a cinnamon stick for a tasty, warming drink. Mix it with Vermont vodka or rum, or add it to your favorite recipe.

The folks at Vermont Switchel practice sustainability, helping to support Vermont's working landscape. Future plans include new flavor choices with the introduction of a concentrate that will require less packaging. The Vermont Switchel Company is happy with the increase in "loyal sippers" who enjoy a product that is part of our agrarian heritage.

The Hardwick Hooch

Serves 2

"Vermont Switchel has some of the finest neighbors in Hardwick. This cocktail is made with just three ingredients—all Vermont made and within 1,000 feet of each other." —*Susan Alexander, owner, Vermont Switchel Company, LLC*

4 ounces switchel
½ ounce Sumptuous Yellow Ginger syrup from Sumptuous Syrups of Vermont
2 ounces Barr Hill vodka from Caledonia Spirits
Ice
2 apple slices, about ⅛ inch thick

Combine the switchel, yellow ginger syrup, and vodka in a cocktail shaker filled with ice. Shake several times. Strain into two martini glasses. Garnish with apple slices.

Recipe from Vermont Switchel Company, LLC

PROFILE

Chai Wallah

Neil Harley, owner of Chai Wallah, has traveled extensively throughout the world. While backpacking in India, he had the opportunity to sample many cups of delicious chai freshly made on the spot by chai wallahs.

Chai is an authentic Indian spiced aromatic milky tea drink, also known as masala chai. Virtually a mainstay of Indian culture, chai is a blend of spices, most commonly cardamom, cinnamon, ginger, cloves, and black pepper. Having worked as a chef in the United Kingdom for many years, Neil felt at home in the kitchen when experimenting with and creating his own chai blend.

Chai Wallah is a Vermont certified organic processor using 100 percent organic spices and Fair Trade organic teas. Neil buys his spices whole and grinds them in small batches to maintain freshness and potency. All of the company's products are from India, Indonesia, and Guatemala. The business is run out of his home in Guilford, Vermont, and he hopes to move to a larger facility when space opens up.

This enterprising businessman has a website that sells chai spice on its own for those who prefer to add their own tea or use the spice to flavor hot chocolate, rice pudding, or homemade ice cream. For folks who like their spice in one mix, the spice blend is offered with a full-bodied 100 percent organic Fair Trade certified Assam tea. Other choices include green tea chai and caffeine-free rooibos chai. Products can be purchased at many local food co-ops throughout New England as well as from the company's website. After spending time in India and Nepal "sitting" with local chai wallahs, Neil returned to Vermont and perfected his five-spice chai recipe blended with various teas. All of his teas are the highest and freshest quality; at Chai Wallah you will find no back stock on the shelf losing flavor.

Hot Mulled Cider (Chai-der)

Makes ½ gallon

Leftover mulled cider can be stored in the refrigerator for up to 3 days. Gently reheat or serve over ice. For a deliciously simple holiday drink, add a generous splash of apple brandy, bourbon, or rum to each guest's mug.

- 2 tablespoons organic chai spice (not tea), such as Chai Wallah
- 1-inch piece of ginger, peeled and cut into thin slices
- ½ tablespoon orange zest (preferably from an unwaxed orange)
- ½ gallon fresh organic apple cider or unfiltered apple juice
- 1 orange, thinly sliced

Place the chai spice, ginger, and orange zest in a double layer of cheesecloth tied with kitchen twine. Set aside. Pour the apple cider in a gallon-size pot and bring to a near boil over medium-high heat. Turn off the heat. Add the chai spice sachet and steep, partially covered, for 15 minutes. Discard the sachet and strain the cider through a fine-mesh strainer into a clean pot or heat-resistant glass bowl. Ladle the cider into mugs and top with an orange slice. Serve warm.

Recipe from Chai Wallah Company

CHAPTER 10

DESSERTS

Fresh Raspberry Sorbet

Makes about 4½ cups

This light and fruity homemade sorbet is the quintessential summer crowd-pleaser—at its best when there's a bumper crop of freshly picked ripe raspberries from your garden, pick-your-own farm, or at your local farmers' market. "Simply said, this is one of my favorite summertime treats." *—Adam Hausmann, owner, Adams Berry Farm*

5 cups fresh raspberries
1¼ cups organic cane sugar
1 cup water, preferably filtered or distilled
1 teaspoon pure vanilla extract
2 tablespoons freshly squeezed lemon juice
Fresh mint leaves

Bring the raspberries, sugar, and water to a boil in a medium-size saucepan over medium-high heat. Reduce the heat to a simmer and cook until most of the berries have fallen apart, about 3 minutes.

Strain the raspberry mixture through a cheesecloth–lined fine-mesh strainer, pressing on the berries with the back of a large spoon, into a clean container to remove the seeds. When the berry mash is cool enough to handle, gather up the corners of the cheesecloth and gently squeeze out any excess juice into the container with the raspberry syrup. Add the vanilla and lemon juice, stirring until well combined. Refrigerate for at least 2 hours.

Pour the sorbet mixture into an ice cream maker and freeze according to the manufacturer's direction. Transfer the sorbet to a large airtight container and freeze until the sorbet is firm, approximately 3 hours. Scoop the sorbet into bowls and top each serving with a mint leaf.

Recipe from Adam's Berry Farm
Photograph (page 298) by Oliver Parini

PROFILE

Liz Lovely, Inc.

Liz Scott grew up spending summers with her grandmother in the Midwest. Young Liz spent many hours in her grandmother's welcoming kitchen helping to bake all kinds of delicious delights. The ingredients used were picked daily from the family's backyard garden. Each day would always end with a freshly baked dessert made from selections such as rhubarb, black walnuts, and a variety of juicy berries. Liz reminisces, "Just the smell of sugar being whipped with butter (now palm nut oil) takes me back to that wonderful time and place."

When Liz changed her eating habits to vegan, the one thing she missed, and craved most, each day was a really good cookie. Creating the perfect cookie for herself, as well as anyone else who was struggling with the same issues, became her passion. She started her business in a tiny apartment near Philadelphia, but soon outgrew the surroundings. After moving to Waitsfield, Vermont, Liz restarted her business, aptly named Liz Lovely. Her product seemed the perfect choice, as she explains, "Everyone loves cookies, they are an everyday indulgence you don't have to feel guilty about!"

As of May 2016, the company was comprised of 92 percent women. Liz clarifies, "Being a female-run company was a happy accident." Liz Lovely cookies are made with only the highest quality non-GMO ingredients. There are eight soft cookie flavors: Oatmeal Raisin, Cowgirl Chocolate Chip, Ginger Snapdragons, Snicker Dudes, Triple Choc Mint, Cowboy-Oatmeal Walnut Chocolate Chip, Peanut Butter Classics, and Chocolate Moose Dragon, plus four flavors of cookie truffles. The cookies are all made in small batches using artisan techniques and only the freshest ingredients, all of which offer the buyer a unique taste experience. The company only makes cookies that are certified non-GMO, kosher, vegan, and gluten-free. Liz feels that she is supporting Vermont's mission of eating fresh and eating local while also offering sustainable jobs and a product that is certified non-GMO.

The company self-sells and distributes their cookies, which can also be purchased online. Liz calls Vermont, "A beautiful, magical place with people who are independent thinkers and food that just tastes better." The perfect place for the Liz Lovely company to call home!

Pecan Tassies

Makes 24

Growing up, pecan tassies were a staple at Liz's house around the holidays. These yummy delights are the classic holiday cookie. Flaky pastry filled with gooey, sweet pecan pie filling—a mini pecan pie that can be eaten in one bite! Special tassie pans are needed for this recipe, but the end result is so worth the extra effort.

Dough

3 ounces cream cheese substitute, such as Tofutti cream cheese, at room temperature
⅓ cup plus 3 tablespoons organic red palm fruit oil*
1 tablespoon water
½ cup plus 2 tablespoons plus 1½ teaspoons rice flour
3 tablespoons plus 1½ teaspoons potato starch
1 tablespoon plus 2 teaspoons tapioca flour
½ teaspoon xanthan gum

Filling

1½ teaspoons Ener-G Foods egg replacer
2 tablespoons water
¾ cup organic light brown sugar
1 tablespoon organic red palm fruit oil*
1 teaspoon pure vanilla extract
⅛ teaspoon sea salt
⅔ cup chopped pecans
Rice flour, to flour the work surface

Position two racks in the upper and lower thirds of the oven and preheat to 325 degrees Fahrenheit. Set aside two ungreased tassie pans or two mini (1¾-inch diameter) muffin tins.

To make the dough: In the bowl of a stand mixer fitted with the paddle attachment, add the dough ingredients and beat on medium-high speed until dough just comes together. Scrape the dough onto a sheet of plastic wrap, flatten into a disk, and wrap in plastic wrap. Chill the dough in the refrigerator for 1 hour.

While the dough is chilling, make the filling. In a small bowl, add the egg replacer then slowly whisk in the water until smooth. With an electric mixer on medium speed, beat together the egg replacer mixture, sugar, oil, vanilla, and salt, until smooth, scraping down the sides of the bowl as needed.

On a lightly floured surface, roll the dough into 24 1-inch balls and press into the bottoms and sides of the cups in the tassie pans or mini muffin tins. Place ½ teaspoon of the chopped pecans into each cup. Spoon a slightly heaping teaspoon of the filling into each cup, then top the filling with approximately ½ teaspoon of pecans. Place the tassie pans on a baking sheet and bake until the filling begins to bubble and the cookies are set in the center, about 25 minutes. Let cool completely in the pans before carefully unmolding.

**Before using the organic red palm fruit oil, place the jar of oil in a pan of warm water for a few minutes. Pour the oil through a fine-mesh sieve to remove any seedy bits.*

Recipe from Liz Lovely, Inc.

Note: The tassies may be stored in a single layer in an airtight container for up to 1 week, or place in freezer bags or a plastic container and freeze for up to 1 month.

PB & Chocolate Whoopie Pies

Makes 45 pies

Liz loves bringing these delectable treats to a party. They are so much easier to transport than cupcakes, and everyone still gets their own personal cake. The irresistible combination of peanut butter and chocolate is sure to be well received, just don't plan to take home any leftovers!

Cookies

¾ cup plus 1½ tablespoons organic red palm fruit oil*
2 cups organic cane sugar
1 tablespoon Ener-G Food egg replacer
⅓ cup plus 1½ tablespoons water, divided
1 tablespoon white vinegar
2 cups almond milk
2 teaspoons pure vanilla extract
2⅓ cups rice flour
¾ cup potato starch
⅓ cup tapioca flour
1 teaspoon xanthan gum
1½ cups unsweetened cocoa powder, sifted
1 teaspoon salt
1 tablespoon baking soda
1 teaspoon aluminum-free baking powder

Filling

1⅓ cups creamy natural peanut butter
¾ cup plus 1 tablespoon plus 1½ teaspoons organic red palm fruit oil*
2 tablespoons plus 1½ teaspoons water
1½ cups confectioners' sugar

Position two racks in the upper and lower thirds of the oven and preheat the oven to 400 degrees Fahrenheit. Line two baking sheets with parchment paper. Set aside.

To make the cookies: In a bowl of a stand mixer fitted with the paddle attachment, add the palm fruit oil and sugar and beat on medium speed until fluffy.

In a small bowl, add the egg replacer, then slowly whisk in 1½ tablespoons water until smooth.

In a medium bowl, whisk together the vinegar and almond milk; set aside.

Add the egg replacer mixture, ⅓ cup water, vanilla, and almond milk mixture to the sugar mixture. Using the mixer guard, beat on medium speed until well combined. The mixture will have a curdled texture. Add the remaining dry ingredients and mix on low speed until well incorporated, scraping down the sides of the bowl as needed.

Scoop 45 tablespoon-size mounds of cookie dough and place them 2 inches apart on the prepared baking sheets. Bake until the cookies are puffed and spring back when touched, about 11 minutes. Cookies should be soft to the touch but not wet. Repeat until all the dough has been used. Using a metal spatula, carefully transfer the cookies to cooling racks and allow to cool to room temperature, about 30 minutes.

To make the filling: In a bowl of a stand mixer fitted with the paddle attachment, beat the peanut butter, palm fruit oil, and water on high speed until smooth and creamy. Add the confectioners' sugar and combine on medium speed. Mix once more on high speed until smooth and fluffy.

To assemble the pies: Spread a heaping tablespoon of the filling onto the flat side of 1 cookie. Sandwich a second cookie on top. Repeat with the remaining cookies and filling.

**Before using the organic red palm fruit oil, place the jar of oil in a pan of warm water for a few minutes. Pour the oil through a fine-mesh sieve to remove any seedy bits.*

Recipe from Liz Lovely, Inc.

Notes:

- This recipe makes more filling than you will need for the cookies. It can be used as icing for cupcakes.
- Cookies are best when eaten on the day they are made. To enjoy the most flavor, serve at room temperature. Cookies will keep for up to 2 days when refrigerated; make sure to place in a single layer in an airtight container. To freeze, individually wrap each cookie in plastic wrap and place in a freezer-safe bag or container. Allow frozen cookies to thaw in the refrigerator, then bring to room temperature before serving.
- Adding vinegar to the almond milk is a great vegan substitute for buttermilk.

PROFILE

Willow Brook Farm

Nathaniel "Nattie" Emmons and his wife, Molly Willard, grew up in Vermont, but they are relatively new to the farming business. They began their farming careers in 2014 with the establishment of Willow Brook Farm. Knowing that they had a lot to learn, the couple joined the Northeast Organic Farming Association's two-year Vermont Journey Farmer Program, which is designed to help new farmers learn the organic certification process, along with marketing and business management skills. Having an organic veteran from NOFA mentor them has been a tremendous source of support.

They are now certified organic, growing produce and medicinal herbs on 5 acres. Medicinal herbs are cultivated, processed, and stored differently than vegetables, allowing the farm an income that extends past the growing season. The farm offers CSA memberships, sells at the Peacham Farmers' Market, and has a farm stand outside of Peacham Village. There are two greenhouses located next to the family's home, with the majority of vegetables being grown a mile down the road near their farm stand. The owners also sell wholesale throughout the Northeast Kingdom. They focus on specific crops to meet consumer demand.

Molly is a botanist and teaches vegetable production at Vermont Technical College, while Nattie manages the farm. Molly reflects, "My parents always said that if you're going to live in Vermont, you're going to have to think about what it is you're going to be able to do to live in Vermont." Nattie and Molly Emmons seem to have done just that!

Apple-Raspberry Pie

Serves 8

"This is a family recipe that has been passed down from generation to generation. My great-grandmother would always make two pies when company would come to visit. One of the pies was a prank, its unpleasant taste causing her guests to wonder how to react politely. Then she would present the delicious pie that was intended for dessert. She loved to get a laugh!" —*Molly Willard, owner, Willow Brook Farm*

Crust

4 ounces unsalted butter, at room temperature
⅛ cup cold water
1¼ cups all-purpose flour, plus more for rolling
⅛ teaspoon kosher salt

Apple-Berry Filling

4 cups mixed fruit, such as 2 cups of apples (peeled, cored, and cut into ⅛-inch-thick slices), 1 cup of raspberries, and 1 cup of blueberries
¼ cup all-purpose flour
3 tablespoons pure Vermont maple syrup, such as Boney Woods Maple
1 tablespoon fresh lemon juice
⅛ cup organic cane sugar
2 tablespoons butter, cut into small pieces

Crumble Topping

¾ cup all-purpose flour
¾ cup organic cane sugar
¼ cup packed organic light brown sugar
½ cup rolled oats
1 teaspoon ground cinnamon
½ teaspoon freshly grated nutmeg
4 ounces cold unsalted butter, cut into small pieces

Vanilla ice cream, for serving, optional

Preheat the oven to 350 degrees Fahrenheit.

To make the crust: Place the butter in a medium bowl and, using your fingers, work the water into the butter until light and fluffy. Add the flour and salt and mix until a sticky ball of dough begins to form. Place a 14-by-14-inch piece of parchment paper on a clean work surface and sprinkle with flour. Turn out the dough onto the parchment paper and sprinkle with additional flour. Top with another sheet of parchment paper and roll out the dough into a 12-inch round. Transfer to a 9-inch pie pan and trim the excess dough, leaving ½-inch hanging over the edge of the pan.

To make the filling: Combine the fruit and flour in a large bowl. Stir in the maple syrup, lemon juice, and sugar until well combined. Pour the fruit into the pie crust and dot around the top of the pie with the butter pieces.

To make the crumble topping: In a medium bowl, combine the flour, sugars, rolled oats, cinnamon, and nutmeg. Using your fingers, work in the butter until the mixture is crumbly and forms pea-size lumps. Sprinkle the crumble topping evenly over the fruit.

Place the pie on a baking sheet and bake until the fruits are fork tender and the filling is bubbling, about 65 minutes. Transfer the pie to a cooking rack and let cool completely before serving. Serve warm with scoops of vanilla ice cream, if desired.

Recipe from Willow Brook Farm
Photograph by Oliver Parini

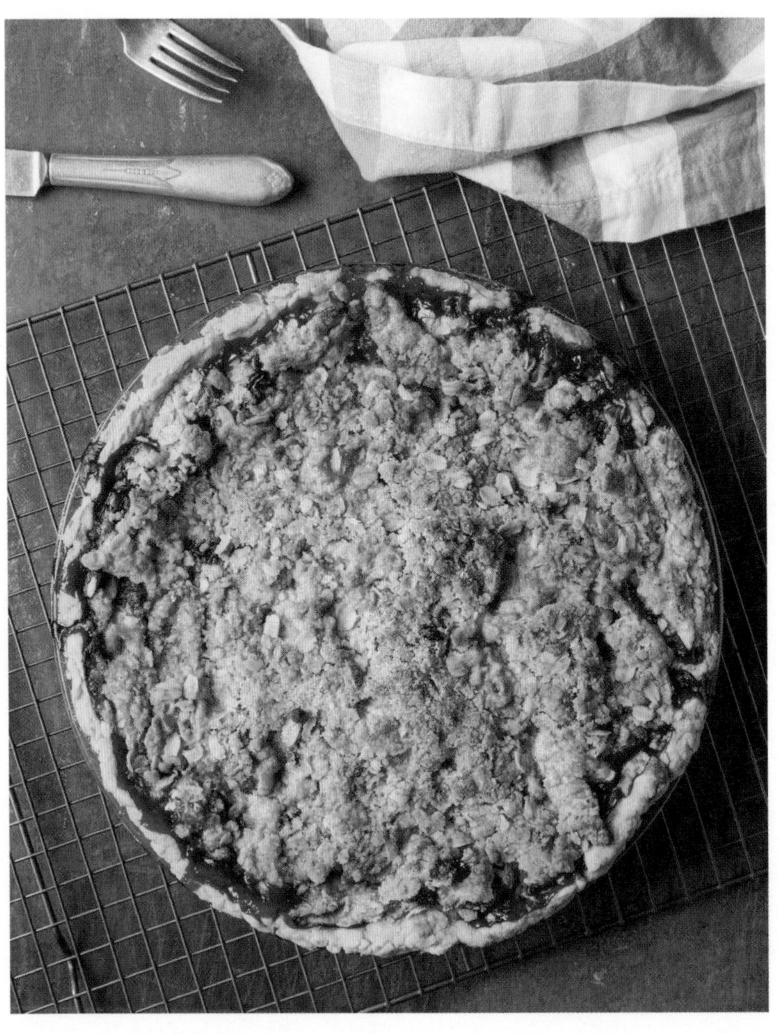

Walden Heights Nursery & Orchard

PROFILE

Walden Heights Nursery & Orchard specializes in certified organic heritage variety fruit trees, bushes, cold-hardy plants for orchards, and edible landscaping for home and garden. They offer hundreds of organic apple tree varieties, as well as pears, grapes, cherries, plums, hops, small fruit, and unusual fruits. Todd Parlo, owner of the nursery and orchard, grew up in the Finger Lakes region of New York, known as apple and grape country. His decision to move to Vermont was based upon the Green Mountain State's farming philosophies, which closely aligned with his own, supporting responsible stewardship of the land and promoting a landscape that is healthy for both people and the ecosystem.

Becoming an organic farmer worked well with Todd's ideology on how farming should be done. As he describes his choice, "I wouldn't say I became an organic farmer, rather I decided to farm according to my own ethics, [which] just happened to fit in the category labeled organic." His business is located in Caledonia County on land converted from a poor-quality forest. The 12 acres is home to hundreds of species of plants, including a test arboretum of approximately 600 apple varieties, a production apple and berry orchard, and a propagation nursery where the organic plants are created from seeds.

Todd's decision to grow fruit was predicated on need. He saw that the local farming community was doing little with growing apples and felt that his crop would fill this void with little competition. While the business is certified organic, they try to go beyond organic standards, with sustainability a major focus. The nursery does not utilize tractors, so there's no compaction of the soil due to heavy equipment. Few fossil fuels are used, plants are propagated on-site, and there's limited use of soil inputs since they fertilize with farm-produced compost.

Fruit and cider are sold at the farm and are included in the orchard's CSA. Walden Heights Orchard products are also marketed to restaurants, local stores, and co-ops. These co-ops have boldly tried the farm's aronia, gooseberries, or apple pear varieties, helping to expand the food horizons and health of those who buy them. As Todd says, "Food deserves respect in the healthy choices we make, the way food is produced, and the creativity we use when embracing its alchemy. Food is a wonderful pathway to discovery."

Sensible Sorbet

Serves 2–3

"The gist of this dessert is in creating both a delicious treat and a truly healthy addition to the diet. We chose the addition of high vitamin and antioxidant fruits like aronia, gooseberry, and red currant with traditional favorites like blueberry and blackberry." *—Todd Parlo, owner, Walden Heights Nursery & Orchard*

½ cup aronia berries
½ cup blueberries
½ cup gooseberries
½ cup blackberries
½ cup red or white currants
½ cup apple cider
¼ cup organic cane sugar
Fresh mint leaves

Bring the berries, apple cider, and sugar to a boil in a medium saucepan over medium-high heat. Reduce the heat to a simmer and cook until most of the berries have fallen apart, about 3 minutes.

Strain the berry mixture through a cheesecloth–lined fine-mesh strainer, pressing on the berries with the back of a large spoon, into a clean container to remove the seeds. When the berry mash is cool enough to handle, gather the corners of the cheesecloth and gently squeeze out any excess juice into the container with the berry syrup. Refrigerate for at least 2 hours.

Pour the sorbet mixture into an ice cream maker and freeze according to the manufacturer's directions. Transfer the sorbet to a large airtight container and freeze until the sorbet is firm, approximately 3 hours. Scoop the sorbet into bowls and top each serving with a mint leaf.

Recipe from Walden Heights Nursery & Orchard

Note: Cranberries can be substituted for aronia berries; the gooseberries can be replaced with rhubarb; and the currants can be replaced with raspberries—just adjust the sugar amount accordingly.

Heirloom Diversipie

Serves 8

"This pie is all about diversity in the main ingredient, that being apples. Instead of propping up America's staple with sweeteners, spices, and other such detriments, we supply the flavor with the pome. However, for those who prefer a sweeter pie, add maple syrup to the filling to suit your taste. In our orchard at Walden Heights, we have hundreds of apple varieties, but all of us have access to a wide selection every fall if we look around. Check the farmers' markets and online for availability." —*Todd Parlo, owner, Walden Heights Nursery & Orchard*

Crust

1½ cups organic all-purpose flour or organic white pastry flour
½ cup organic whole wheat flour or oat flour
2 tablespoons organic cane sugar
½ teaspoon salt
¾ cup organic lard or unsalted butter, cold and cut into small pieces
Ice water, as needed

Filling

8 assorted apples (about 3 pounds), such as russets, macs, and the nutty, peeled, cored, and cut into ¼-inch-thick slices (see page 313 for apple variety recommendations)
3 tablespoons organic all-purpose flour
2 tablespoons pure maple syrup, optional
¼ teaspoon ground cinnamon
⅛ teaspoon ground nutmeg
⅛ teaspoon salt
1 large egg, lightly beaten
Coarse sugar
Vanilla ice cream or whipped cream

To make the crust: Preheat the oven to 400 degrees Fahrenheit. Combine the flours, sugar, and salt in a large bowl. With a pastry cutter or your fingers, cut the lard into the flour until the mixture begins to form pea-size pieces. Add the ice water, 1 tablespoon at a time, as needed, mixing until the dough just comes together. Do not overmix. Turn the dough out onto a lightly floured work surface and form into two disks. Wrap in plastic wrap and chill in the refrigerate for 15 minutes.

On a clean, floured surface, roll one disk into a 12-inch round. Transfer to a 9-inch pie pan and trim the excess dough, leaving a ½-inch overhang.

To make the filling: In a large bowl, toss the apples, flour, maple syrup (if using), cinnamon, nutmeg, and salt until evenly coated. Spoon the apple mixture into the crust.

Roll the second disk of dough out on a floured surface into a 12-inch round and place it over the apple filling. Trim the excess dough along the edge, leaving a ½-inch overhang. Fold the edges of the dough under, then crimp to seal. Brush the top with the egg. Cut several slits in the top of the crust and sprinkle with coarse sugar.

Place the pie on a baking sheet and bake until the apples are tender and the filling starts to bubble, about 65 minutes. You may need to cover the perimeter of the crust with a foil collar to prevent it from overbrowning. Transfer the pie to a cooling rack and let cool completely. Serve with a scoop of ice cream or a dollop of whipped cream.

Recipe from Walden Heights Nursery & Orchard

Heirloom Apple Recommendations for Apple Pie

Haralson—This is the orchard's old standby, due not just to its nice sweet-tart balance, but because it keeps its shape nicely in baking. Arkansas Black and Grimes Golden will work as substitutes for body.

Sweet Sixteen—Think cherry lollipop and you will understand the taste in this one. Another option is a well-ripened Arlie's Redflesh, which presents a noteworthy watermelon flavor to the mix.

Russet—Most have a syrupy high sugar contribution in these rough-skinned fruits. We prefer Golden Russet, but Roxbury, Hunt, Jordan, and others will suffice.

The Redfleshed—Almata and Redfield are two varieites, but there are many. These add a blast of red color, more nutrition, and a welcome tartness.

Cox's Orange Pippin—A classic full-flavored English heirloom, citrus notes being just one of the undertones. Many of its offspring have similarities, like Kidd's Orange Red, Holstein, and Karmijn de Sonneville.

Ellison's Orange—This is one of a host of spicier apples, with the anise flavor predominating. Beacon and Fenouille Gris are others with this attribute.

The Fruity—Sunrise apple will show off its grape notes, Ribston Pippin its pear, Mantet or Chenango Strawberry their strawberry flavors, and Pitmaston pineapple its, well, pineapple.

The Nutty—Chestnut Crab, Hudson's Golden Gem, Orleans Reinette, Zabergau Reinette, and Pomme Gris are just a few that develop the rich flavor of nuts.

The Macs—The traditional heirloom mac will work here, but any of its progeny, like Niagara or Lobo, but particularly Fameuse, the parent and superior to McIntosh for flavor and adding a creaminess to the firmer apples in the recipe.

Note: In order to ensure you are obtaining GMO-free apples, choose both organic (organic standards prevent the use of GMOs) and heirloom or unusual apples, which are not slated by the industry for genetic modification. The first GMO apples released in the United States were the Arctic series, Golden Delicious, and Granny Smith. Next for release are GMO Fuji and Gala. Note that these are all popular run-of-the-mill varieties. Under United States law, sellers are not required to label them as genetically modified.

From Walden Heights Nursery & Orchard

PROFILE

Moonlight Farm

The owner of Moonlight Farm, Nate Lewis, believes that farms today are becoming more specialized, unlike the nineteenth and early twentieth century, when farming was a lot more diversified. A prime example of this theory is his farm in Waterbury Center, Vermont. His is a small operation that grows certified organic strawberries, blueberries, raspberries, and garlic. He also produces heirloom vegetable seeds as part of a movement to preserve genetic diversity and develop varieties that are well suited to the region. Most of his products are sold at Hunger Mountain Co-op in Montpelier, Pete's Greens in Waterbury Center, as well as via the Internet.

Nate's mother, a prolific gardener, encouraged him when he was young to spend time playing around her garden learning about different plants and how they are grown. When he was an Environmental Conservation major at the University of New Hampshire, he took a job at the organic farm on campus. While working there, Nate quickly learned that he had strong instincts for growing crops. After graduation, he went on to a full-time job at an organic farm north of Boston, where he learned the business side of farming. It quickly became apparent to Nate that he wanted to start a business of his own, with pastoral Vermont being the perfect place to do so.

After moving to Vermont, Nate and his wife, Chelsea Bardot Lewis, realized that there were already a lot of great farmers in the marketplace, so they set out to find their own niche, one that would allow their products to stand out from the rest. They discovered that garlic is well suited to the area, a staple that can be enjoyed almost all year long. The couple admit that growing organic fruit requires a great deal of work, but for them the end result makes it all worthwhile. They find it extremely rewarding to work with chefs who are passionate about the quality of the fresh strawberries, raspberries, blueberries, and garlic that the farm supplies them with. It gives the owners of Moonlight Farm a great deal of pleasure to know that their produce will be turned into memorable culinary adventures. The farm is certified by Vermont Organic Farmers, its owners dedicated to shepherding the organic movement into the next generation.

Blueberry-Almond Sour Cream Cake

Serves 8

This recipe comes from Nate Lewis's mother, who is a wonderful baker and gardener. Nate developed his green thumb by spending summers with her in their garden. The fresh blueberries keep this cake nice and moist. Serve the cake on its own or with a dollop of whipped cream. Any leftover cake should be covered and refrigerated.

Crust
6 tablespoons butter, softened
½ cup organic cane sugar
1 large egg
1 teaspoon pure vanilla extract
1 teaspoon pure almond extract
1½ cups all-purpose unbleached flour
2 teaspoons aluminum-free baking powder

Blueberry Filling
3 cups fresh or frozen blueberries
½ cup organic cane sugar
1½ tablespoons cornstarch
⅛ teaspoon freshly grated nutmeg

Almond Topping
2 large eggs
½ cup organic cane sugar
2 cups sour cream
1 teaspoon pure vanilla extract
1 teaspoon lemon zest (preferably from an unwaxed lemon)
⅓ to ½ cup thinly sliced almonds

Confectioners' sugar for dusting

Preheat the oven to 350 degrees Fahrenheit. Grease a 9-inch springform pan. Set aside.

To make the crust: In a medium bowl, cream the butter and sugar together with an electric mixer on medium speed until light and fluffy, scraping down the sides of the bowl as needed. Beat in the egg, vanilla, and almond extract until well blended, scraping down the sides of the bowl as needed. Stir in the flour and baking powder until the dough starts to come together. Continue to mix with your hands until you have a consistent dough. Press the dough firmly into the bottom of the prepared springform pan.

To make the blueberry filling: In a separate medium bowl, gently toss the blueberries, sugar, cornstarch, and nutmeg together. Pour the blueberry mixture evenly over the dough.

To make the almond topping: In a clean medium bowl, using an electric mixer on medium speed, beat together the eggs, sugar, sour cream, vanilla extract, and lemon zest until well

combined. Pour over the blueberry filling and smooth the top with a rubber spatula. Sprinkle the almonds evenly over the top.

Bake until the top is golden brown and the filling is set, about 55 minutes. Transfer the pan to a wire rack and allow the cake to cool completely.

To unmold the cake, run a knife around the edge of the pan to loosen and gently release the sides from the pan. Set the cake, supported by the springform base, onto a cake plate. Dust with confectioners' sugar and serve at room temperature or chilled.

Recipe from Moonlight Farm
Photograph by Oliver Parini

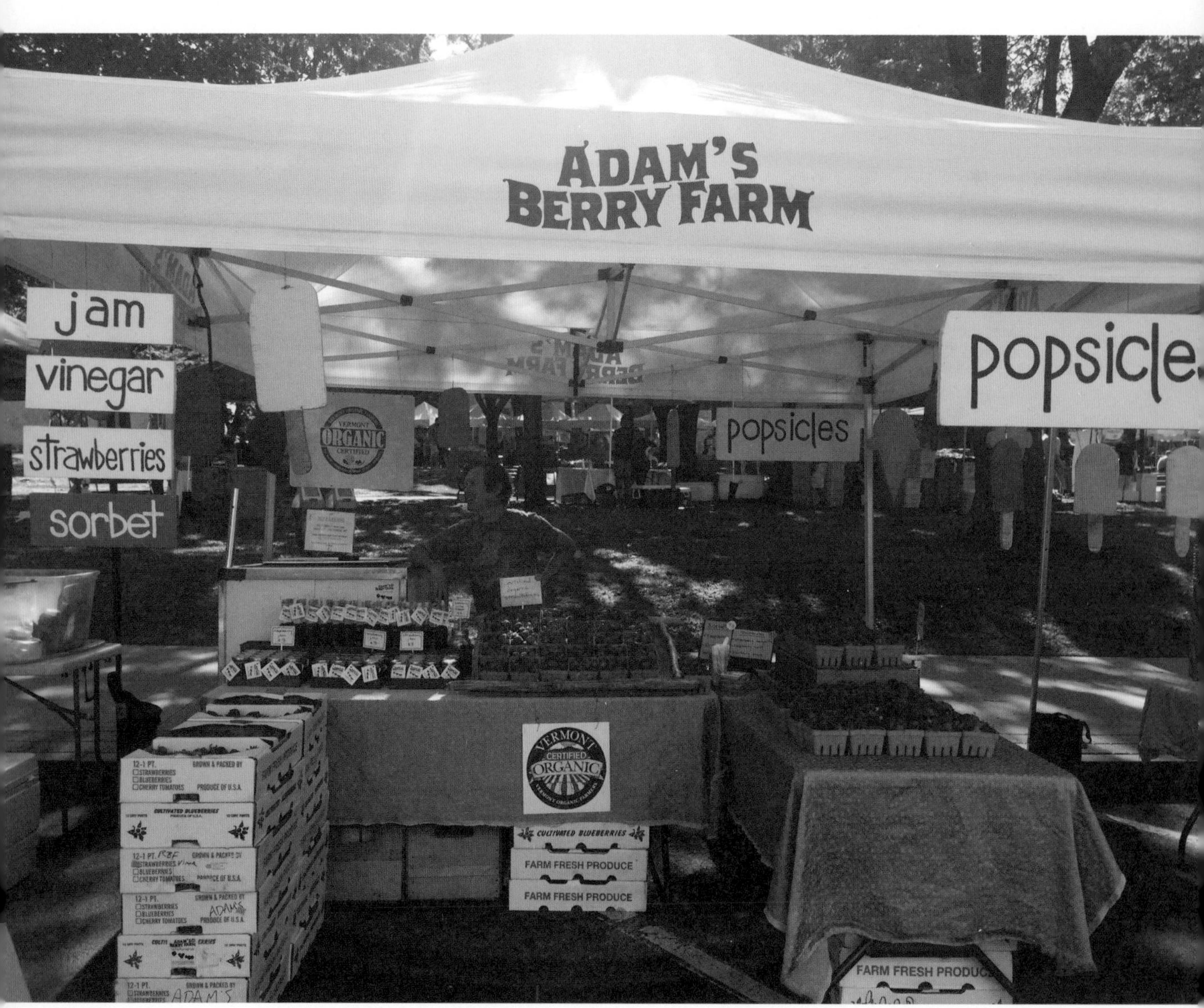
ADAM'S BERRY FARM
jam
vinegar
strawberries
sorbet
popsicles
popsicle
VERMONT CERTIFIED ORGANIC
CULTIVATED BLUEBERRIES
FARM FRESH PRODUCE
FARM FRESH PRODUCE

Adam's Berry Farm

In 2001, Adam Hausmann started his berry farming venture with a scant 300 plants. He soon learned that the growing season in Lincoln, Vermont, was "mouse-sized" and decided to expand his horizons to Burlington's Intervale Center, where he applied to be part of their farm incubation program. Problems with continual flooding and crop loss brought him to his current location in Charlotte, Vermont. Thanks to the help of the Vermont Land Trust and the Farmland Access Program, in 2012 Adam was able to purchase a piece of conserved farmland. The farm offers fertile soil and gorgeous views from its hilltop location, taking visitors back in time to yesteryear Vermont.

The focus of the farm is producing certified organic strawberries, raspberries, and blueberries. They also grow a variety of currants, gooseberries, kiwis, table grapes, and a small selection of stone fruits. For Adam, the goal of the farm is quite simple: to create a sense of community through food and berries. He greatly values the interactions and relationships with the people who purchase the farm's products and support its livelihood.

Adam says, it all comes down to the question of, "Would we want to eat it ourselves and feed it to our families?" This philosophy led to the use of certified organic practices. These efforts are rewarding to both Adam and his employees, who believe that the food we consume has a direct impact on the environment and the future.

The farm offers pick-your-own berries from June through the middle of October, an activity that is very popular with local families. Those who prefer to buy their berries from the farm stand can also find homemade chutneys, local honey, blueberry wine, vinegar, farm-made sorbets, frozen berries, multicolored eggs, and low-sugar jams. Ninety percent of Adam's berries are distributed within a 15-mile radius through restaurants and food markets and, during the growing season, at the Burlington Farmers' Market.

Adam and his employees enjoy the opportunity to interact with their customers, talking about the farm's organic growing practices and providing those who visit a chance to see a working farm in action. It is their belief that these interactions will encourage people to return to Adam's Berry Farm and buy directly from other farmers, farmers' markets, and local independent stores, thereby helping the Vermont economy to thrive. Adam works with a number of like-minded businesses that support sustainable agriculture and the thought process of knowing how your food is grown and where it comes from. He values his relationships with local restaurants and their creative chefs who never cease to amaze him with their adventurous spirit. For Adam and those at Adam's Berry Farm, the importance of local relationships within the food community is what it's all about: supporting local foods and an active working landscape for future generations.

Photograph courtesy of Adam's Berry Farm

ADAM'S
BERRY FARM

Homemade Strawberry-Lemon Fruit Pops

Makes 10–12 fruit pops

These pretty homemade fruit pops are fun to make! "This is one of the simplest and most popular pops we make for farmers' markets. It is always refreshing and it consistently brings joy to our customers faces." —*Adam Hausmann, owner, Adam's Berry Farm*

Simple Syrup

Makes approximately 1⅛ cups

¾ cup organic cane sugar

¾ cup water

Fruit Pops

4 cups fresh strawberries, hulled and coarsely chopped

¾ cup simple syrup

4 tablespoons freshly squeezed lemon juice

¼ teaspoon finely grated lemon zest (preferably from an unwaxed lemon)

6 strawberries, hulled and cut into thin slices, optional

To make the simple syrup: Pour the sugar and water into a small saucepan and bring to a simmer over medium heat. Remove from the stovetop and allow to cool completely.

To make the fruit pops: Puree the strawberries in a blender until smooth. Add the simple syrup and lemon juice in a slow and steady stream. Add the lemon zest and pulse until combined. Arrange 4–5 strawberry slices, if using, inside 3-ounce ice pop molds. Carefully, pour the strawberry puree into each chamber up to ¼-inch below the top of each mold. Cover and insert wooden sticks or spoons. Place them in the freezer and freeze until solid, at least 8 hours or overnight.

Recipe from Adam's Berry Farm

Photograph courtesy of Adam's Berry Farm

Strawberry-Rhubarb Crisp

Serves 5

"Each year, Woodbelly's first flush of catering events coincides with the ramps, trout lilies, and other wild greens appearing in the woods. Then the rhubarb and strawberries arrive and we make this dessert." —*David Huck, owner, Woodbelly Pizza*

Topping

2 tablespoons unsalted butter
2 tablespoons pure maple syrup
1 cup rolled oats
¼ teaspoon fine sea salt

Filling

2 tablespoons unsalted butter
Zest of ½ orange
Juice of 1 orange
7 ounces fresh rhubarb, diced into 1-inch pieces (about 1¾ cups)
2 tablespoons organic cane sugar
7 ounces strawberries, hulled (about 1½ cups)
1 teaspoon pure vanilla extract
⅛ teaspoon salt

Whipped cream or vanilla ice cream
Fresh mint leaves

Preheat the oven to 375 degrees Fahrenheit.

To make the topping: Melt the butter on a quarter-sized baking sheet or in an oven-safe skillet in the oven. Remove the baking sheet from the oven and add the maple syrup. Stir in the oats and salt until well combined. Return the baking sheet to the oven and toast the oats, stirring every 5 minutes, making sure to break up the mixture with a spatula each time, until golden brown and dry, about 15 minutes. Adjust the seasonings with additional salt and maple syrup, if desired.

To make the filling: Melt the butter in a medium saucepan. Add the orange zest and juice, rhubarb, and sugar and cook, stirring occasionally, until the rhubarb is fork tender but retains its shape, about 10 minutes. Remove from heat and allow to cool for 4 minutes.

While the rhubarb is cooling, prepare the strawberries. Cut the strawberries in half vertically, and then horizontally. Gently fold the strawberries into the rhubarb mixture. Stir in the vanilla and salt. Adjust seasonings with additional sugar and salt if desired.

To assemble: Evenly divide the fruit filling into five 4-ounce canning jars up to the collar line, then top with about 2½ tablespoons of the topping. Top with a dollop of whipped cream or a scoop of ice cream. Garnish with fresh mint leaves. Serve at once.

Recipe from Suzanne Podhaizer for Woodbelly Pizza
Photograph from iStockphoto.com

PROFILE

Champlain Valley Creamery, Ltd.

Champlain Valley Creamery is known for its certified organic award-winning cheese. The company produces a variety of cheeses, including fresh, soft-ripened and hard aged selections. Owner and head cheese maker Carleton Yoder started the business in 2003. He moved to Vermont after receiving a master's degree in food science from Virginia Tech. After making cider for six years, it became obvious to Carleton that a lifetime in the cider business was not for him. With cheese making as a minor hobby, he decided to embark on a career that had a local focus and started Champlain Valley Creamery. The company is located in Middlebury, Vermont's industrial park, its center of operations in a building equipped with solar panels that keep electrical consumption at net zero.

Carleton purchases the milk for his cheese from the Blissful Organic Dairy. The milk comes from a single herd of crossbred Jersey and Holstein cows in nearby Bridport, Vermont. He has been hauling milk from that farm back to his creamery in 10-gallon milk cans since day one. It is immediately processed with an impressive timeline of 25 minutes from cow to vat, and then to cheese by the end of the workday.

Most of the cheese is fresh and short-aged, so according to FDA rules it needs to be pasteurized. The company uses a low and slow method of batch, or vat, pasteurization. Champlain Valley Creamery is certified organic by Vermont Organic Farmers.

The company produces Old Fashioned Organic Cream Cheese, Organic Champlain Triple (a soft-ripened triple crème), Organic Queso Fresco (a traditional fresh Mexican cheese), Organic Smoked Queso (hickory-smoked fresh cheese), and Pyramid Scheme (an ash-ripened triple crème). Carleton and his small crew are always experimenting and hope to add more selections soon. Carleton says, "Cheese making is hard work, but we strive to let the milk, cream, culture, salt, and mold shine through. It is equal parts art and science."

Since his wife, Moira Cook, came on board in 2010, the business is now a family affair. Their cheeses are sold at retailers throughout New England and New York. Fresh from the farm to the table!

Old-Fashioned Organic Cheesecake

Serves 12

Champlain Valley Creamery's award-winning Old Fashioned Organic Cream Cheese is made without stabilizers or preservatives from cultured fresh organic cow's milk and cream. It has the perfect balance of creaminess and tanginess. It is delicious on bagels, as a sandwich spread, or simply on its own.

Graham Cracker Crust

2 cups finely ground graham crackers or cookies of your choice
6 tablespoons unsalted butter, melted

Cheesecake

1½ pounds Champlain Valley Creamery's Old Fashioned Organic Cream Cheese, softened
1 cup organic cane sugar
5 large eggs, room temperature
1 teaspoon freshly grated lemon zest (preferably from an unwaxed lemon)
1 teaspoon pure vanilla extract
¼ teaspoon salt
1 cup sour cream, room temperature

Whipped cream, optional
Assorted fresh berries, optional

Preheat the oven to 325 degrees Fahrenheit. Spray a 9-inch springform pan with nonstick cooking spray.

To make the crust: In a medium bowl, mix the graham cracker crumbs with butter. Press the cookie crumbs gently into the bottom of springform pan. Bake until the crust is firm, about 15 minutes. Transfer to a cooling rack and let cool to room temperature. When the springform pan is cool enough to handle, set the pan on a large piece of aluminum foil and fold up the sides around the pan. Set in a large roasting pan.

To make the cheesecake: With an electric mixer on medium speed, cream together the cream cheese and sugar, scraping down the sides of the bowl as needed. Add the eggs, one at a time, beating until just combined. Add the lemon zest, vanilla extract, and salt and beat until smooth, scraping down the sides of the bowl as needed. Fold in the sour cream. Pour the filling over the crust and smooth the top with a rubber spatula.

Pour enough hot water in the roasting pan to come halfway up the sides of the springform pan. Bake for 30 minutes, rotate the roasting pan a half-turn, and bake for an additional 30 minutes. The cheesecake's center will slightly jiggle when you gently shake the pan.

Let the cheesecake rest in the turned-off oven for 40 minutes with the oven door slightly ajar. Carefully remove the cake from the water bath and let cool completely on a cooling rack. Loosely cover with plastic wrap and allow to chill in the refrigerate for at least 4 hours or overnight.

To unmold the cheesecake, run a hot, thin, non-serrated knife around the edges of the pan to loosen and gently release the sides from the pan. Set the cheesecake, supported by the springform base, onto a cake plate. Top with fresh berries and a dollop of whipped cream, if desired, and serve.

Recipe from Champlain Valley Creamery. Ltd.
Photograph by Oliver Parini

PROFILE

Revolution Kitchen

Each time Debra and Peter Maisel visited their children at college in Burlington, Vermont, the couple would puzzle over the absence of vegetarian eateries in the area. As restaurant owners themselves, they believed that there would be strong support for a higher-end vegetarian establishment in that community. After their daughter graduated from college and decided to remain in the Green Mountain State, the couple opted to move to Vermont as well. Utilizing their twenty years of experience preparing vegetarian dishes in the five restaurants they have owned, the Maisels opened their sixth restaurant in 2013, their first in Vermont. The Revolution Kitchen is located in the heart of bustling Burlington. Peter, a graduate of the Natural Gourmet Institute in New York City, and Debra, a self-taught baker and chef, are happy to be part of the lively downtown scene.

The restaurant's menu is vegetarian and vegan friendly. Dishes are inspired by Asian flavors and Vermont ingredients with daily specials that include Thai, Spanish, Mexican, and Italian selections. The menu is constantly changing in order to bring diners fresh, organic, and natural ingredients sourced from local food producers. The couple believes in the importance of cooking with produce that is grown without the use of pesticides, "clean food."

Revolution Kitchen is stylishly decorated with graceful, welcoming decor. The open kitchen offers guests a rare opportunity to observe the culinary process at work, allowing the wafting scent of searing vegetables to give diners a preview of the day's delicious, healthy dishes. Guests can choose from a variety of starters, salads, sandwiches, and dinners. The dessert menu changes nightly, reflecting the season's bounty. It is interesting to note that one of the dessert favorites at Revolution Kitchen is their banana cream pie, a scrumptious delight that took Debra many years to perfect.

Debra and Peter believe in crafting food that guests of their restaurant feel good about eating. To this end, they are using the very best ingredients that Vermont has to offer and, in the process, changing the way people view vegetarian fare. You don't have to be a vegan or vegetarian to appreciate the cuisine at the Revolution Kitchen; many an omnivore may be found enjoying one of their savory creations. Drop by and see for yourself!

Maple Vanilla Cake with Almond Buttercream Frosting and Maple-Candied Pecans

Serves 10–12

Spelt is an ancient strain of wheat with a unique nutty, complex flavor that is slightly sweeter and milder than whole wheat. Spelt flour has a great nutritional profile—packed with protein, fiber, and a complex of B vitamins.

Cake

3½ cups organic spelt flour
2 cups organic raw sugar
2 teaspoons baking soda
¼ teaspoon salt
1 cup canola oil
1½ cups almond milk
½ cup pure maple syrup
2 teaspoons pure vanilla extract

Skillet Maple-Candied Pecans

Makes 1 cup

1 cup pecan halves
¼ cup pure maple syrup

Almond Buttercream Frosting

1½ cups vegan buttery sticks, such as Earth Balance, softened
4½ cups organic confectioners' sugar, sifted
2 teaspoons pure vanilla extract
3 tablespoons almond milk

Preheat the oven to 350 degrees Fahrenheit. Lightly grease two 9-inch round cake pans and line with parchment paper. Set aside.

In a large bowl, sift together the flour, sugar, baking soda, and salt.

In another large bowl, whisk together the oil, milk, maple syrup, and vanilla extract until well combined. Stir into the dry ingredients until just combined, being careful not to overmix.

Pour the batter evenly into the prepared pans and smooth the tops with a rubber spatula.

Bake until a toothpick inserted into the center comes out clean, about 25 minutes. Set the cake pans on a cooling rack and let cool completely before frosting.

To make the skillet maple-candied pecans: Heat a dry medium-size skillet over medium heat. Add the pecans and maple syrup and cook, stirring constantly, until the syrup starts to crystallize and stick to the pecans. Pour the nuts onto parchment paper and let cool and harden for 15 minutes.

While the pecans are cooling, make the frosting. In the bowl of a stand mixer with the paddle attachment, whip the butter substitute on medium speed for 7 minutes, scraping down the sides of the bowl as needed. Add the sugar, vanilla extract, and milk and mix on low speed, scraping down the sides of the bowl as needed, until just blended. Increase the speed to medium and continue to whip until light and fluffy.

When the cakes have completely cooled, place the first cake, top-side up, on a cake stand. Using a spatula, spread 1 cup of the frosting evenly over the top and just beyond the edge of the cake, adding more frosting as needed. Place the second layer on top, top-side down. Frost the top and sides of the cake. Top with caramelized pecans.

Recipe from Revolution Kitchen
Photograph by Brent Harrewyn

PROFILE

Four Springs Farm

Located on a west-facing hillside in the town of Royalton, Vermont, you'll find picturesque Four Springs Farm. Owner Jinny Hardy Cleland purchased the 70 acres in July of 2001 with plans to create an organic farm with a strong learning component. The farm is named after the year-round springs that are found on the property.

Organic fruits, vegetables, and herbs are the central part of the farm. These are sold directly to locals through a CSA program, a farmers' market, and several area stores. The farm's beautiful greenhouse-grown pansies, early harbingers of spring, are offered for sale to the public. Additional flower varieties, herbs, and vegetables are grown for farm use. The meat and eggs from organically raised poultry are used in the farm's Buttermilk Bakery and WildBerry Catering businesses. The bakery is primarily in operation during the winter months, when the workload on the farm has lessened. Jinny loves to bake a variety of cookies, delicious rolls, and bread, which she sells to a few local stores and those folks who stop by to place an advance order.

In 2009, the farm started WildBerry Catering, a licensed kitchen that offers meals to small groups that visit the farm to camp or attend one of the farm's events. Under the umbrella of WildBerry Catering is found a line of jams and jellies. Both the catering company and the line of jams and jellies feature ingredients that are grown at Four Springs or neighboring farms.

Enhancing the overall mission of the farm is the campground and learning center that opened in 2004. The center welcomes the public to visit and see what is happening on small farms today. Four Springs's Immersion Experiences are two-week residential programs for high school students that offers a hands-on approach to learning about a homesteading lifestyle, including how to grow and harvest crops and care for livestock.

Families are invited to stay in the rustic cabins found on the property or set up camp at one of the tent sites. Spectacular views while being one with nature in a quiet New England retreat—the perfect formula for a vacation to remember!

Clabber Rhubarb Cake

Makes two 8-inch round cakes

"Clabbering milk is very easy, but it must be done with raw milk, not pasteurized milk, because the pasteurization process kills off the bacteria needed to make the milk clabber. To get raw skim milk, allow the milk to sit in the fridge for a day, then skim off the cream layer that rises to the top. To clabber the skim milk, leave it in the fridge for 10 days, shaking every now and then. Little beads will start to form in the milk. When the beads are suspended in the milk and are clearly seen through the side of the jar, the milk is clabbered. A faster way to do it is to allow the skim milk to sit out on the counter for 2–3 days at room temperature. The milk will start to clabber more quickly. After clabbering, the milk can be refrigerated again for up to a week or so before use. In a pinch, you can substitute buttermilk or sour cream for soured raw milk." —*Sarah Strauss, recipe tester*, The Vermont Non-GMO Cookbook

½ cup shortening
1½ cups organic brown sugar
1 large egg
2 cups organic all-purpose flour
1 teaspoon baking soda
¼ teaspoon ground ginger
1 cup soured (clabbered) raw skim milk
½ teaspoon finely grated lemon zest (preferably from an unwaxed lemon)
1 tablespoon fresh lemon juice
1 teaspoon pure vanilla extract
2 cups fresh finely chopped rhubarb
Organic confectioners' sugar
Vanilla ice cream or whipped cream

Preheat the oven to 350 degrees Fahrenheit. Lightly grease and flour two 8-inch round baking pans with nonstick cooking spray. Set aside.

In a large bowl, using an electric mixer on medium speed, cream together the shortening and brown sugar until smooth. Add the egg, scraping down the sides of the bowl as needed and beating until just smooth.

In a medium bowl, sift together the flour, baking soda, and ginger. In a third bowl, combine the milk, lemon zest and juice, and vanilla. Add the dry ingredients alternately with the milk mixture to the sugar mixture and beat until smooth. Fold in the rhubarb. Pour the batter into the prepared pans and bake until the tops are golden brown and a toothpick inserted into the center of the cakes comes out clean, about 45 minutes.

Let the cakes cool in the pans on a cooling rack for 20 minutes. To unmold, run a knife around the edges of the pans to loosen the cakes. Set the cakes on cake plates. Dust with confectioners' sugar. Serve cake with a dollop of whipped cream or a scoop of vanilla ice cream.

Recipe from WildBerry Catering at Four Springs Farm

PROFILE

Lake Champlain Chocolates

Jim Lampman, founder of Lake Champlain Chocolates (LCC), has always had a passion for chocolate. As a restaurant owner in the early 1980s, he would frequently buy fancy chocolates as holiday gifts for his staff. When his pastry chef confessed that he thought the chocolates were far from perfection, Jim challenged him to do better. He did, and the rest is history. The hand-rolled truffles that were created as a result of this dare had a rich chocolaty flavor that the others failed to equal in taste and quality. Soon thereafter, Jim realized he was about to embark on an exciting new chapter of his life.

Within a year, the restaurant was sold and LCC was created in 1983, and Jim, after all this time, still considers it a sweet labor of love. The company began with a small group of people who were willing to work for chocolate. They launched their venture with truffles, then expanded the product line to include: Chocolates of Vermont, Five Star Bars, sea salt caramels, hot chocolate, organic chocolate, and the ever-popular Chocolate of the Month Club. All of their chocolate is kosher certified and Fair Trade.

Growing from a small factory selling truffles wholesale to a few specialty stores, in 1998 the company moved to a 24,000-square-foot facility on Pine Street in Burlington, Vermont. LCC believes in using a craftsman's approach to chocolate, which requires creativity, patience, and mastery for each handmade piece. The company introduced European flavors and tastes, using Vermont ingredients to create chocolates that rival those made in Belgium and Switzerland. They are committed to using non-GMO ingredients. For the past 30 years, the company has made it their mission to find the best and freshest ingredients from local farmers and producers. LCC never adds preservatives, extenders, or additives to any of its chocolates.

In March 2013, LCC earned "Fair Trade for Life - Social and Fair Trade Certification." Fair Trade means that the best ingredients are sourced from trusted partners, each person in this process being treated and compensated fairly. The company's organic chocolate bars are the first of their products to be labeled Fair Trade Certified. Determined to make a difference, LCC has relationships with cacao growers in Guatemala and the Dominican Republic, working with them to improve the quality of the cacao they produce as well as their livelihoods.

Today, LCC products are found in 2,000 specialty stores, natural food co-ops, gift shops, upscale hotels and inns, as well as at the company's three Vermont retail stores. The family-owned business recently transitioned to the second generation—siblings Eric Lampman and Ellen Lampman Reed now serve as president and vice president, respectively. The Lampman family recognizes that, "The choices we make affect people, our product, and our planet; as a result, we are committed to developing more organic products and to source only non-GMO ingredients." By doing so, the LCC family is striving to make an impact on local and global communities. *Theobroma cacao*, the scientific name of the cacao tree, means "food of the gods." Without a doubt, one taste of Lake Champlain Chocolates will prove that to be oh so true!

The Ultimate Chocolate Cake

Serves 10

"This cake really is the ultimate, especially when frosted with our Mocha Buttercream Frosting. Our favorite organic Fair Trade unsweetened cocoa powder is Dutch-processed for optimal baking, which simply means its acidity had been reduced so it can impart nothing but serious full-chocolate flavor and color. The Mocha Buttercream Frosting is devilishly good, particularly when applied liberally to this cake! **Note:** There are no eggs in this recipe." —*Meghan Fitzpatrick, PR and communications, Lake Champlain Chocolates*

Cake

3 scant cups all-purpose flour, plus extra for flouring pan
2 cups organic cane sugar
1 cup organic unsweetened baker's cocoa powder
2 teaspoons baking soda
1½ teaspoons salt
2⅓ cups warm water
1¼ cups unsalted butter, melted, plus extra for greasing pan
2 tablespoons distilled white vinegar
2 teaspoons pure vanilla extract

Mocha Buttercream Frosting

1 cup unsalted butter, softened
4 cups organic confectioners' sugar
½ cup organic unsweetened baker's cocoa powder
2 teaspoons instant coffee granules dissolved in ¼ cup hot water, slightly cooled

Preheat the oven to 350 degrees Fahrenheit. Butter and flour a 10-inch tube pan. Set aside.

To make the cake: In a large bowl, sift together the flour, sugar, cocoa powder, baking soda, and salt.

In a medium bowl, whisk together the water, butter, vinegar, and vanilla. Stir into the dry ingredients until just combined, being careful not to overmix. Pour the batter into the prepared pan and smooth the top with a rubber spatula. Set on the middle rack in the oven and bake until a toothpick inserted into the center comes out clean, about 50 minutes. Allow the cake to cool in the pan for 10 minutes, then unmold and allow to cool completely before frosting.

To make the frosting: In the bowl of an stand mixer with the paddle attachment, whip the butter on medium speed for 7 minutes, scraping down the sides of the bowl as needed. Add the

sugar, cocoa powder, and 2 tablespoons of coffee and mix on low speed, scraping down the sides of the bowl as needed, until just blended. Add additional coffee to taste, if desired. Increase the speed to medium and continue to whip until light and fluffy.

Recipe from Lake Champlain Chocolates
Photograph by Oliver Parini

Runamok Maple

Eric Sorkin and his wife, Laura, moved to Vermont in 1999 with the desire to start an organic farm in a state that supported the type of agriculture they believed in. It was truly culture shock for the two suburbanites, who at first struggled to adapt to a rural way of life that was completely foreign to them. Now suburbia seems light-years away, and their home, which is tucked away in the middle of the woods, is accepted as the most natural way to live one's life.

After nine years of farming, the Sorkins needed a change. Because of the excellent sugar bush found on their property, they saw more opportunity with maple than farming. The decision was made to switch from vegetables to maple syrup, one of Vermont's greatest products.

The business, Runamok Maple, is located on the western slope of Mt. Mansfield, the state's highest mountain. Co-owners Eric and Laura both have degrees in environmental management and share a strong conservation ethic that blends beautifully with their company and ecology. Eric has built the business from the ground up with support from Laura, who divides her time between raising their children, growing a few commercial crops, and her career writing about food and farming.

In the maple industry, folks work all year long preparing for approximately 20 good sugaring days. Out of these days, there are only two or three sap runs that result in the most prized syrup of the season. Throughout the sugaring season, the flavor of the syrup varies due to temperature, moisture, and other acts of nature, which necessitates constant tasting to determine when the syrup has reached the peak of flavor. Since this is usually the syrup that sugar makers bottle for themselves, it is called "the sugar maker's cut."

Depending upon the time of year, the company employees 10–20 workers. To obtain the pure maple syrup, this busy team must tap 81,000 trees by hand, repeating the process each year. It requires about six weeks to make a year's worth of product, so there's no time for sleeping on the job. One season, the crew managed to get 2,000,000 gallons of sap out of the trees and to the sugarhouse—an unbelievable act of teamwork! Note that it takes about 40 gallons of sap to make 1 gallon of maple syrup.

Runamok produces nine different flavors of maple syrup in addition to their Sugarmaker's Cut. They have created a collection of infused, smoked, and barrel-aged maple syrup and are constantly working on new recipes to highlight the unique flavors in their product. One of their gift boxes, which contains bottles of Bourbon Aged, Cinnamon Vanilla Infused, and Hibiscus Infused syrup, was selected as one of Oprah's Favorite Things in 2016. Their products are sold online and in specialty stores.

All of Runamok's products are real maple—no artificial flavors or preservatives are added. Everything is organic, created in small batches using only the best ingredients. They are certified organic by Vermont Organic Farmers and are the first sugar bush to have their woods certified Bird-Friendly by Audubon Vermont.

Photograph by Oliver Parini

Maple Pudding

Serves 6

"I am often asked what the best application for maple syrup in cooking is, and the answer is easy: pair with dairy. Butter, milk, cream, even yogurt, bring out the best in maple. Maple pudding is an excellent example of how much maple and cream elevate each other. Serve it with an oatmeal or cinnamon cookie and you have the best maple-dairy-nirvana delivery system I can think of."
—Laura Sorkin, co-owner, Runamok Maple

2 cups whole milk, divided
1 cup heavy cream
1 cup pure maple syrup
⅛ teaspoon salt
¼ cup cornstarch
2 large egg yolks
3 tablespoons unsalted butter
1 teaspoon pure vanilla extract
Whipped cream
Cookies

Pour 1 cup of milk, the cream, maple syrup, and salt into a medium saucepan, whisking until well combined. Cook this mixture over medium heat until it just begins to steam, about 8 minutes, then turn off the heat.

Place the cornstarch in a medium bowl. In a slow and steady stream, whisk in the remaining cup of milk until the cornstarch mixture is completely smooth. Whisk in the egg yolks until well combined. In a slow and steady stream, whisk in 1 cup of the hot milk mixture into the egg mixture to temper them. Slowly whisk the egg mixture into the remaining hot milk mixture on the stovetop. Whisking constantly, cook the mixture over medium-low heat until it thickens to the consistency of a thick cake batter, about 7 minutes. Remove from the heat and whisk in the butter and vanilla until well combined. Ladle the mixture into six 6-ounce ramekins. Cover each ramekin with plastic wrap, making sure the plastic wrap is touching the top of the pudding. Let cool to room temperature, then chill in the refrigerator until completely cooled and set, at least 2 hours or overnight. Top with a dollop of whipped cream and serve with a cookie of your choice.

Recipe from Runamok Maple
Photograph by Oliver Parini

Note: If you like skin on your pudding, do not cover with plastic wrap before cooling in the refrigerator.

PROFILE

Vermont Raw Nut Butter

Seo Lee, the owner of Vermont Raw Nut Butter, was born and raised in South Korea. Moving with his family to Virginia in the 1980s, he grew up seeking a countrified lifestyle. Feeling that the state of Vermont would offer him the way of life he desired, Seo moved to the Green Mountain State in 1999 after graduating from college. During his first five years in Vermont, he worked on a certified organic vegetable farm and became an avid consumer and supporter of organic and local products.

He decided to start his own business in 2010, launching the Vermont Raw Nut Butter Company, which now produces six varieties of raw nut butter. The products include Tahini (made with 100 percent raw certified organic sesame seeds), Almond, Peanut, Cashew, Macadamia, and Coconut Raw Nut Butter. Each selection contains 100 percent raw certified organic nuts. All of the nut butters have only one ingredient, except for the Macadamia Butter, which has a little cashew butter added for texture.

A granite stone grinder is used in the process, mashing the nuts for 8–10 hours at a time. Due to the nature of the granite that is used during this procedure, the temperature never rises above 98 degrees Fahrenheit. This method produces a product that is creamier and smoother than typical nut butter products. Vital essential fatty acids, minerals, and other important nutrients remain intact.

Seo supports the non-GMO movement and personally stands behind every one of his products. His raw nut butter has no added trans fats and is 100 percent vegan and gluten-free. Seo's products are being used by a number of Vermont chefs and may also be found at various juice bars in the Burlington, Vermont, area, as well as at Healthy Living and various farm stores throughout the state.

Maple Cashew Butter Balls

Makes about 48

These delicious, melt-in-your mouth little white cookies have a crumbly, nutty texture! They are quite fragile and need to be treated carefully when being covered with sugar.

2 cups almond flour, plus extra for rolling the balls
1 cup Vermont Raw Nut Butter Cashew Butter
¼ teaspoon sea salt
1 cup unsalted butter, cut into small pieces, softened to room temperature
3 tablespoons pure maple syrup
½ teaspoon pure vanilla extract
1 cup organic confectioners' sugar

In the bowl of a stand mixer with the dough hook attachment, mix the flour, cashew butter, and salt on medium speed until well combined; the mixture will have a crumbly texture, about 3 minutes.

Using an electric mixer on medium speed, cream together the butter, maple syrup, and vanilla until fluffy. Add this to the cashew butter mixture and mix until just combined.

Scrape the paste-like dough into a medium bowl, cover with plastic wrap, and chill in the refrigerator until firm, at least 1 hour.

While the dough is in the refrigerator, preheat the oven to 300 degrees Fahrenheit. Line 2 baking sheets with parchment paper and set aside.

Using lightly floured hands and working in small batches, quickly roll out the dough into 1-inch balls. Place the balls 1 inch apart on the prepared baking sheets. **Note:** A lightly floured disher scoop with a volume of 1 tablespoon or 2 lightly floured tablespoons also works well to form the dough into balls.

Bake until the cookies feel dry on the outside but still soft on the inside, about 25 minutes. Allow the cookies to cool on the baking sheets for 10 minutes.

While the cookies are cooling, place the confectioners' sugar in a shallow pie pan. Working in batches, place the cookies in the pie pan and carefully coat them evenly with the sugar. Transfer to a cooling rack to cool completely. Sprinkle with additional sugar, if desired, and serve.

Recipe from Vermont Raw Nut Butter

Dark Chocolate Almond Butter Cups

Makes 12

These almond butter cups are a great twist on an old classic. The dark chocolate is filled with antioxidants, and the orange zest provides a subtle citrus undertone.

Cups

7 ounces organic dark chocolate 70% Cacao, coarsely chopped

Virgin coconut oil cooking spray

Filling

½ cup Vermont Raw Nut Butter Almond Butter
2 tablespoons honey
2 tablespoons pure maple syrup
1½ teaspoons finely grated orange zest (preferably from an unwaxed orange)
½ teaspoon pure vanilla extract
¼ teaspoon plus ⅛ teaspoon Himalayan fine pink salt, divided
1 tablespoon organic peanuts, crushed

Place the chocolate in a microwave-safe bowl and melt in the microwave in 30-second increments, stirring in between, until melted and smooth, about 2 minutes.

Line a 12-cup mini muffin tin with mini paper liners. Lightly spray the liners with cooking spray. Set aside.

Spoon about 1 teaspoon of the chocolate into the bottom of each liner. Using a small pastry brush, evenly coat the cupcake liners with chocolate. Place in the freezer until the chocolate has hardened, about 10 minutes.

While the chocolate is hardening, make the filling. Using an electric mixer on medium speed, mix together the almond butter, honey, maple syrup, orange zest, vanilla, and ⅛ teaspoon of salt, until smooth.

Spoon 1 heaping teaspoon of the almond butter mixture into each muffin cup and smooth the tops with the back of a spoon.

Top with another 1½ teaspoons of chocolate over the top of each muffin cup, making sure to completely cover with chocolate.

Sprinkle the remaining ¼ teaspoon of salt evenly over the top of the cups. Garnish each with peanuts. Refrigerate until set, at least 30 minutes.

Store in a covered container at room temperature or refrigerate.

Recipe from Vermont Raw Nut Butter

Note: The filling makes more than you will need for the butter cups. Spread the extra filling on toast, pancakes, or waffles.

Sweet Potato Pie

Serves 8

This sugary, custardy dessert has a lighter and more airy texture than its pumpkin pie relative! Garnish with a dollop of crème fraiche for a hint of tangy creaminess.

Pie Filling

3 sweet potatoes
Extra virgin olive oil
1 14-ounce can sweetened condensed milk
¼ cup organic brown sugar
2 eggs, lightly beaten
2 tablespoons freshly squeezed orange juice
1 teaspoon cinnamon
1 teaspoon ground ginger
½ teaspoon salt

Graham Cracker Crust

1½ cups graham cracker crumbs (about 10–12 graham crackers)
3 tablespoons organic brown sugar
½ teaspoon ground ginger
⅛ teaspoon kosher salt
5 tablespoons unsalted butter, melted
Crème fraiche, optional

Spray a 9-inch pie pan with nonstick cooking spray and set aside. Preheat the oven to 425 degrees Fahrenheit. Line a baking sheet with foil. Set aside.

To make the pie filling: Rub the potatoes with oil. Place the potatoes on the prepared baking sheet. Season with salt and pepper to taste. Using the tines of a fork, pierce the potatoes 6–8 times. Bake until the potatoes are fork tender, about 50 minutes. Let the potatoes rest for 10 minutes, then slice in half and scoop out the flesh into a medium bowl. Add the condensed milk, brown sugar, eggs, orange juice, cinnamon, ginger, and salt. Mash with an old-fashioned masher until smooth. Adjust seasonings with salt to taste.

While the potatoes are baking, make the graham cracker crust. Place the graham crackers, brown sugar, ginger, and salt in a food processor and pulse until well combined. While the machine is running, add the butter in a slow, steady stream until well combined.

Preheat the oven to 350 degrees Fahrenheit. Press the graham cracker mixture gently into the bottom and sides of the prepared pie pan. Carefully pour the potato filling over the crust and smooth the top with a rubber spatula. Bake in the oven until the pie has set, about 45 minutes. Allow the pie to cool to room temperature before cutting. Serve with a dollop of crème fraiche, if desired.

Recipe from JJ Hapgood General Store & Eatery

Tip: The pie filling makes more than you will need for this recipe. Ladle the leftover filling into lightly greased ramekins right under the rim. Place on a baking sheet and bake at 350 degrees Fahrenheit, uncovered, until puffed and firm to the touch, approximately 20 minutes. Garnish with a dollop of crème fraiche. Serve warm with your favorite cookie.

PROFILE

Vermont Village Cannery

Back in the 1970s, a group of community-minded Vermonters began sourcing apples from abandoned apple orchards—apples that grew wild, tended by the seasons and weather. These folks developed a cooperative in 1975 and started making cider and batches of applesauce in their communal kitchen, selling the products locally. After a while, a community cannery was built in Barre, Vermont, with the help of local grant money; all products that passed through the facility were FDA approved.

As the natural food market began to change in the 1990s, evolving into the organic food movement, the cannery adapted with the times. The Vermont Organic Farmers' Group spearheaded the development of the country's first natural organic certification program, which led to the cannery being certified as an organic processor in 1996. When it became apparent that a worker-owned cooperative was no longer financially feasible, the Vermont Village Cannery was born, with new investor-owners coming on board. During this period, the company introduced its new line of certified organic applesauce, apple cider vinegar, and apple butter. The apples they use are GMO-free, high-quality fruit that is grown for its superior flavor.

The business is committed to producing a product that supports local organic farmers and the environment. The fruit that is used is grown without the use of chemical fertilizers, synthetic pesticides, or herbicides. Each year the cannery is inspected by a third-party USDA-certified organic inspector, with all aspects of the process carefully examined to ensure compliance with organic standards.

At the cannery, applesauce is made in small batches the old-fashioned way, cooked in small kettles using the whole apple, including the peel. There is no water or sugar added to this process. The applesauce is gluten-free and kosher certified and does not contain tree nuts, peanuts, or preservatives. The Vermont Village Cannery is a strong supporter of the state's GMO labeling law, believing that consumers should have the right to know what is in their food. Their products are sold in co-ops and grocery stores throughout the region and beyond—just look for the Vermont Village Organic label.

Oatmeal Raisin Cookies

Makes about 3 dozen

To reduce the fat in these cookies, natural applesauce was substituted for some of the butter.

1¾ cups quick cooking oats
1½ cups all-purpose flour
1 teaspoon aluminum-free baking powder
1 teaspoon baking soda
1 teaspoon salt
1 teaspoon ground cinnamon
¼ teaspoon ground nutmeg
½ cup unsalted butter, softened, plus extra for greasing baking sheets
1 cup packed organic brown sugar
½ cup organic cane sugar
1 egg, lightly beaten
¾ cup unsweetened applesauce, preferably Vermont Village
1 cup semi-sweet chocolate chips
1 cup raisins
1 cup chopped walnuts

Preheat the oven to 375 degrees Fahrenheit. Lightly grease three baking sheets. Set aside.

In a medium bowl, stir together the oats, flour, baking powder, baking soda, salt, cinnamon, and nutmeg.

Using an electric mixer, in a large bowl, cream together the butter and sugars on medium speed until fluffy. Add the egg and applesauce, scraping down the sides of the bowl as needed, beating until well blended. Add the flour mixture, mixing until well combined. Fold in the chocolate chips, raisins, and walnuts.

Drop the dough, about 2 tablespoons per cookie, 3 inches apart on the prepared baking sheets. Bake until light golden brown, about 10 minutes. Allow the cookies to cool on the baking sheets for 5 minutes, then transfer to cooling racks to cool completely.

Recipe from Village Cannery of Vermont
Photograph by Emily Esslinger

Farmhouse Chocolates + Ice Cream

Erlé LaBounty is a Vermonter through and through. This was never more evident than when his family moved down the road from his grandfather's dairy and thirteen-year-old Erlé took on the responsibility of trekking to the farm each day after school to lend a hand. After graduating from his high school's culinary program in 1999, he decided to forego family tradition and pursue his love of cooking, making a life-changing decision to attend the New England Culinary Institute in Montpelier, Vermont; he graduated in 2001.

Holidays were always an occasion for Erlé to pursue his favorite pastime, making chocolates. He loved working with chocolate, helping his mother create beautifully molded delicacies for family members and friends. This passion led to the founding of his company, Farmhouse Truffles, in 1998. The business was named in honor of his grandparents' farmhouse, the place where his chocolate making career began.

Eliza La Rocca met Erlé when she moved to Woodstock, Vermont, to work with authors, restauranteurs, and vintners Deirdre Heekin and Caleb Barber; Erlé had worked for Deirdre and Caleb for six years when he was fresh out of culinary school. Eliza and Erlé married in 2012, and she began helping with various aspects of the chocolate company. Her hard work and perseverance have transformed the small part-time business into a full-time operation. She has been the driving force behind the ice cream portion of the company, and thus the change to the current company name, Farmhouse Chocolates + Ice Cream. The focus on ice cream began when Eliza decided to create a chocolate sorbet to sell at local farmers' markets during the hot summer months. The refreshing, cold sorbet was a totally awesome idea that turned out to be a huge success.

The sorbet's triumph led them to invest in new specialty equipment and a relocation to their own commercial kitchen, one that is large enough to accommodate all of their production needs. Here the couple can create their handmade small-batch products, with enough space left over for retail sales. Using organic milk and non-GMO cream from local farms, local eggs, and seasonal produce, Eliza pasteurizes each batch in-house, crafting each flavor from start to finish. The kitchen facility is located in the town of Bristol, Vermont, not far from scenic Lake Champlain.

Erlé continues to create superior chocolates using the finest local and seasonal ingredients combined with organic, Fair Trade, soy lecithin-free dark chocolate. La Rocca and LaBounty have carefully crafted their packaging to feature recycled, compostable, and recyclable materials.

The owners of this wonderful company are doing their utmost to support the local economy. Simply stated, their mission is: "At Farmhouse Chocolates + Ice Cream, we live to bring joy to our customers by making chocolates, ice cream, and sorbets that are simple but sublime, using the highest quality local and organic ingredients. We're not in it to get rich, we're in it for the love of good, beautiful things, carefully sourced and made with love—blow-your-mind, make-your-day, lift-your-spirits treats made from real food!"

Salted Caramel Sauce

Makes about 3¼ cups

This sauce is delicious drizzled over ice cream, flan, or coffee. "You can keep the salted caramel sauce in your refrigerator for up to 2 months if kept in the back, where it's the coldest. My husband and I are both pretty trim, and we always make our caramel products with butter and cream. You are making caramel sauce; it's not supposed to be healthy! We strongly recommend using local, full-fat ingredients." —*Eliza La Rocca, co-owner, Farmhouse Chocolates + Ice Cream*

1 stick salted butter, sliced into ½-inch-thick pieces, at room temperature
2 cups organic cane sugar
1¼ cups organic or local, non-GMO heavy cream, warmed
¾ teaspoon coarse sea salt
¼ teaspoon pure vanilla extract

In a 2-quart heavy-bottomed saucepan, melt the butter over medium heat. Using a wooden spoon, add the sugar and stir just enough so that it does not clump or stick to the bottom of the pan. Continue stirring every 30 seconds or so, until the sugar has completely melted and the caramel turns a light amber color, about 10 minutes. Carefully remove the saucepan from the heat and in a very slow and steady stream add in half of the cream while whisking vigorously. Carefully and slowly whisk in the remaining half of the cream until thoroughly combined. Stir in the salt and vanilla. Adjust seasonings with salt to taste.
Enjoy immediately or refrigerate for later use.

Recipe from Farmhouse Chocolates + Ice Cream
Photograph by Oliver Parini

Note: Allow the caramel sauce to come to room temperature before refrigerating. You can make the caramel sauce in advance, just warm it up in the microwave or on the stovetop prior to adding to your sipping chocolate.

Vermont Amber Organic Toffee

Elizabeth Feinberg started making toffee as a holiday gift for teachers, friends, and family back in 2005. Much to her surprise, folks continued to ask her to bring the delicious toffee to parties, dinners, and all manner of occasions. They just couldn't seem to get enough of the yummy treat! When people began inquiring where they could buy her toffee, an idea blossomed and the decision was made to commence experimenting with new toffee flavors to test the retail market and determine if her confections would generate a positive response.

During a toffee tasting and sharing event held at a local store, a helpful grocery manager told Elizabeth, "Make your toffee organic, and I will put it on the shelf." Since the business was new, the change to organic was a relatively easy process . . . and the rest is history!

Vermont Amber Organic Toffee is made from a few simple ingredients: organic butter, organic evaporated cane juice, organic brown rice syrup, and kosher salt. Its creator acknowledges that she uses a savory approach when making her product: quite simply, remove the chocolate, spread the toffee thin, and add flavor. She is very grateful for her two daughters, who do a lot of the taste testing.

The company offers a variety of scrumptious flavors: Salted Sesame, Pumpkin Seed Chipotle (some kick to this one), Coconut, Cacao Nib, Ginger Cookie, Tomato Terrific, and No Bits Just Plain Toffee. The company's signature toffee, Fennel Seed, received the 2017 Good Foods Award for Confections. This award celebrates confections that are produced using locally grown, natural, minimally processed ingredients.

Elizabeth, her two daughters, and an assortment of four-legged friends call White River Junction, Vermont, home. Her company is based at the Hotel Coolidge in White River Junction's cozy downtown area. Elizabeth emphasizes that she strives to keep Vermont Amber Organic Toffee a local business, staying true to creative organic food and her farmers' market roots. The toffee is sold at various markets and co-ops throughout the state and may also be found at the Woodstock Farmers' Market and Dan & Whit's Country Store in Norwich, Vermont.

The creator of Vermont Amber Organic Toffee has traveled quite a distance from her pastry chef and schoolteacher beginnings to where she finds herself today, a Good Foods Award winner who makes an organic toffee product that keeps folks coming back for more. Elizabeth loves the challenge of creating new flavors, adding complexity to simple ingredients that are crafted in small batches. These crispy, crunchy pleasures give their creator a chance to "express her culinary point of view" by making a certified organic product that delights the taste buds. As those who have sampled Vermont Amber Organic Toffee say, "Once you start eating it, it's impossible to stop!"

Organic Cacao Nib Cookies

Makes about 74

"Smoked salt is preferred however; coarse sea salt or kosher salt is a fine substitute. Alternatively, dough may be rolled into a log to slice and bake at a later time. It will keep refrigerated for up to 10 days, or freeze for longer storage." *—Elizabeth Feinberg, owner, Vermont Amber Organic Toffee*

1½ cups cacao nibs
2½ cups organic all-purpose flour
¾ teaspoon baking soda
1 cup organic unsalted butter, at room temperature
1½ cups organic cane sugar
1 tablespoon organic pure vanilla extract
1 teaspoon coarse sea salt, such as smoked sea salt
2 large organic eggs
1 tablespoon finely grated fresh zest from 1 large orange or clementine

Preheat the oven to 375 degrees Fahrenheit. Line two baking sheets with parchment paper. Set aside.

Heat a medium skillet over medium heat. Add the cacao nibs and toast, stirring occasionally, for 5 minutes. Set aside to cool. Once cooled, place the cacao nibs in a zipper-lock bag and lightly crush with a rolling pin or heavy can or jar.

In a medium bowl, combine the flour and baking soda. Set aside.

Beat the butter on medium speed until fluffy. Add the sugar, vanilla, and salt and cream together on medium speed until smooth. Add the eggs, one at a time, scraping down the sides of the bowl as needed, beating until well blended. Add the flour mixture in three batches, mixing the cacao nibs and zest into the last batch of flour. Mix on low speed until well combined.

Scoop up the dough into small balls using a tablespoon-size scoop. Place the balls onto the prepared baking sheets about 3 inches apart. Bake until light golden brown, about 12 minutes. Allow the cookies to cool on the baking sheets for 5 minutes, then transfer to cooling racks to cool completely.

Recipe from Vermont Amber Organic Toffee

La Garagista Farm + Winery

With their mission to care for the land in creative and natural ways, the owners of La Garagista Farm and Winery share in and support the food and agriculture of their Barnard, Vermont, community. Their land, which is located on Mount Hunger, is part of a small homestead that has been farmed for more than 200 years. The property is now used to produce alpine wine and apple cider.

Owners Caleb Barber and Deirdre Heekin care for the farm and its diverse agriculture, growing vegetables, fruits, flowers, nuts, and herbs for the past 19 years. They also grow hybrid grapes, which are a cross between vinifera grapes and hardier native American species, for their winery. The home farm contains a small cultivated apple orchard and several wild apple trees. The fruit from these trees is used for making cider.

About 17 apple varieties are involved in cider production, resulting in their farmhouse-style cider. The farm's cider is made in the same way that farmers made theirs many years ago—having a barrel of cider and drawing from it during the year, and when there was a little left in the bottom of the barrel, they would add new juice on for the next vintage fermentation. This process would go on each year, creating a mixture of all the vintages. Following this same formula, the farm's first vintage was created in 2010, and each subsequent year they have added another. It took seven years to release their first cider.

Deirdre is a self-taught sommelier, first making wine at home in 2006 as part of an educational experiment. In 2007, she purchased and planted 100 vines obtained from a small Vermont nursery, and the winery was born. La Garagista Winery opened its doors in 2010 with the creation of its first vintage wine. The couple happily shares tasks and responsibilities; Deirdre is wine grower, organizer, writer, photographer, flower farmer, and designer. Caleb, on the other hand, is the gardener, cook, builder, mechanic, and philosopher. The couple's varied interests and skill sets play off each other, creating a winning combination.

Along with the home farm vineyard, they also lease and farm two vineyards in the Champlain Valley, one outside of Vergennes and another in West Addison. Time is divided between the three vineyards, taking into consideration the different needs of each. The winery does both single varietal wines and blends, but only within each particular parcel; fruits from different vineyards are not blended. This method is used to highlight the difference between the parcels and the character of each terroir. The wines themselves are an expression of the season and may show variations within the same vintage. The winery makes approximately 12 different cuvees, a mixture of sparkling and still, red, white, orange, and rosé.

Biodynamic methods are used for growing, which incorporate organic, permaculture, companion planting, and soil regeneration. The owners work from the soil up, developing the natural flora in their vineyards to help improve soil health. With much hard work, ingenuity, and dedication, Deirdre and Caleb have taken their wines from the vineyards of Vermont to the markets of New York, Boston, California, Montreal, and the United Kingdom. The next step is to keep up with the growing demand for their very popular wines.

Photograph from iStockphoto.com

Torta con l'Uva (Grape Cake)

Serves 12–15

"The two of us come at this recipe from different sources of inspiration. Deirdre is reminded of a luncheon at an old domaine in Champagne during the 1950s, a story told in an old book about that region; the luncheon ended with a grape tart. I am always reminded of a small store in Piemonte, Italy, where we ate this cake that had apples baked into it. It was a beautiful cake to behold, simple and delicious. We serve it during our wine harvest—for breakfast, after lunch, as an afternoon pick-me-up, when the grapes at our home farm are plentiful and ripe. I tend to gravitate toward black grapes with seeds, although we often use thinly sliced apples for a variation." —*Caleb Barber, co-owner, La Garagista Farm + Winery*

2 cups all-purpose flour, plus extra for flouring pans
2 tablespoons aluminum-free baking powder
1 teaspoon salt
½ pound butter, softened, plus extra for greasing pans
1½ cups organic cane sugar
5 large eggs, whites and yolks separated
4 cups fresh wine grapes or Concord grapes, destemmed, rinsed, and dried

Preheat the oven to 375 degrees Fahrenheit. Butter and flour a 10-by-15-inch sheet cake pan, shaking off any excess flour. Set aside.

In a medium bowl, combine the flour, baking powder, and salt. Set aside.

In the bowl of a stand mixer, cream together the butter and sugar on medium speed until light and fluffy. Add the egg yolks and beat, scraping down the sides of the bowl as needed, until well combined. Add the flour mixture and mix on medium-low speed until well combined.

In a medium bowl, beat the egg whites with an electric mixer on high speed until stiff peaks form. Fold gently into the batter in three additions, leaving the last addition of whites just mixed in; the batter should be very streaky with the eggs whites.

Pour the batter into the prepared pan—the batter should be no more than ½-inch deep—and smooth the top with a rubber spatula. Evenly distribute the grapes over the batter, then gently press them all the way to the bottom of the pan. The batter will come up about halfway up the grapes.

Place the pan in the center of the middle oven rack and bake until the cake turns a nice golden color on top and a toothpick inserted into the center comes out clean, about 40 minutes. Let the cake cool in the pan for 10 minutes before cutting into squares and serving.

Recipe from La Gargagista Farm + Winery
Photograph courtesy of La Garagista Farm + Winery

Note: The batter will be very dry, almost cement like, right before the egg whites are added. The first two additions of the whites allow for saturating the batter, and the third is left streaky. This cake is meant to be a shallow sheet cake, about 1 inch or a little higher once baked.

Dark Chocolate and Sea Salt Cookies

Makes 30

"These cookies are everything that a cookie should be: tender, but crumbly, salty, yet chocolaty, rich, and gooey. The sea salt and dark chocolate combination make these more special than your average chocolate chip cookie. This dough can be frozen (sans sea salt topping) and it will bake well, making it one of our favorite freezer cookies. Make a double batch and freeze half so you can pop out one or a dozen from the freezer when unexpected guests show up or a cookie craving strikes! Be sure to top with the sea salt before baking." —*Ali Hartman, owner, MKT: Grafton*

1 cup organic butter
2 large eggs
1½ cups organic light brown sugar
1 tablespoon pure vanilla extract
3¼ cups all-purpose flour
1¼ teaspoons aluminum-free baking powder
1½ teaspoons kosher salt
2 cups dark chocolate chunks or chips
Sea salt flakes

Preheat the oven to 325 degrees Fahrenheit. Generously grease two baking sheets and set aside.

In a small saucepan, melt the butter over medium heat. Set aside and let cool to room temperature.

In the bowl of a stand mixer, beat the eggs lightly on medium speed. Add the sugar and vanilla and beat until well combined. Add the butter, mixing until all ingredients are well incorporated and creamy.

In a large bowl, mix together the flour, baking powder, and kosher salt. Working in batches, use a rubber spatula to fold the dry ingredients into the wet ingredients. Fold the chocolate into the batter.

Roll the dough into 2-inch balls and drop them on the prepared baking sheets about 3 inches apart. Top with sea salt flakes. Bake until the cookies are set in the middle and lightly golden brown around the edges, about 15 minutes. Allow the cookies to cool on the baking sheets for 5 minutes, then transfer to cooling racks to cool completely.

Recipe from MKT: Grafton

Note: Feel free to bake the cookies right away; however, you'll have a more flavorful cookie if you let the dough rest in the refrigerator for at least 1 hour.

Conversion Charts

METRIC AND IMPERIAL CONVERSIONS

(These conversions are rounded for convenience)

Ingredient	Cups/Tablespoons/ Teaspoons	Ounces	Grams/Milliliters
Butter	1 cup/ 16 tablespoons/ 2 sticks	8 ounces	230 grams
Cheese, shredded	1 cup	4 ounces	110 grams
Cornstarch	1 tablespoon	0.3 ounce	8 grams
Cream cheese	1 tablespoon	0.5 ounce	14.5 grams
Flour, all-purpose	1 cup/1 tablespoon	4.5 ounces/0.3 ounce	125 grams/8 grams
Flour, whole wheat	1 cup	4 ounces	120 grams
Fruit, dried	1 cup	4 ounces	120 grams
Fruits or veggies, chopped	1 cup	5 to 7 ounces	145 to 200 grams
Fruits or veggies, puréed	1 cup	8.5 ounces	245 grams
Honey, maple syrup, or corn syrup	1 tablespoon	.75 ounce	20 grams
Liquids: cream, milk, water, or juice	1 cup	8 fluid ounces	240 milliliters
Oats	1 cup	5.5 ounces	150 grams
Salt	1 teaspoon	0.2 ounces	6 grams
Spices: cinnamon, cloves, ginger, or nutmeg (ground)	1 teaspoon	0.2 ounce	5 milliliters
Sugar, brown, firmly packed	1 cup	7 ounces	200 grams
Sugar, white	1 cup/1 tablespoon	7 ounces/0.5 ounce	200 grams/12.5 grams
Vanilla extract	1 teaspoon	0.2 ounce	4 grams

OVEN TEMPERATURES

Fahrenheit	Celsius	Gas Mark
225°	110°	¼
250°	120°	½
275°	140°	1
300°	150°	2
325°	160°	3
350°	180°	4
375°	190°	5
400°	200°	6
425°	220°	7
450°	230°	8

Directory

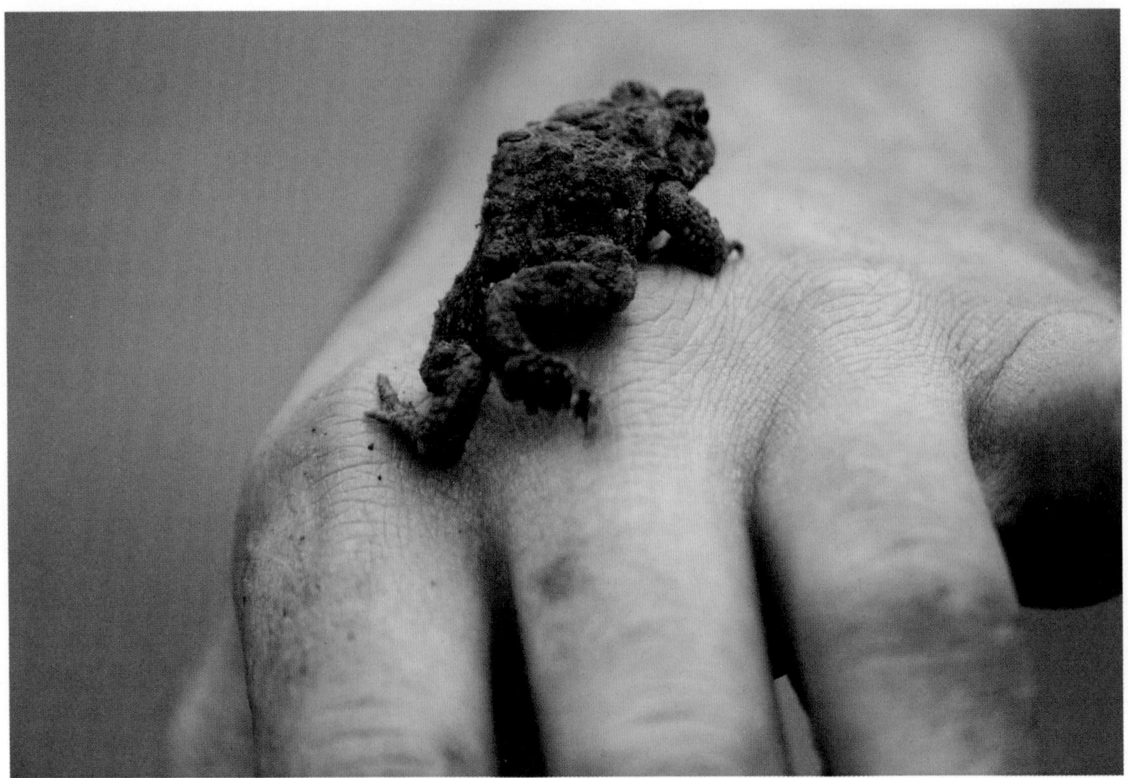

Photograph by Tristan Von Duntz

Eateries and Producers

Adam's Berry Farm
Telephone: 802-578-9093
Website: www.adamsberryfarm.com

Artisan Restaurant Tavern & Garden at Four Columns Inn
Telephone: 802-365-7713
Website: www.fourcolumnsvt.com

Bear Roots Farm
Telephone: 802-760-0495
Website: www.bearrootsfarm.com

Ben & Jerry's Homemade, Inc.
Telephone: 802-846-1500
Website: www.benjerry.com

Benito's Hot Sauce
Telephone: 802-730-6823
Website: www.benitoshotsauce.com

Brotbakery
Telephone: 802-370-4077
Website: www.brotbakery.com

Buffalo Mountain Food Co-operative & Café
Telephone: 802-472-6020
Website: www.buffalomountaincoop.org

Burelli Farm
Telephone: 802-595-2572
Website: www.burellifarm.com

Butternut Mountain Farm
Telephone: 802-888-5900
Website: www.butternutmountainfarm.com

Cedar Circle Farm & Education Center
Telephone: 802-785-4737
Website: www.cedarcirclefarm.org

Chai Wallah
Telephone: 802-257-4435
Website: www.chai-wallah.com

Champlain Valley Creamery, Ltd.
Telephone: 802-989-7361
Website: www.cvcream.com

Coleman Brook Tavern at Okemo Mountain Resort
Telephone: 802-228-1430
Website: www.okemo.com

Earthwise Farm and Forest
Telephone: 802-234-5524
Website: www.earthwisefarmandforest.com

El Cortijo Taqueria Y Cantina
Telephone: 802-497-1668
Website: www.cortijovt.com

Elmer Farm
Telephone: 802-388-3848
Website: www.elmerfarm.com

Farmhouse Chocolates + Ice Cream
Telephone: 802-349-6228
Website: www.farmhousechocolates.com

The Farmhouse Group
Telephone: 802-497-1026
Website: www.farmhousegroup.com

The Farmhouse Tap & Grill
Telephone: 802-859-0888
Website: www.farmhousetg.com

Footprint Farm, LLC
Telephone: 802-453-6628
Website: www.footprintfarmvt.com

Four Springs Farm
Telephone: 802-763-7296
Website: www.fourspringsfarm.com

Freighthouse Market & Café
Telephone: 802-626-1400
Website: www.thelyndonfreighthouse.com

Full Moon Farm, Inc.
Telephone: 802-598-2036
Website: www.fullmoonfarminc.com

Full Sun Company
Telephone: 802-377-3541
Website: www.fullsuncompany.com

Golden Well Farm & Apiaries
Telephone: 802-870-0361
Website: www.goldenwellfarm.com

Green Rabbit, LLC
Telephone: 802-363-1431
Website: www.greenrabbitvt.com

Guild Tavern
Telephone: 802-497-1207
Website: www.guildtavern.com

Health Hero Farm
Telephone: 802-378-5033
Website: www.healthherofarm.com

High Mowing Organic Seeds
Telephone: 802-472-6174; 866-735-4454
Website: www.highmowingseeds.com

The Inn at Round Barn Farm
Telephone: 802-496-2276
Website: www.theroundbarn.com

Jersey Girls Dairy & Farm Store
Telephone: 802-875-6576
Website: www.jerseygirlsdairy.com

JJ Hapgood General Store and Eatery
Telephone: 802-824-4800
Website: www.jjhapgood.com

Juniper Bar & Restaurant, Hotel Vermont
Telephone: 802-651-5019
Website: www.hotelvt.com

KC Wright
Telephone: 603-498-2424
Website: www.pitchforkstotablespoons.blogspot.com

Kettle Song Farm
Telephone: 802-223-8410

Kismet, LLC
Telephone: 802-223-8646
Website: www.kismetkitchens.com

La Gargagista Farm + Winery
Telephone: 802-291-1295
Website: www.lagaragista.com

Lake Champlain Chocolates
Telephone: 802-864-1808
Website: www.lakechamplainchocolates.com

Liz Lovely, Inc.
Telephone: 802-496-6390
Website: www.lizlovely.com

Mad River Distillers
Telephone: 802-496-6972
Website: www.madriverdistillers.com

Marigold Kitchen Pizza
Telephone: 802-445-4545
Website: www.marigoldkitchen.info

Meadows Bee Farm
Telephone: 802-874-4092
Website: www.meadowsbeefarm.com

Meeting Place Pastures
Telephone: 802-462-3759
Website: www.meetingplacepastures.com

Mighty Food Farm
Telephone: 781-307-6801
Website: www.mightyfoodfarm.com

Mint Restaurant and Tea Lounge
Telephone: 802-496-5514
Website: www.mintvermont.com

MKT: Grafton
Telephone: 802-843-2255
E-mail: www.mktgrafton.com

Moonlight Farm
Telephone: 978-479-4163
Website: www.moonlightfarmvermont.com

Naked Acre Farm
Telephone: 774-212-2177
Website: www.nakedacrefarm.com

Nitty Gritty Grain Company of Vermont
Telephone: 802-425-4544
www.nittygrittygrain.com

NOFA Vermont
Telephone: 802-434-3821
Website: www.nofavt.org

Non-GMO Project
Telephone: 360-255-7704
Website: www.nongmoproject.org

Pangea Farm, LLC
Telephone: 917-447-4352
Website: www.pangea.farm

Pascolo Ristorante
Telephone: 802-497-1613
Website: www.pascolovt.com

Pedalbarrow Farm
Telephone: 802-758-2019

Pingala Café & Eatery
Telephone: 802-540-0110
Website: www.pingalacafe.com

Revolution Kitchen
Telephone: 802-448-3657
Website: www.revolutionkitchen.com

Runamok Maple
Telephone: 802-644-9366
Website: www.runamokmaple.com

Rural Vermont
Telephone: 802-233-7222
Website: www.ruralvermont.org

Shadow Creek Farm
Milton, VT 05468

Someday Farm
Telephone: 802-362-2290
Website: www.somedayfarmvt.com

Stowe Street Café
Telephone: 802-882-8229
Website: www.stowestreetcafe.com

Sweet Simone's
Telephone: 802-336-2126
Website: www.sweetsimones.com

3 Squares Café
Telephone: 802-877-2772
Website: www.threesquarescafe.com

1000 Stone Farm
Telephone: 703-901-2922
Website: www.1000stonefarm.com

Three Crow Farm
Telephone: 802-644-1522
Website: www.threecrowsfarm@gmail.com

Tonewood Maple
Telephone: 802-496-5512
Website: www.tonewoodmaple.com

Tourterelle Restaurant & Inn
Telephone: 802-453-6309
Website: www.tourterellevt.com

Trattoria La Festa
Telephone: 802-253-8480
Website: www.trattoriastowe.com

Valentine Farm
Telephone: 802-881-1645
Website: www.valentinefarmvt.wordpress.com

Vermont Amber Organic Toffee
Telephone: 603-738-7460
Website: www.vermontamber.com

Vermont Fresh Network
Telephone: 802-434-2000
Website: www.vermontfresh.net

Vermont Public Interest Research Group (VPIRG)
Telephone: 802-223-5221
Website: www.vpirg.org

Vermont Raw Nut Butter
Website: www.VermontRawNutButter.com

Vermont Switchel Company, LLC
Telephone: 802-522-5898
Website: www.vtswitchel.com

Village Cannery of Vermont
Telephone: 802-479-2558
Website: www.vermontvillageapplesauce.com

The Village Roost Café & Marketplace
Telephone: 802-464-3344
Website: www.villageroost.com

V Smiley Preserves
Website: www.vsmileypreserves.com

Walden Heights Nursery & Orchard
Telephone: 802-563-3012
Website: www.waldenheightsnursery.com

Williamsville Eatery
Telephone: 802-365-9600
Website: www.WilliamsvilleEatery.com

Willow Brook Farm
Telephone: 802-592-3214
Website: www.willowbrookfarmvt.com

Woodbelly Pizza
Telephone: 802-522-3476
Website: www.woodbellypizza.com

Woodbury Game Birds
Telephone: 802-282-6123
Website: www.woodburygamebirds.com\

Wood's Market Garden
Telephone: 802-247-6630
Website: www.woodsmarketgarden.com

Woodstock Inn & Resort
Telephone: 802-457-1100
Website: www.woodstockinn.com

Photographers

Brent Harrewyn— Hoverfly Photography
Telephone: 802-233-1002
Website: www.hoverflyphotography.com

Brian Crumley
Telephone: 917-698-5938

Brie Passano Photography
Telephone: 917-497-2076
Website: www.briephotography.com

Dave Allen
West Chesterfield, NH 03466
Website: www.old-maps.com

Photograph by Tristan Von Duntz

Evi Abeler
Telephone: 917-346-6414
Website: www.eviabeler.com

Golden Aura Photography by Emily Esslinger
Website: www.goldenauraphotography.com

Kelly Fletcher Photography
Telephone: 802-345-7653
Website: www.kellyfletcherphotography.com

Okemo Mountain Resort
Telephone: 802-228-1430
Website: www.okemo.com

Stephanie Challis Photography
Telephone: 972-900-2400
Website: www.stephaniechallisphotography.com

Tristan Von Duntz Photography
Telephone: 802-595-3457

Photograph by Oliver Parini

Index

C

D

E

F

N

O

P

Q

R

S

T

U

V

W

Y

Z

About the Author

Tracey Medeiros is the author of *The Connecticut Farm Table Cookbook*, *The Vermont Farm Table Cookbook*, and *Dishing Up Vermont*. She writes "The Farmhouse Kitchen: A Guide to Eating Local" column for *Edible Green Mountains* magazine and is also a freelance food writer, food stylist, and recipe developer and tester. She is often seen on various television cooking segments preparing one of her favorite recipes while sharing helpful culinary tips with the viewing audience. Tracey travels regionally as a guest speaker and cooking instructor, emphasizing her commitment to the sustainable food movement by using locally produced fresh ingredients to create dishes that are healthy and delicious. Learn more at: www.traceymedeiros.com. The author and her family reside in the Green Mountain State.

Map of Vermont 1814 Amos Doolittle from Carey's General Atlas of the World Library of Congress www.old-maps.com